The Effective Deposition:
Techniques and Strategies That Work

The Effective Deposition:
Techniques and Strategies That Work

Revised Second Edition

David M. Malone
Attorney at Law
Washington, D.C.

Peter T. Hoffman
Professor of Law
University of Nebraska
Lincoln, Nebraska

NATIONAL INSTITUTE FOR TRIAL ADVOCACY

Reproduction Permissions
National Institute for Trial Advocacy
Notre Dame Law School
Notre Dame, Indiana 46556
(800) 225-6482   Fax (219) 271-8375
nita.1@nd.edu   www.nita.org

Malone, David M. and Peter T. Hoffman, *The Effective Deposition: Techniques and Strategies That Work*, Revised 2d ed. (NITA, 2001).

ISBN: 1-55681-682-0

Library of Congress Cataloging-in-Publication Data

Malone, David M., 1944-
   The effective deposition : techniques and strategies that work / David M. Malone, Peter T. Hoffman.-- rev. 2d ed.
      p. cm. -- (NITA practical guide series)
   Includes index.
   ISBN 1-55681-682-0
      1. Depositions--United States. I. Hoffman, Peter T. II. Title. III. Series.

KF8900 .M34 2001
347.73'72--dc21

2001031579

To

The Memory of
Robert F. Hanley,
My Teacher and Friend
— D.M.M.

Sarah and Alice
— P.T.H.

The cases and incidents described in this text are drawn from the authors' imaginations, based upon experience. The names are not intended to refer to any living persons or actual companies, except that we have occasionally used the names of teaching colleagues to heighten their interest in reading our work. Many of the names selected for the fictitious characters are Lithuanian, to show respect and support for the successful Lithuanian freedom movement.

Contents

Chapter Four
PLANNING AND SCHEDULING DEPOSITIONS

Chapter Five
PREPARING TO TAKE THE DEPOSITION

Chapter Six
BEGINNING THE DEPOSITION

Chapter Seven
QUESTIONING TECHNIQUES

Chapter Eight
STYLE, ORGANIZATION, AND OTHER MATTERS

Chapter Nine
USING DOCUMENTS

Chapter Ten
CONCLUDING THE DEPOSITION

Chapter Eleven
OBNOXIOUS OR OBSTRUCTIONIST DEFENDING COUNSEL

Chapter Twelve
PROTECTIVE ORDERS AND APPLICATIONS TO THE COURT

PART THREE: DEFENDING DEPOSITIONS
Chapter Thirteen
PREPARING THE WITNESS TO BE DEPOSED

PREFACE

The year 2000 brought another series of amendments to the Federal Rules of Civil Procedure, most relating to the conduct of discovery in the federal courts. This second revised edition incorporates the 2000 amendments and discusses how these changes affect the taking of depositions. Since the publication of the first edition of this book, much has changed about deposition practice. The 1993 and 2000 amendments to the Federal Rules of Civil Procedure have resulted in what some would say are radical modifications in the way all discovery, not just depositions, are conducted in the federal courts. We have endeavored to incorporate all of these changes into the revised second edition of *The Effective Deposition*.

As with the first and second edition, a number of individuals deserve special thanks for their assistance in bringing the revised second edition of *The Effective Deposition* to reality. John Maciejczyk was an editor of exceptional ability and diplomacy in the editing of the second edition. His efforts are well appreciated. Deanne Siemer, Managing Director of Wilsie Co., LLC; Frank Rothschild of the Hawaii Bar; Anthony Bocchino, NITA's Editor in Chief; and Tom Singer of the Indiana Bar—all outstanding NITA teachers—have allowed us to incorporate several of their thoughts about the taking of depositions. As with previous editions, we also have the benefit of the many helpful comments and suggestions made by the thousands of participants and faculty who have used the book in NITA deposition programs around the country. These suggestions have been invaluable and have resulted in many important improvements to the book. Needless to say, any errors remain ours and are not attributable to others.

PART ONE:

THE LAW

Chapter One

MECHANICS OF TAKING AND DEFENDING DEPOSITIONS

"Mechanics will kill you."
— Warren S. Radler, Trial Attorney

Few hard and fast rules control the conduct of depositions; yet you must carefully observe the few that do exist so that the product of the deposition, the transcript, is valid and useful months or years later when the witness or his memory is perhaps long gone.

The mechanics of taking and defending depositions are quite simple, but to avoid mistakes you must be thoroughly familiar with the applicable rules. Small or inadvertent mistakes can cost money and time, and prevent the use of valuable deposition testimony on behalf of your client. To avoid such mistakes, you should carefully read and study the rules and statutes applicable to discovery in your jurisdiction.

The Federal Rules of Civil Procedure were amended in 1993 and again in 2000, resulting in several dramatic changes in the way discovery is conducted. While the Federal Rules or some variation of them have been adopted by the vast majority of the states, many have not yet chosen to adopt some or all of the 1993 and 2000 Amendments. To further complicate matters, a substantial number of state and federal courts have adopted local rules supplementing or modifying the rules concerning discovery. One important change wrought by the 2000 Amendments is that U.S. District Courts can no longer modify or opt out of many of the discovery rules. Because of the many variations between jurisdictions in the rules governing depositions, you must carefully check the rules in your own jurisdiction. This book will discuss how to take and defend depositions under the Federal Rules as they existed through the year 2000, as well as note any changes due to the 2000 Amendments. Since many states still follow the pre-1993 version of the Federal Rules concerning discovery, the practice under the pre-1993 version will be discussed as well.

1.1 WHOSE DEPOSITION MAY BE TAKEN?

You may take the deposition of any person, including witnesses who are not parties to the action.[1] While most other discovery devices such as interrogatories are limited to parties alone, depositions may be taken of anyone who you believe may have knowledge of relevant information. In addition to non-party witnesses, depositions may be taken of the parties to the action, agents and employees of the parties, former parties, and, in special circumstances, the attorneys of the parties. Although this is normally not done, a party expecting to be unavailable for trial and wanting her testimony presented through a deposition may even take her own deposition. Corporations can be deposed through their officers, directors, and managing agents, and organizations generally may be deposed through their designees. Note, however, that you must seek leave of court to take the deposition of a person confined in prison.[2]

1.2 RULE 30(B)(6) DEPOSITIONS

Many times, employees or agents of corporations, partnerships, governmental agencies, or associations such as labor unions have valuable information relevant to some issue in a case, but you may not know the identity of the particular person in the organization with that information. Or, more than one person has the necessary information, with each knowing something pertinent. While you could take a series of depositions until you have identified and deposed the person or persons with the required information, the Federal Rules of Civil Procedure provide an easier and more efficient method.

Under Rule 30(b)(6) you may notice the deposition of a corporation, partnership, association, or governmental agency and designate the matters on which examination is requested without naming a particular person to be deposed. The organization must then designate the witness or witnesses who consent to testify on behalf of the organization and will testify about the designated matters. The designated witness or witnesses should be able to testify as to matters known or reasonably available to the organization concerning the designated topics. In other words, the organization must make reasonable efforts to find and present the requested information through a witness of its choosing.

---

1. Fed.R.Civ.P. 30(a)(1).
2. Fed.R.Civ.P. 30(a)(2).

1.3   TIMING

Under Rule 26(d), no discovery is permitted in most cases until after the parties have conferred to plan discovery pursuant to Rule 26(f), and this includes depositions.[3] The purpose and timing of the conference are discussed in § 4.1. Certain unusual, or very routine types of cases, which would not benefit from having the parties confer are exempt from this prohibition.[4] The prohibition on discovery until after the parties have conferred can be modified by an order within the case or by agreement of the parties, but the U.S. District Courts may no longer by local rule change the timing of discovery. The prohibition on discovery can also be disregarded if the notice of deposition contains a certification, with supporting facts, that the witness is expected to leave the United States and be unavailable for examination in this country unless deposed before the parties have conferred.[5] However, a deposition taken before the parties have conferred because the witness is leaving the United States cannot be used against a party who shows that it was unable through the exercise of diligence to obtain counsel to represent it at the deposition.[6] By the same token, depositions can only be used against parties who had notice of their taking.[7]

Under the pre-1993 version of the Federal Rules of Civil Procedure, depositions could be taken any time after the commencement of the action and before trial without leave of court, with three exceptions. Leave of court is required: first, when the plaintiff seeks to take a deposition prior to the expiration of thirty days after service of the summons and complaint on any defendant;[8] second, when the witness is confined in prison;[9] and third, when the taking of the deposition is contrary to any court order or local court rule.

Under the pre-1993 version, even when the deposition is being taken by the plaintiff within thirty days of the service on a defendant of the summons and complaint, leave of court is not required if: the defendant has first noticed the taking of a deposition or has otherwise sought discovery;[10] or the witness is about to go out of the district where the action is pending and more than 100 miles from the place of trial; or

---

3. The 2000 Amendments to Rule 26(d) and (f) have changed the requirement that the parties meet to discuss discovery and other issues to require now that the parties confer on these issues.

4. Fed.R.Civ.P. 26(a)(1)(E) and (f).

5. Fed.R.Civ.P. 30(a)(2)(C).

6. Fed.R.Civ.P. 32(a)(3).

7. Fed.R.Civ.P. 32(a).

8. Fed.R.Civ.P. 30(a) (amended 1993).

9. *Ibid.*

10. *Ibid.*

the witness is about to embark on a sea voyage and will be unavailable for examination unless a deposition is taken within the thirty-day period.[11] If the defendant is unable to obtain a lawyer through diligent efforts taken during the thirty-day period, the deposition cannot be used against that defendant.[12] Similarly, if not all defendants have been served with the summons and complaint before the deposition is taken, the deposition may only be used against those parties who were present at, represented at, or received notice of the deposition.[13]

1.4 PRIORITY

The concept of priority—the party first noticing the taking of deposition has a right to complete the taking of that deposition before the opponent may take a deposition—has been abolished under the Federal Rules of Civil Procedure. Now, no such priority exists in discovery and either party may notice a deposition even though a previously noticed deposition has not yet been completed. Further, the Rules have also abolished the priority given until 1993 under Rule 30(a) to defendants who could notice depositions at any time, while prohibiting plaintiffs from taking depositions until thirty days after service of the summons and complaint or until the defendant has sought discovery.

1.5 SCHEDULING OF THE DEPOSITION

As a matter of convenience and courtesy, most depositions are scheduled by agreement among the parties. By cooperating, you can avoid conflicts in both the lawyer's and the witnesses' schedules, and you can avoid the expense of motions to reschedule the time for the deposition. Several courts, by local rules, require that, before noticing a deposition, the parties must attempt to arrive at a mutually agreeable date. Absent agreement, the date set in the notice of deposition will control unless a witness or a party objects and moves for a protective order rescheduling the deposition.[14]

---

11. Fed.R.Civ.P. 30(a) and 30(b)(2) (amended 1993).
12. Fed.R.Civ.P. 30(b)(2) (amended 1993).
13. Fed.R.Civ.P. 32(a) (amended 1993).
14. Fed.R.Civ.P. 26(c)(2). See chapter 12, "Protective Orders and Applications to the Court."

A party may object to the deposition date or time.[15] A non-party may also timely move to quash a subpoena if it "fails to allow reasonable time for compliance."[16] The motion is brought in the court issuing the subpoena (which must, of course, be a court which had personal jurisdiction of the intended deponent since non-parties are not automatically subject to the jurisdiction of the forum court).

1.6   GIVING NOTICE OF THE DEPOSITION

Rule 30(b)(1) requires that the party intending to take the deposition give written notice of the deposition to all other parties to the action. The notice must state the following: the time and place for taking the deposition; the name and address of each person to be examined if known or, if not known, a general description sufficient to identify the witness or the particular class to which the witness belongs. Further, if a subpoena duces tecum is to be served on the witness, the notice must include or attach a list of the materials in the subpoena that are to be produced at the deposition. The notice of deposition may list more than one witness to be examined. Finally, Rule 30(b)(2) requires that the notice state the method by which the testimony is to be recorded: stenographic, videotape, or audiotape.

The notice requirements for Rule 30(b)(6) depositions (where a corporation, partnership, association, or governmental agency is required to designate a witness or witnesses to testify about specified topics) are the same as for other depositions, with two differences—the notice must designate with reasonable particularity the matters on which examination is requested, and no witness is specified by the notice-giver. Except for 30(b)(6) depositions, no rule requires that the notice designate the subject matter of the deposition.

1.6.1   Time requirements for giving notice.

Rule 30(b)(1) does not require a specific number of days notice of a deposition. Indeed, all that is required is "reasonable notice." Rule 32(a) suggests that eleven days is sufficient "reasonable notice."[17] However,

---

15. *Ibid.* Rule 32(a) states that a deposition may not be used against a party who, having received less than eleven days' notice of the deposition, has promptly filed a motion for a protective order under Fed.R.Civ.P. 26(c)(2) and the motion is pending at the time the deposition is held. Fed.R.Civ.P. 32(a).

16. Fed.R.Civ.P. 45(c)(3)(A)(i). Also see, Fed.R.Civ.P. 45(c)(1) (providing for the award of costs and other relief for imposing undue burden and expense on a subpoenaed witness).

17. Fed.R.Civ.P. 32(a) states that a deposition shall not be used against a party who received less than eleven days' notice of the deposition and who promptly moved for a protective order under Fed.R.Civ.P. 26(c)(2), when the motion was still pending at the time designated for the deposition.

the Advisory Committee Notes add that this provision "is not intended to signify that eleven days' notice is the minimum advance notice for all depositions or that greater than ten days should necessarily be deemed sufficient in all situations." In short, sufficient notice depends on the circumstances of each case. Upon motion, the trial court may enlarge or shorten the notice time required[18] and may, as part of a protective order or scheduling order under Rule 16(b), impose a specific notice requirement on the parties.[19]

Because of the strong policy encouraging agreement on dates, there should be little occasion for formal motions practice concerning the adequacy of notice.

1.6.2 Service of the notice of deposition.

The party taking the deposition must serve the notice of deposition on every party to the action.[20] The notice should be served on a party's attorney if he is represented or on the party himself if he is proceeding pro se. Service may be made by either personal service on the attorney or party, or by first-class mail addressed to the attorney's or party's last known address. Personal service is accomplished by: delivering a copy to the attorney or party; leaving the copy at the attorney's or party's office with a clerk or other person in charge; leaving it in a conspicuous place in the office; or, if the office is closed or there is no office, leaving it at the attorney's or party's residence with someone of suitable age and discretion who is living there.[21]

1.7 GEOGRAPHIC LOCATION OF THE DEPOSITION

A deposition may be taken at any location to which the parties and the witness agree. If no agreement can be reached, as discussed below, the geographic location depends to a large extent on whether the witness is a party or non-party.

1.7.1 Parties.

A party may schedule a deposition for any location subject to the court's power under Rule 26(c)(2) to grant a protective order designating a different place. The burden is on the party wishing to change the location from that given in the notice of deposition, but the courts appear to have developed some general rules governing where

---

18. Fed.R.Civ.P. 30(b)(3).
19. Fed.R.Civ.P. 26(c)(2) and 26(f).
20. Fed.R.Civ.P. 30(b)(1).
21. Fed.R.Civ.P. 5.

depositions can be taken. In addition, several federal courts have adopted local court rules governing the place of taking of depositions.

1.7.2 Plaintiffs.

A defendant may take the deposition of a plaintiff in the geographic area where the plaintiff resides, has a place of business, is employed, or where the action has been brought. The courts have found many exceptions to this rule and look at the realities of the situation such as relative financial burdens on any of the parties.

1.7.3 Defendants.

Plaintiffs usually must depose defendants in the geographic area of their residences, places of business, or employment. Again, courts usually do not enforce this general rule when to do so would result in an injustice or undue financial hardship.

1.7.4 Corporations.

You usually may depose corporate officers, directors, or managing agents at the principal place of business for the corporation, as well as where they live. Depositions of mere employees or agents are treated the same as any other non-party witness—their depositions must occur within 100 miles of the place where the witness resides, is employed, or regularly transacts business in person.

1.7.5 Non-parties.

The place of deposition for a non-party is governed principally by Rule 45(c)(3)(A)(ii) concerning subpoenas. That rule states that the target of a deposition subpoena may be required to attend only within 100 miles from the place where the person resides, is employed, or regularly transacts business.

A party may always agree with a witness for the witness's deposition to be taken at some place other than where the witness can be subpoenaed. Many times, it may well be more efficient to agree to pay the witness's expenses for coming to another location than for the parties' attorneys to journey to the witness. But where no such agreement is possible, Rule 45 dictates the location of the deposition.

1.8 NUMBER OF DEPOSITIONS

The Federal Rules of Civil Procedure impose two separate and distinct limitations on the number of depositions that parties may take in a case. First, Rule 30(a)(2)(A) limits plaintiffs, defendants, and third party defendants to ten depositions per side unless the parties have stipulated in writing to a different number or the court has given leave for a greater number. Note that the restriction is on the number of depositions per side, not per party. The planning conference and scheduling conference are usually the places where the parties discuss different limitations among themselves and with the court.[22] The U.S. District Courts, with the 2000 Amendments, may no longer use local rules to set a different limit on the number of depositions permitted, but they may still establish different limits by court order in a particular case.

Rule 30(a)(2)(b) establishes the second limitation and states, in effect, that a person can only be deposed once absent a stipulation or court order.

In jurisdictions which follow the pre-1993 version of the Federal Rules of Civil Procedure, a party may ask the court to limit the number of depositions by a motion for a protective order under Rule 26(c).

1.9 LENGTH OF DEPOSITIONS

The 2000 Amendments impose a seven-hour, one-day time limitation on the length of depositions.[23] Note that under this limitation, the seven hours must occur on one day rather than extending over two or more days. The court may, by order within a particular case, impose a different limitation on a specific witness or on all the depositions in a case, but may no longer alter the length by local court rule. The parties may also alter the time limits by written stipulation. (A statement of the stipulation included in the deposition record would be sufficient to satisfy this requirement of a "writing.") Additional time may be allowed by the court if needed for fairness or if the deposition is impeded or delayed for any reason. Only actual deposition time is counted and not the time necessary for reasonable breaks and lunch.[24] In a 30(b)(6) deposition,[25] each designated witnesses' testimony is counted as a separate deposition for purposes of calculating time (although it is reasonable to wonder whether this is consistent with the Advisory Committee's opinion that a Rule 30(b)(6) deposition counts as one deposition, despite the designation of multiple witnesses).

---

22. See § 4.1.
23. Fed.R.Civ.P. 30(d)(2).
24. Advisory Committee Notes to Rule 30.
25. See § 1.2.

In jurisdictions following the pre-1993 Federal Rules of Civil Procedure, the length of depositions can be limited by a protective order under Rule 26(c).

1.10 COMPELLING THE WITNESS'S ATTENDANCE

The procedure for compelling a witness to attend his deposition depends on whether the witness is a party; an officer, a managing agent, or director of a party; or a non-party.

1.10.1 Parties.

Any party may require an individual party to appear at a deposition by merely serving a notice of deposition on the party-deponent and the other parties. Any party may also require an officer, director, or managing agent of a party to attend its deposition by merely serving a notice of deposition,[26] but the notice must name or adequately describe the witness and state that the witness is an officer, director, or managing agent.[27]

1.10.2 Non-parties.

Absent an agreement to appear voluntarily, non-party witnesses may be required to attend their depositions only if subpoenaed.[28] The subpoena, in addition to requiring the witness to appear, may also command the witness to produce designated documents and other evidence.[29]

ISSUANCE OF SUBPOENA

Any attorney may issue and sign a subpoena if the subpoena is for an action pending in a court in which the attorney is authorized to practice, or if the attorney is authorized to practice in the federal district court of the district where the deposition is scheduled to be taken.[30] In other words, if the case was filed in the Northern District of Texas, a Northern District of Texas attorney may sign a subpoena directed to a deponent who is within the Northern District or within 100 miles of the court. If in that same case a deponent is located in the District of New Jersey, the Texas attorney may sign the subpoena, which issues from the New Jersey district court, the court having personal jurisdiction over the deponent. A subpoena from the Texas court could not "reach" the New Jersey deponent. Clerks of any U.S.

---

26. Fed.R.Civ.P. 37(d).
27. *El Salto, S.A. v. PSG Co.*, 444 F.2d 477 (9th Cir. 1971).
28. Fed.R.Civ.P. 30(a)(1).
29. Fed.R.Civ.P. 45(a)(1).
30. Fed.R.Civ.P. 45(a)(2) and (3).

District Court have blank subpoenas available. While clerks of district courts may issue signed, blank subpoenas, there is no reason to resort to this more difficult procedure when attorneys themselves may sign and issue subpoenas. The attorney taking the deposition should fill in on the subpoena the name of the district in which the deposition is to be taken, as stated in the notice of deposition, as well as the other requested information, and sign the subpoena to complete issuance.

SERVICE OF THE SUBPOENA

Anyone eighteen years or older and not a party to the action may serve the subpoena, but the server must take reasonable steps to avoid imposing undue burden or expense on the witness. Unlike the service of the notice of deposition or even the summons commencing the action, subpoenas cannot be served by mail; only personal service is acceptable. The server must deliver the subpoena to the witness and concurrently tender one day's witness fees and mileage allowance (unless the subpoena is issued on behalf of the United States or one of its officers or agencies). The witness fee in effect at the time of this writing is $40.00 per day including the time necessary for going to and from the place of the deposition.[31] If the witness travels by common carrier, then the most economical rate reasonably available must be paid as long as the method used was reasonable and the shortest practical route was followed.[32] If the witness travels by private car, the General Services Administration mileage rates (currently at $0.30 per mile) should be used.[33] The clerks of the U.S. District Courts usually have information about current rates.

When serving a corporation or organization with a subpoena, for instance for a Rule 30(b)(6) deposition, the server should leave the subpoena with an officer or a managing or general agent to ensure that the corporation receives actual notice.

Following service, the party responsible should file a proof of service with the clerk of the district court, but in practice this is not often done unless a witness has failed to appear for his deposition and contempt proceedings are being brought. The proof of service should state the name of the person served, the date, and the manner of service, and be signed by the person who made the service.

GEOGRAPHIC LIMITATIONS ON SERVICE

A deposition subpoena may only be served within: the district of the court from which the subpoena has issued; 100 miles of the place of the deposition; or the state where the deposition is to occur if the state has a

---

31. 28 U.S.C. § 1821(b).
32. 28 U.S.C. § 1821(c)(1).
33. 28 U.S.C. § 1821(c)(2).

statute or court rule authorizing such service. The court may also authorize extended service of the subpoena if there is a federal statute permitting such.[34]

1.11 REQUIRING DOCUMENTS TO BE BROUGHT TO THE DEPOSITION

Generally, you will want to have documents or other tangible evidence produced prior to a deposition so that you can be completely familiar with the material before having to question about it. Rule 34 (for parties) and Rule 45 (for non-parties) establish the procedure for requiring the production of tangible evidence. The mechanics of these rules, as applied to the non-deposition production of evidence, are beyond the scope of this discussion, but sometimes, because time is short or production will occur some distance away, you will want to schedule the production as part of deposition.

1.11.1 Parties.

You can arrange the production of documents and other tangible evidence by a party-witness at a deposition by agreement of the parties or by serving a notice to produce pursuant to Rule 34. While some confusion exists about the issue, Rule 30(b)(5)[35] suggests that a notice to produce is the exclusive means of requiring the production of evidence by a party at a deposition. The notice to produce must be served on every party to the action and is usually served with the notice of deposition.

1.11.2 Non-party witnesses.

You may require a non-party deposition witness to produce documents and other tangible evidence at a deposition by using a subpoena duces tecum. Rule 45 contains the requirements for a subpoena duces tecum. While a subpoena duces tecum can be issued and served entirely separate from the taking of a deposition, the subpoena commanding the witness to appear at a deposition may also command the witness to bring and produce documents and other tangible items of evidence for inspection.

The procedure for issuing a subpoena duces tecum is the same as that given above for the issuance of a subpoena *ad testificandum* but the notice of deposition will be different. When a subpoena duces tecum has been served on a witness, you must attach to, or include in, the notice a

---

34. Fed.R.Civ.P. 45(b)(2).

35. "The notice to a party deponent may be accompanied by a request made in compliance with Rule 34 for the production of documents and tangible things at the taking of the deposition. The procedure of Rule 34 shall apply to the request."

designation of the materials to be produced as set forth in the subpoena.[36] The easiest and most convenient method of doing this is to refer to the subpoena duces tecum in the notice of deposition and attach a copy of the subpoena to the notice which is then served on the other parties to the action.

1.12 THE DEPOSITION ITSELF

1.12.1 Before whom may the deposition be taken?

Depositions conducted in the United States, its territories, and its insular possessions may be taken before any person authorized to administer oaths either by the laws of the United States or of the place in which the action is pending or before a person appointed by the court in which the action is pending.[37] In practice, the deposition is taken before a court reporter who is also a notary public. Although the rules permit the deposition officer and the person recording the testimony to be two different persons, economy and efficiency usually dictate that one person serve both functions. The parties may stipulate to having the deposition taken before a non-notary or someone who, for instance, is an employee of one of the lawyers.[38] In other words, if the reporter does not show up for a deposition, the parties could agree that a secretary in the office could take the deposition in shorthand. Special rules, contained in Rule 28(b), govern the taking of depositions in foreign countries.

1.12.2 Recording of the deposition.

Under Rule 30(b)(2) the party noticing the deposition may choose the method of recording the testimony: sound, sound-and-visual, or stenographic (i.e., audiotape, videotape, and stenographic). The party taking the deposition shall state the method of recording in the notice of deposition and shall bear the expense of the recording. A party may also arrange for a non-stenographic deposition to be transcribed. Any other party, at its own expense and after giving notice to the witness and other parties, may designate another method of recording in addition to the method given in the notice of deposition.[39] While the party noticing the deposition is free to choose any method of recording the deposition, Rule 32(c) requires the presentation of deposition testimony in videotape or audiotape format, where available and when requested by any party, unless the use is solely for impeachment.

---

36. Fed.R.Civ.P. 30(b)(1).
37. Fed.R.Civ.P. 28(a).
38. Fed.R.Civ.P. 28(a) and 29.
39. Fed.R.Civ.P. 30(b)(3).

Under the pre-1993 version of the Federal Rules of Civil Procedure, depositions are to be taken stenographically unless the parties have stipulated or the court has ordered that another method be used.[40] The stipulation or order shall designate the person before whom the deposition is to be taken, the manner of recording, preservation and filing of the deposition, and any other provisions necessary to assure that the recorded testimony will be accurate and trustworthy.[41]

The recording is usually done by the deposition officer, who is a notary public, but the rules permit it to be done by someone acting under the officer's direction and in the officer's presence.[42] Of course, as noted above, the parties can stipulate otherwise.

1.12.3 Conduct of the deposition.

The rules governing the conduct of depositions are relatively few. Under the pre-1993 version of the Federal Rules of Civil Procedure, the deposition officer is only required to put the witness under oath. However, the current rules established several other requirements. Under Rule 30(b)(4) the deposition officer shall begin the deposition with a statement on the record that gives (1) the officer's name and business address, (2) the date, time, and place of the deposition, (3) the name of the witness, and (4) an identification of all persons present. The deposition officer shall also swear the witness on the record. At the end of the deposition, the officer shall state on the record that the deposition is complete and shall also recite any stipulations between counsel concerning the custody of the transcript or recording and exhibits as well as any other matters which have been agreed upon. Videotape and audiotape depositions have some further requirements that are discussed in chapter 18.

Examination and cross-examination may proceed as permitted at trial as provided by the Federal Rules of Evidence.[43] Under Rule 30(c) other witnesses cannot be excluded from the deposition room without first obtaining a protective order under Rule 26(c)(5). All objections made at the deposition to the qualifications of the officer taking the deposition, the manner of taking it, the evidence presented, the conduct of the deposition, or any other objection to any aspect of the proceedings are to be noted by the officer on the deposition record,[44] but the deposition shall proceed with the testimony being taken subject to the objections.[45]

---

40. Fed.R.Civ.P. 30(b)(4) (amended 1993).

41. Fed.R.Civ.P. 30(c) (amended 1993).

42. *Ibid.*

43. See Fed.R.Evid. 6. Rule 30(c) states that the Federal Rules of Evidence shall apply with the exception of Rules 103 (rulings on evidence) and 615 (exclusion of witnesses).

44. Fed.R.Civ.P. 30(c).

45. *Ibid.*

Rule 30(d)(1) requires that any objection to evidence made during the deposition be stated concisely and in a non-argumentative and non-suggestive manner. Thus, for example, the classic objection, "You can answer, if you know," is made explicitly impermissible. Further, you can instruct a witness not to answer a question only when necessary to preserve a privilege, to enforce a previous court order limiting examination ("counsel may ask the witness about liability but not damages"), or to seek an order limiting or terminating the deposition.

Any documents or other exhibits produced during the deposition are to be marked for identification and annexed to the deposition if any party requests it. Copies may be substituted for the originals if requested by the witness as long as the witness provides copies and the parties have an opportunity to compare the copies with the originals. The copies will thereafter serve as the originals. The court has the power to require the originals to be attached if there is reason for doing so.[46]

Of course, under Fed.R.Evid. 102, photographic, xerographic or electronic duplicates, "duplicate originals," are as admissible as the actual original item, for nearly all purposes. For reasons of economy, one or more of the parties may choose not to attend the deposition, but instead to serve written questions in a sealed envelope to the party taking the deposition. The party taking the deposition is required to transmit the questions to the officer conducting the deposition, who shall propound the questions to the witness and record the answers verbatim.[47] As a tactical matter, such an approach is ordinarily used only when the witness is willing to cooperate with the party submitting the questions so the answers may be prepared in advance.

A related procedure is to take the entire deposition by written questions. The procedures are set forth in Rule 31 and are usually used when the witness is distant but is willing to cooperate, or the matters upon which examination is to occur are routine, such as authenticating a document.

The parties may also agree, by a stipulation in writing or by a court order, that the deposition be taken by telephone or, under Rule 30(b)(7), other remote electronic means such as satellite television.[48] However, you should generally make use of a telephone deposition when you do not think it necessary to observe the witness's demeanor and the cost of attending the deposition is relatively high.

---

46. Fed.R.Civ.P. 30(f)(1).
47. Fed.R.Civ.P. 30(c).
48. Fed.R.Civ.P. 30(b)(7).

1.12.4 Stipulations.

The Federal Rules of Civil Procedure permit the parties to stipulate in writing that a deposition may be taken before any person, at any time or place, in any manner, and when so taken may be used like any other deposition.[49] As a practical matter, the parties, if on working terms, will stipulate to most matters concerning depositions rather than petition the court for some form of relief or protective order.

1.12.5 Post-deposition requirements.

Following the conclusion of the deposition, the deposition officer and the parties have several further obligations:

> 1. Under Rule 30(e), review, correction and signature must be requested by the witness or a party before completion of the deposition, or else they are waived. Once the request is made, and the transcript is available, the witness has thirty days to review the deposition. Under the pre-1993 version of the Federal Rules of Civil Procedure, the witness has the opportunity for review, correction and signature unless the parties and the witness waive that opportunity.[50]

> 2. The witness then has thirty days to make any changes in the form and substance of the deposition and to provide a statement of any reasons for the changes.[51] Such changes are not limited by the rule to errors in transcription made by the reporter; if the witness misheard the question, for example, she may change her answer (although, of course, the original answer remains in the original transcript, for whatever use is appropriately made of it at trial); indeed, if the questioning attorney misspoke, but the witness answered the intended (not the spoken) question, the witness may change the question, and that would actually make the transcript more accurate than any other change.

> 3. In jurisdictions following the pre-1993 version of the Federal Rules of Civil Procedure, the witness shall sign the deposition unless the parties have waived signing or the witness is ill, cannot be found, or refuses to sign. If the deposition is not signed within thirty days of it being given to the witness, the deposition officer shall sign it and include a statement of the reasons for the failure to sign. If the witness gives a reason for refusing to sign, this must be stated as well.[52]

---

49. Fed.R.Civ.P. 29.
50. Fed.R.Civ.P. 30(e).
51. *Ibid.* See § 15.1.
52. Fed.R.Civ.P. 30(e) (amended 1993).

4. The deposition officer shall certify that the witness was duly sworn by the officer and that the deposition is a true record of the witness's testimony.[53] Under Rule 30(e), the certificate should also state whether a witness or one of the parties requested the witness to review the deposition and shall attach any changes made by the witness to the questions or answers.

5. Unless otherwise ordered by the court, the deposition officer is to place the deposition in an envelope or package, seal the envelope or package, endorse the title of the action on it, mark it with "Deposition of (give name of witness)," and file it with the court.[54] Many courts by local court rule no longer require (or permit) the filing of discovery,[55] and Rule 30(f)(1) alternatively permits the officer to send the deposition to the attorney who arranged for the transcription or recording, normally the deposing attorney, who is then required to keep it safely.

6. Under Rule 30(f)(2), the officer shall retain a copy of the recording of a videotape or audiotape deposition or the notes of a stenographic deposition.

7. The party taking the deposition is to give prompt notice to all other parties of the filing of the deposition.[56]

8. The officer is to furnish copies of the deposition to any party requesting one upon payment of a reasonable charge therefor.[57]

---

53. Fed.R.Civ.P. 30(f)(1).
54. *Ibid.*
55. Fed.R.Civ.P. 5(d).
56. Fed.R.Civ.P. 30(f)(3).
57. Fed.R.Civ.P. 30(f)(2).

PART TWO:

TAKING DEPOSITIONS

Chapter Two

PURPOSES OF TAKING DEPOSITIONS

"Ignorance never settles a question."
— Disraeli

Each side in a litigation has a number of discovery devices available: interrogatories, document subpoenas, requests for admissions, requests for production, orders for physical and mental examinations, informal (non-judicial) investigations, and of course, depositions. Among these, depositions are the most effective device for learning the theories and approaches an opponent is entertaining. The opportunities provided by depositions—to follow up, to probe, and to challenge—account for their effectiveness and popularity.

Having decided that depositions are the best method of obtaining the particular information you are seeking, your next step is deciding the purposes for which you are taking the deposition. Broadly speaking, there are three overlapping reasons to take depositions: first, to gather information; second, to perpetuate testimony; and third, to facilitate settlement. While these purposes are not mutually exclusive, knowing the reasons or objectives for taking the deposition allows you to organize and phrase your questions in a way that maximizes your effectiveness.

2.1 GATHERING INFORMATION

The most common reason to take a deposition is to gather information. You want to know what is going on in the case, what are the facts, how the events occurred, what the other side knows, what the weaknesses are in your own case, where the flaws exist in the opponent's case, and so on. In short, the deposition is being taken for the purpose of discovery. Several different reasons exist for gathering information in a case, as will be discussed below.

2.1.1 Finding out what you don't know.

Typically you ask questions in a deposition to find out what you do not already know. The reason you ask questions is to expand your knowledge of the case. Why did the defendant collide with your party's car? What damages does the plaintiff claim to have suffered from alleged price-fixing activities? And so on. You ask questions of witnesses to discover the facts and positions in the case.

2.1.2 Confirming what you think you know.

Often, based on documents and what your clients and friendly witnesses have told you, you think you know what happened in a case. Even though you are confident of your knowledge, that does not mean that the other side's witnesses agree with the version of events your witnesses presented. A second purpose for taking depositions is to confirm what you think you know. If the opposing witnesses agree with your witnesses, then you can have greater confidence that this will be an undisputed area at trial; perhaps stipulations on those points will be possible. On the other hand, if the witnesses disagree, you will know this before trial when you still have an opportunity to marshal the proof in favor of your version of the facts, or to adjust your theories and themes to the new facts. The worst possible scenario is for you to find out at trial, when you can do little to meet the situation, that what you thought was undisputed is actually hotly contested. Depositions save you from this problem.

2.1.3 Testing out legal and factual theories.

At the discovery stage of a case each side will not only be trying to figure out what happened, but also will be attempting to develop a legal and factual theory for presenting the case to the court in the most persuasive light. Because it is the discovery phase of the case, the parties are exploring which theory will work best. Part of this exploration process is not only to determine an attractive legal theory, but also to determine whether the necessary facts exist to support the legal theory.

Your legal theory depends on the existence of certain key facts as well as a host of supporting ones. As part of the information-gathering aspect of discovery, you will seek to elicit facts which support your own legal theory and weaken your opponent's theory. Let's take a typical personal injury case where the plaintiff claims the defendant's negligence was the direct and proximate cause of the plaintiff's injuries resulting from the collision between the two sides' automobiles. The defendant, in turn, claims contributory negligence on the part of the plaintiff. The plaintiff's factual theory is that the defendant was speeding just prior to the accident, while the defendant claims the plaintiff ran a red light.

During discovery each side will not only seek admissions that support its own theory of the case, but will also try to find weaknesses and flaws in the opponent's theory. The plaintiff will try to gain whatever evidence it can of the defendant's speeding as well as gain admissions to weaken the defendant's claim of contributory negligence. The defendant will do the exact opposite. For instance, the plaintiff may have found out that the defendant was not looking at the speedometer at the time of the accident and had not looked at it for the last two blocks. Instead, the driver was looking at some roadside construction. From this information, the plaintiff has an admission that supports its case (failing to look at the speedometer), and has identified a weakness in the defendant's case (defendant cannot say whether the plaintiff ran the red light because he was looking at the construction). Other areas may not have proved to be so fruitful and now the plaintiff knows not to pursue these on cross-examination of the defendant at trial. It may turn out, after discovery is completed, that certain key facts do not exist to support the plaintiff's theory or to weaken the defendant's theory. If that is the case and no alternative theory remains viable, the plaintiff may have to dismiss the action or settle on the best terms possible.

One of the main information-gathering functions of depositions is to test factual theories. Each side is attempting to determine which theories will work and which should be abandoned, as well as how its opponent's theories can be weakened or destroyed.

2.1.4 Preparing for trial.

By using depositions to test legal and factual theories, you are also using them to prepare for trial. One of the cardinal rules of almost all cross-examination is never ask a question to which you do not know the answer. Depositions are where you find out the answer. If the answer during the deposition was favorable to your legal and factual theory, then it is a safe question to ask on cross-examination of the witness at trial. If the witness changes his answer at trial from what was given in the deposition, then you have the deposition available for impeachment. On the other hand, if the answer at the deposition was unfavorable, then you know the question is one that should not be asked at trial.

Another rule of cross-examination is to ask only questions that do not contain characterizations or subjective terms. For instance, most trial lawyers would not ask a question on cross-examination of the opposing party such as "Just before the accident were you going very fast?" (unless it can be followed up with questions showing how fast the opponent was going). The witness can honestly answer such a question with a "No" if he believes he was going fast, but not "very" fast, or does not believe he was going fast even though he was traveling well over the speed limit. But depositions are safe places to ask such questions. If the witness agrees with the characterization during the deposition, then you can safely ask the question during cross-examination. Even if the witness does not agree with the characterization during the deposition, you may obtain the underlying facts supporting the characterization so you can make the argument to the jury at the conclusion of the trial. Thus, at deposition you could ask, "Why don't you think you were going too fast?" and then press the witness for all of the bases for that position. Those bases may turn out to be illogical, or attackable, or patently incredible, and cross-examination at trial might then display the deposition facts.

In short, depositions are the time for you to try out possible lines of cross-examination. You can use those that are successful at trial, and drop those that are not. For this reason, many trial lawyers prepare their cross-examinations from the depositions in the case, and most of them at least start their preparation with the depositions, and then move to other useful materials and approaches, such as contemporaneous statements in documents, "803(18) learned treatises," and the witness's personal incredibility.

2.2 PRESERVING TESTIMONY

In addition to gathering information, you can use a deposition to preserve testimony. The reasons you might want to preserve testimony will be discussed, but you should note that while the goals of information gathering and preserving testimony overlap to some extent, they may also conflict. For example, as part of your preparation for trial, you are probably interested in fully exploring the strengths of your opponent's case so that you can better attack those strengths through your own witnesses. But, by exploring those strengths you are also preserving the testimony for use by your opponent if any of its witnesses should prove to be unavailable for trial. Generally, preservation (or *de bene esse*) depositions are noticed to preserve the testimony of one's own witnesses who may not be available for trial (due to age, travel, or illness, for example); if the other side's witnesses wind up unavailable, you might not have the benefit of deposition admissions, but you don't have the detriment of their entire direct testimony, either. As a practical matter, however, you will normally be deposing the significant witnesses for the other side, for discovery purposes, because you cannot risk having to face them at trial without having deposed them; as a result, the pretrial testimony will be preserved, good and bad, and the benefit of discovery usually outweighs the detriment of preservation.

2.2.1 Locking in testimony.

Let's face it, not all witnesses are as fully respectful of the truth as we might wish. In fact, some are out-and-out liars, while others, to be charitable, merely have memory problems. Depositions provide control over witnesses who deviate from their prior deposition testimony by providing a means of punishing them at trial through impeachment or by encouraging truthful recollection by using the deposition to refresh their memories. Depositions freeze the witness's story; the witness can deviate from it only at her peril.

2.2.2 Substitute for live testimony.

If a witness becomes "unavailable" for any reason—death, illness, being beyond the subpoena power of the court, forgetfulness, or by claiming a privilege—the Federal Rules of Civil Procedure[1] as well as Federal Rules of Evidence[2] permit you to use the witness's deposition testimony as a substitute for live testimony. Depositions become critically important when a witness is elderly, in danger of disappearing prior to the trial, lives a great distance from the court, or for any other reason is not likely to be able to testify at trial. In addition, a court will receive deposition testimony as substantive evidence when it is offered as an admission of a party opponent,[3] impeachment by a prior inconsistent statement,[4] or a prior consistent statement.[5] While often not as persuasive (or interesting) as live testimony, deposition testimony is usually better than no testimony at all.

2.2.3 Basis for temporary injunctive relief and motions.

Litigants frequently use depositions to support applications for preliminary injunctions as well as motions, primarily motions for summary judgment. Used in this way, depositions substitute for affidavits or declarations, particularly since you may find it impossible to obtain a signed and sworn statement from a hostile witness or affiliate of the opposing party.

---

1. Fed.R.Civ.P. 32(a)(3).
2. Fed.R.Evid. 804.
3. Fed.R.Evid. 801(d)(2); Fed.R.Civ.P. 32(a)(2).
4. Fed.R.Evid. 801(d)(1)(A); Fed.R.Civ.P. 32(a)(1).
5. Fed.R.Evid. 801(d)(1)(B).

2.3 FACILITATING SETTLEMENT

Depositions facilitate settlement in three ways: permitting evaluation of the witness and attorney, opening lines of communication, and punishing the witness.

2.3.1 Evaluating the witness and attorney.

Face-to-face confrontation in a deposition permits each side to evaluate the witness being deposed and make judgments about the credibility of the witness and how the judge or jury will perceive the testimony. When the witness comes across as especially believable or unbelievable, it affects the settlement value of the case. In addition, each side will also make judgments about the abilities of opposing counsel that will influence the amount at which a case will settle.

2.3.2 Opening lines of communication.

The deposition setting provides an opportunity for counsel to talk with each other. A deposition may be the first time the two sides have had the opportunity to talk seriously other than over the telephone. At depositions of the principals in the case, if serious settlement discussions do occur, the availability of the parties will sometimes facilitate a quick settlement.

2.3.3 Punishing the witness.

While not an ethically permissible basis for taking a deposition, a potential result of rigorous cross-examination during a deposition is that a party or key witness finds the whole experience so distasteful and unpleasant that settlement occurs on favorable terms for the other side. The witness or party may simply say that she is not going to go through the same experience again at trial and she may persuade or instruct counsel to settle. By the same token, a deposition may end up consuming so much of a party's or witness's time that the further demands of preparation for trial and the trial itself may not be an acceptable cost. Again, punishing the witness is not ethically permitted as the purpose for taking a deposition,[6] but it is frequently a by-product of a deposition taken for other, legitimate reasons.

As will be discussed later in this text, the objectives of a deposition will determine, to a large extent, how you approach the questioning of a witness. If you are primarily attempting to obtain admissions for a summary judgment motion, the way in which you phrase questions and the order in which you ask them is often completely different than if you are trying to find out exactly what a witness knows. Even if you have multiple objectives, you must still determine which are more important

---

6. Fed.R.Civ.P. 11.

for those situations when they come into conflict. For these reasons, you should think carefully in advance about the purposes for which you are taking a deposition.

Chapter Three

ADVANTAGES AND DISADVANTAGES OF DEPOSITIONS

"Pickaxe, shovel, spade, crowbar, hoe and barrow,
Better not invade, Yankees have the marrow."
— Samuel Woodworth

Depositions are the most powerful discovery device available to a litigator, but certainly not the only one. Just as a shovel is sometimes preferable to a hoe, other types of discovery may be better suited than a deposition for acquiring the necessary information in a particular case. Depositions are excellent for obtaining some types of information and less effective for other types. Before deciding to take a deposition, you must decide whether depositions are the best discovery device considering the case, the type of witness, and the type of information being sought. To make this decision, you must understand the advantages and disadvantages of depositions.

3.1 ADVANTAGES

There are many advantages to using depositions as a discovery device.

3.1.1 Unfiltered information.

Depositions allow you to hear the opposing party's story in his own words, rather than filtered through the editorial judgment of opposing counsel. Since you are not allowed to talk with the opposing party without opposing counsel's permission, information is only available through depositions, interrogatories, and requests for production and for admission. With interrogatories, opposing counsel usually obtains the necessary information from the client and edits the answers to provide the least amount of useable information that is still responsive to the question. The information provided by the opposing party to his attorney and what is actually put down on the paper in response to the interrogatory often have scant resemblance to each other.

On the other hand, the witness himself answers at a deposition. The opposing counsel may influence the answer by careful preparation of the witness and by advice during the deposition, but to a large extent what you hear are the witness's own answers, minimally edited by opposing counsel. The opportunity to actually talk to the opposing party is remarkable, and may allow the questioning attorney to ask questions like, "What did you think of our last settlement offer?" and "What are you prepared to do to get us to drop this case?" which are questions that would never draw responsive answers if asked through interrogatories.

3.1.2 Opinions, mental impressions, and subjective information.

Because the witness answers your questions directly and the answers are not filtered through opposing counsel, your questions can elicit the witness's opinions, mental impressions, and subjective information. Contrast this with interrogatories, the other major discovery device, where the answer is edited by a lawyer and you cannot easily ask follow-up questions. For example, consider a typical interrogatory and the answer that might be given:

> Interrogatory No. 22: Please describe in detail how the accident occurred.

> Answer: The defendant's automobile collided with the plaintiff's automobile.

Such an interrogatory will almost always draw garbage as a response. Opposing counsel will often edit any response to provide as little useful information as possible. Now contrast this with a deposition:

Q. Tell me how the accident occurred.

A. Well, the other car hit me.

Q. Okay, let's back up. Where were you when you first saw the plaintiff's car?

A. I was east of the intersection of Kirby and Mattis.

Q. How far east?

A. About fifty feet.

Q. What lane were you in?

A. The curb lane.

Q. How fast were you going?

A. About fifteen miles per hour.

Q. Why were you going so slow?

A. The light looked like it was about to change.

And so on.

Depositions are the only useful discovery device for obtaining spontaneous or interpretive information such as how an incident occurred, the details of a conversation, or the recollection of an eyewitness. Such matters as mental impressions, the details of emotional reactions, or anything to do with thought processes are best obtained through depositions, which provide you the ability to probe the witness's knowledge and memory.

3.1.3 Ability to follow up.

When an answer to an interrogatory is evasive or does not provide the requested information, you have only the choices of bringing a motion to compel or accepting the response given. Even worse, you must compose all the questions in advance. If the answers reveal new information that you want to know more about, you may be out of luck. It is difficult to ask a follow-up interrogatory, since it frequently draws objections. In any event, any answers are at least thirty days away.

Depositions, on the other hand, allow you to follow up a question with other questions until you are satisfied that you have thoroughly exhausted an area. For instance, evasive or non-responsive answers can be quickly attacked forcing the witness to answer:

Q. Where were you when this conversation was going on?

A. Do you mean at the beginning or end?

Q. Let's take both. Where were you at the beginning?

A. I was over by the door.

Q. Where were you at the end?

A. I was still by the door.

Q. Did you ever move away from the door during the conversation?

A. No.

Q. Who started the conversation?

A. It just started.

Q. Well, who said the first word?

A. I did.

Your ability to follow up is also important when a line of questions suggests new leads. Perhaps something about the way the witness answered or looked indicates there is more than the answer alone suggests. For instance, if a witness pauses unusually long or starts the answer in a hesitating way, this often hints that you should ask follow-up questions. Sometimes the phrasing of the answer will suggest a lead:

Q. Did she say anything about the contract?

A. Not at that time.

Q. Was something said about the contract at another time?

Interrogatories rarely provide such hints and, when they do, follow-up is difficult.

3.1.4 Spontaneous answers.

Depositions allow you to get a witness's unrehearsed response without allowing a long period of time to reflect on the answer. Contrast this again with interrogatories, where a party will have a minimum of thirty days to think about how to phrase the answer in its least damaging form. Of course, witnesses can rehearse answers to expected questions in a deposition, but your ability to attack a subject from several different angles means the witness will eventually have to answer spontaneously.

3.1.5 Fast moving.

Depositions can be scheduled and taken upon "reasonable notice" to the other side.[1] By contrast, interrogatories, the next most commonly used discovery device, need not be answered until thirty days after their service (prior to the 1993 amendments, the defendant had up to forty-five days after service of the summons and complaint in which to answer).[2] When you need information quickly, depositions are the method to use.

Speed is particularly important when you want to find out a witness's story—while memories are fresh and have not started to fade. For example, in a personal injury case you may want to find out what the witnesses recall about the accident early in the case when recollection is better, rather than waiting until shortly before trial, several months or years later. Similarly, when witnesses are likely to die or disappear, depositions obtain their stories while they are still available.

The fast moving nature of depositions also becomes important when you are bumping up against discovery deadlines or a trial date. The

---

1. Fed.R.Civ.P. 30(b)(1) provides only for reasonable notice. What is reasonable will vary from jurisdiction to jurisdiction and from case to case, see § 4.1, but is usually less than the thirty days provided for answering interrogatories. Under Rule 26(d) a party cannot seek discovery from any source until after the planning conference required by Rule 26(f) unless authorized by stipulation or court order, or special circumstances exist. See § 5.1. Under the pre-1993 version of the Federal Rules of Civil Procedure, the plaintiff cannot notice a deposition within thirty days of the service of the summons and complaint unless the defendant first notices one or otherwise seeks discovery or special circumstances exist. Fed.R.Civ.P. 30(a) (amended 1993).

2. Fed.R.Civ.P. 33(a) (amended 1993).

ability to schedule a deposition quickly may allow you to get a witness's story in time for you to prepare for trial. Of course, you can use informal investigation even prior to filing an action, but when quick action is needed, there is nothing faster than a deposition.

3.1.6 Face-to-face confrontation.

Depositions are the only discovery device that allow you to actually meet the opposing party and attorney, and those witnesses who refuse to talk with you on an informal basis. Face-to-face confrontation has several advantages. First, it forces the witness to tell his story while under oath and while facing the opposing party or at least the party's attorney. A party theoretically is also under oath when it answers interrogatories, but, in reality, the oath is frequently glossed over at the time of signing. On the other hand, the circumstances of the swearing and questioning at a deposition often will impress on a witness the importance of truthfulness.

Second, face-to-face confrontation allows you to evaluate the impression the witness will make at trial. Does the witness appear shifty and disingenuous or honest and forthright? Will a jury sympathize with the witness or reject the witness because of his arrogance? You can answer these questions and more, at least preliminarily, by putting the witness through the rigors of a deposition.

Third, depositions allow you to evaluate the abilities and behavior of opposing counsel. You have a chance to see whether the attorney is passive or aggressive, prepared or unprepared, articulate or bumbling, and so on. After the deposition, you are better able to gauge what you are up against.

Finally, depositions provide you with an opportunity to discuss settlement when the opposing attorney and client are together. Many cases are settled following a deposition because it is the first time the attorneys have met face to face and had the chance to evaluate the effectiveness of key witnesses.

3.1.7 Information from uncooperative witnesses.

Outside of court or a deposition, nothing requires a witness to answer a lawyer's or an investigator's questions. In fact, a witness can refuse to say anything to either side. When a witness does refuse to cooperate, the only discovery device available to get that person's story is a deposition. Finally, only depositions and subpoenas for the production of books, documents, and things can be used with non-party witnesses;[3] all of the other discovery devices—interrogatories, requests for admissions, notices to produce—can be used only against a party.

---

3. Fed.R.Civ.P. 45.

3.1.8 Generate fewer objections.

Depositions can be contentious, with the attorneys arguing with each other and seeking the assistance of the magistrate to referee their disputes. Nonetheless, compared to interrogatories, depositions generate fewer objections, and when they are made they do not stop the deposition. The simple fact is that answering interrogatories is one of the most frustrating, boring, and irritating tasks a lawyer is called upon to perform. As a result, it is often much easier to object to an interrogatory than to answer it, especially since you are so angry about having to answer the interrogatory anyway. An objection avoids the need to answer to the extent the interrogatory is objectionable.[4] The attorney posing the interrogatory must then bring a motion to compel.

On the other hand, it is comparatively easy to sit and listen to your witness answer questions. You may be bored, but you rarely have the intense desire to engage in the sophistry that is generated by interrogatories. Even if defending counsel objects, the objections do not excuse the witness from answering. As a result, depositions usually yield far more information than any other type of discovery.

3.2 DISADVANTAGES

Despite the many advantages of depositions as a discovery device, several drawbacks must also be considered.

3.2.1 Failures of memory or lack of knowledge.

Sometimes witnesses cannot remember or never knew the facts about which you are asking. For instance, you ask the president of the Widget Corporation how many widgets were sold in 1998, and the truthful answer may be, "I don't recall." While frustrating, there is not much you can do other than try to refresh the witness's memory in some way. You have no right to ask the witness to look up the information, although often a polite request to do so may be complied with. Even more frustrating is to ask the witness the same question and have the witness tell you that she doesn't know, but some other witness does.

Quite simply, if a witness honestly does not know the answer to a question or cannot remember the answer and nothing refreshes the witness's memory, there is nothing you can do. And when asking for numerical-type information, such as financial data, "I don't remember" is frequently the answer you will receive.

To a certain extent, you can avoid these problems by some advance preparation. The documents containing the necessary information or

---

4. Fed.R.Civ.P. 33(b)(1).

those which can be used to refresh memory may be the subject of a notice to produce or subpoena in advance of the deposition. Another alternative is to schedule a Rule 30(b)(6) deposition, requiring the corporation or other group to designate a witness who is prepared to testify about particular matters.[5]

Often the best approach is to not take a deposition at all, but to send interrogatories requesting the desired information (assuming the information is being sought from an opposing party). Interrogatories search both the files and the memory of a party, and the collective memory of an institutional party, by requiring the party to take all reasonable steps to provide the requested information. "I don't remember" will not suffice if the party can find the information with some reasonable amount of work. Files must be checked, records examined, and other employees asked to provide the necessary information. A deposition cannot do this (unless it is a 30(b)(6) deposition).

3.2.2   Experience with cross-examination.

All but experienced witnesses are anxious about cross-examination. They may become flustered, confused, or nervous. Obviously, this may cause the jury not to believe them. But all of us improve with practice and that is what you are allowing a witness to do—improve with practice—by putting her through the rigors of cross-examination during a deposition. When trial comes, the witness will know what to expect from you and will be better prepared.

3.2.3   Helps to prepare opponent's case.

All attorneys, at one time or another, have had the experience of taking a deposition of a witness and watching the defending attorney scribble down every answer the witness gives. The reason for this may be thoroughness, but often the attorney has not previously interviewed the witness and the answers are as new to her as to you. While you are learning about the case and preparing for trial, so is your opponent.

If you are against a more conscientious opponent who has prepared the witness, you still have forced that attorney to prepare her case better by carefully reviewing the facts and rehearsing the answers. Absent the deposition, your opponent may not have done this work or have done it so close to trial that it would be too late to patch any holes in the testimony.

---

5. See § 1.2.

3.2.4 Expense.

Depositions cost money. Not only must you pay the cost of the court reporter attending the deposition, but when a transcript is desired, as is usually the case, you must pay another charge for this as well. Finally, the time you consume in preparing and taking the deposition must be accounted for, either against the contingent fee or as billable hours. Interrogatories and informal investigation also take time, but out-of-pocket expenses are usually less.

Depositions become even more expensive when travel is involved. You must generally depose non-party witnesses and defendants close to their residence or place of business or employment. Plaintiffs are usually deposed where the litigation is pending or at their residence or place of business or employment.[6] When litigation is national in scope, the travel costs can be prohibitively high. Interrogatories, subpoenas, and requests for admissions, on the other hand, can be sent by mail.

3.2.5 Reveal theories.

The questions you ask at a deposition reveal your legal and factual theories. For instance, if the defendant's questions in a breach of contract case concern the plaintiff's efforts at mitigation, the plaintiff's attorney will be able to guess that failure to mitigate will be one of the defenses raised, and will prepare the plaintiff's case accordingly. Perhaps revealing theories is not a concern because everyone involved knows from the pleadings and the facts of the case what will be raised, but if you are trying to conceal your theory until trial, then you risk revealing your intentions by taking depositions.

3.2.6 Cannot obtain legal theories.

If the plaintiff's attorney asks the defendant in a deposition if she is claiming the plaintiff was contributorily negligent, the defendant's attorney should object that the question calls for a legal opinion. Although the witness should still answer subject to the objection the defendant's attorney will be right. In contrast, while interrogatories cannot ask purely legal questions, they can properly ask for a party's contentions ("Are you contending that the plaintiff failed to mitigate its damages? If so, please state all facts on which you base this contention.").[7]

---

6. See § 1.7.
7. Fed.R.Civ.P. 33(c).

Chapter Four

PLANNING AND SCHEDULING DEPOSITIONS

"The best laid schemes o' mice and men
Gang aft a-gley. . . ."
— Robert Burns

Effective discovery requires planning and coordination. In particular, depositions can be combined with other methods of discovery and with each other. Carefully planned discovery is essential to conducting successful litigation and requires thought about what information is needed to prepare a case for trial or settlement and how best to obtain that information.

4.1 THE DISCOVERY PLAN

The 1993 amendments to the Federal Rules of Civil Procedure have radically transformed how discovery is conducted in those districts that have not opted out of portions of their provisions. One of the most important changes is the meeting between counsel to plan discovery in the case. Amended Rule 26(f) requires all parties to meet, except when ordered otherwise, to draft a discovery plan giving the parties' views and proposals concerning:

1. What changes should be made in the timing, form, or requirements under the mandatory disclosures portion of the rules,[1] including a statements to when the mandatory disclosures were or will be made;

2. The subjects on which discovery may be needed, when discovery should be completed, and whether the parties should conduct discovery in phases or be limited to particular issues;

3. What changes should be made to the limitations imposed by the amended Rules on the number of depositions and interrogatories and whether additional limitations should be imposed; and

4. Whether the courts should enter any protective orders[2] or other orders affecting scheduling and discovery.[3]

---

1. See § 4.2.1.
2. Fed.R.Civ.P. 26(c).
3. Fed.R.Civ.P. 16(b) and (c).

Finally, in the planning meeting the parties must also discuss the "nature and basis of their claims and defenses and the possibilities for a prompt settlement or resolution of the case,"[4] and how to proceed with the mandatory disclosures under amended Rule 26(a)(1).

The parties must submit the results of the planning meeting to the court, which will use it in issuing a scheduling order under amended Rule 16(b) unless the case is of a type exempted under local rules. The scheduling order will set time limits for joining other parties and amending the pleadings, filing motions, and completing discovery. In addition, the scheduling order may modify the times for the mandatory disclosures and supplementing discovery; modify the limits on the extent of discovery; set the dates for any conferences before trial, the final pretrial conference, and the trial date; and make any other appropriate orders.

Depending on the type of case and the results of the planning meeting, some scheduling orders contain detailed timetables for conducting discovery while others do no more than set a cut-off date for when discovery must be completed. Many of the suggestions made in the following pages concerning the sequence and scheduling of discovery may be reflected in the scheduling order or may be left to the parties to develop as the litigation progresses.

The planning meeting should be held as soon as is practicable, but no later than fourteen days before a scheduling conference is held or a scheduling order is due. The court may hold a scheduling conference whenever it chooses, but the scheduling order is to be issued no later than ninety days after the defendant appears or 120 days after the complaint has been served on a defendant. In some federal courts, the scheduling order is issued when the complaint is filed.

The requirement of a planning meeting in amended Rule 26(f) provides you with the opportunity to thoughtfully explore the discovery strategy to be followed in a case. First, check local rules to determine whether the court in which you are litigating has opted out of any of the provisions of the amended Rules. Second, before the meeting you must think through in great detail what discovery you need in the case. Some of the issues you should consider are:

- How many depositions you need;
- What witnesses you should depose;
- In what order should you depose the witnesses;
- If there should be a limit on the length of the depositions;

---

4. Fed.R.Civ.P. 26(f).

- If any special rules are necessary for the taking of the depositions such as excluding other witnesses from the deposition room;
- If the time limits and content of the mandatory disclosures should be modified;
- If other discovery devices such as interrogatories should be used before depositions are taken;
- If the limitation on the number of interrogatories should be waived;
- If there are any special orders needed for the taking of discovery such as a protective order concerning trade secrets;
- If discovery should proceed in phases, either by witnesses or topics, to avoid duplicative discovery and to set the stage for any summary judgment motions;
- If counsel should meet periodically to review and make suggestions for modifying the scheduling order.

The above is merely a suggested list of topics that you should think about before the planning meeting. A particular case may have a longer or shorter list of concerns. Even though several of these topics may concern you, a desire for flexibility in conducting discovery or worries you have about revealing litigation strategy may prevent you from proposing them as part of the discovery plan. This, however, in no way lessens your need to think about them. Effective planning requires that you consider these issues at some point during the course of the case; amended Rule 26(f) merely requires that you do so early in the litigation.

4.2 COORDINATING DEPOSITIONS WITH OTHER DISCOVERY

The first step in coordinating a deposition schedule with other discovery is deciding what information you need to successfully conduct depositions. For example, assume a plaintiff is claiming lost profits as a result of a defendant's failure to purchase the number of signs required under a purchase agreement. You represent the defendant. Based on information from your client, you know that the plaintiff is a small manufacturer of electronic signs. The contract was for the sale of a large quantity of a particular type of electronic sign manufactured by the plaintiff. The plaintiff purchases most of the component parts of the signs from various vendors, which it then assembles into the finished product. The plaintiff's main contribution to the product is the assembly. The plaintiff is a small corporation with a president, a purchasing agent, a bookkeeper/accountant, and a plant foreman.

At this point you know one key defense is to attack the plaintiff's calculation of lost profits, and to prepare for this you intend to take whatever depositions are necessary. What information do you need before taking depositions? A short, but incomplete list might include:

- A list of the vendors of the parts used in manufacturing the signs
- The prices and terms for the purchase of the parts
- Any calculations by the plaintiff of costs and profits for the manufacturing of the signs
- Any accounting records concerning manufacturing expenses
- The name of the employee who decided what parts to purchase

With thought, you could add many more items to this list, but these few illustrate the point.

Once the information needed has been identified, the next question is how to go about getting it. The best answer to that question is to look at the different discovery devices available for use.

4.2.1 Mandatory Disclosures

Absent a stipulation, court order, local rule directing otherwise or opting out from this part of the amendments, parties litigating in jurisdictions that have adopted the 1993 amendments to the Federal Rules of Civil Procedure[5] must disclose, without awaiting a formal discovery request, certain basic information about the case. Specifically, each party shall provide to all other parties in the case:

1. The name and, if known, the address and telephone number of each individual likely to have discoverable information relevant to disputed facts alleged with particularity in the pleadings, identifying the subjects of the information;

2. A copy of, or a description by category and location, of all documents, data compilations, and tangible things in the possession, custody, or control of the party that are relevant to disputed facts alleged with particularity in the pleadings;

3. A computation of any category of damages claimed by the disclosing party, making available for inspection and copying all non-privileged material upon which the computation is based, including materials bearing on the nature and extent of any claimed injuries; and

4. For inspection and copying any insurance agreement that may be available to satisfy all or part of any judgment which may be entered in the action or to indemnify or reimburse for payments made to satisfy the judgment.

---

5. Fed.R.Civ.P. 26(a)(1).

These disclosures are to be made in writing at the initial meeting of the parties under amended Rule 26(f) to discuss the discovery plan for the case, or within ten days after the meeting, unless otherwise stipulated or directed by the court.[6]

The triggering requirement for several of the mandatory disclosures is pleading alleged facts with particularity. Alleging potentially disputed matters with particularity in the complaint or answer can go a long way to assist with discovery. Also, instead of having to send out interrogatories seeking the identity of potential witnesses, to find out whether insurance coverage exists or to seek information about damages computation, parties must now provide this information automatically. Similarly, you may no longer need to request key documents in a case. In many cases you may be able to dispense entirely with interrogatories and requests for production and proceed directly with depositions. But you can only do this if the facts about which you are seeking information have been alleged with particularity in the complaint or answer.

Aggressive counsel may interpret this mandate as requiring only the disclosure of witnesses who have specific information directly demonstrating or disproving particular disputed factual allegations. For example, counsel to bank directors who deny they negligently approved commercial real estate development loans without reviewing underlying appraisals may identify the corporate secretary whose minutes reflect that the board gave careful consideration to the loan. They may not identify the security guard whose records demonstrate that most members of the board departed within fifteen minutes of their arrival. You should expect that witnesses who have information from which reasonable inferences could be drawn regarding disputed facts will be overlooked in the initial disclosures. Therefore, while perhaps accelerating discovery, the mandatory disclosures do not relieve you of the fundamental burden of developing your own proof.

4.2.2 Interrogatories.

Imagine the deposition of the plaintiff's purchasing agent and what could happen:

COUNSEL FOR DEFENDANT:

Q. Now sir, please tell me the name of all vendors from whom the plaintiff purchases parts for use in manufacturing the electronic signs which are the subject of this action.

---

6. See Fed.R.Civ.P. 26(a).

A. Well, let's see. We purchase most of the circuit boards from Zenith, but several of the more specialized ones come from JVC. The sign casings come from a small firm in town, Acucom, and we get some parts from jobbers.

Q. Any other vendors?

A. Oh, sure. We use over thirty vendors, but I know I can't remember them all right now.

Q. Do you have a list of the various vendors?

A. Yes, back at the office.

Q. Counsel, I suggest that you provide me with the list and we finish as much as we can today and then continue the deposition tomorrow after I have a chance to review the list.

COUNSEL FOR PLAINTIFF:

Give me a request in writing and I will take it under advisement. Quite frankly, I see no need to continue this deposition and cause further inconvenience and expense for my client. If you wanted a list of our vendors you knew how to get it without waiting until the middle of this deposition. I will tell you now that I will resist any efforts to resume this deposition at a later time.

The defendant's lawyer prior to this deposition could have avoided all of these problems if before the deposition he had sent the plaintiff a set of interrogatories asking for the names of all vendors supplying parts for the signs. Of course, the interrogatories could also ask for any other information that would be helpful in conducting the deposition such as a description of the parts, the purchase price, quantities, and so on.

Interrogatories are one of the most useful deposition preparation tools because through them, you can obtain information in advance. In factually complex cases, the first wave of discovery routinely consists of interrogatories sent soon after the litigation commences, with the answers to be used, in part, to help prepare for the later depositions. The advantages of using interrogatories in preparing for depositions are several:

Interrogatories can be used to identify factual data and information that a witness is not likely to recall at deposition. As illustrated above, if a witness cannot remember the correct answer to a question there is little the lawyer taking the deposition can do except attempt to refresh the witness's memory. If, however, you have obtained such information by sending interrogatories before the deposition, you can question the witness without concern about memory failures. When you intend to question a deposition witness about objective information in the hands of the opposing party, such as data, calculations, lists, or other information that the witness will not likely recall easily, obtain this information through interrogatories before the deposition.

Interrogatories can help identify potential deposition witnesses and documents. Interrogatories frequently ask about all witnesses who have knowledge of the facts—who attended an event or meeting, participated in a transaction, and so on. Similarly, interrogatories often ask a party to identify all documents referring to a particular event or resulting from a transaction. The purpose of these types of interrogatories is, among other things, to identify potential deposition witnesses and documents which you will ask the opponent to produce. While you can and should ask these same questions at the depositions of key witnesses as a method of confirming the accuracy of the interrogatory answers, these witnesses many times do not have comprehensive knowledge of other witnesses and documents. For instance, the plaintiff's president in our example may know others who attended the meetings that she attended concerning parts orders, but she may not know who attended other meetings when she was not present. Similarly, the defendant in a personal injury case may be unaware of those witnesses to the accident who were later located by his lawyer or a private investigator. The advantage of interrogatories over depositions in identifying witnesses and documents is that the opposing party cannot rely solely on their current memory of facts. Instead, the party answering the interrogatory must make reasonable inquiry of all of its employees and agents and conduct a reasonable search of all records.[7] Remember, however, that if the court has adopted the 1993 amendments to the Federal Rules of Civil Procedure, the mandatory disclosures of amended Rule 26(a) include the names, addresses, and telephone numbers of all individuals likely to have discoverable information relevant to disputed facts alleged with particularity.

Interrogatories can identify who in a company or organization has knowledge about a topic. Imagine again the deposition of the plaintiff's purchasing agent in our breach of contract case. One of the facts you, representing the defendant, wish to know is the name of the person who decided what parts were to be purchased for manufacturing the signs. An obvious method of obtaining this information is for you to ask about it during the purchasing agent's deposition. The response might be something like "I am not sure, but I think it was our president." When you later take the president's

---

7. *Miller v. Doctor's General Hospital*, 76 F.R.D. 136 (D.Okla. 1977); 8 C. Wright & A. Miller, *Civil Procedure* § 2177, n. 22 (West 1994).

deposition, her answer is, "No, it wasn't me. I'm pretty sure it was an outside designer." And so goes the game at increasing expense and inconvenience. Sending a simple interrogatory before the first deposition asking who made the decision about what parts to purchase, would avoid this difficulty and greatly facilitate later discovery.

Of course, you can use a Rule 30(b)(6) deposition[8] to accomplish the same objective by asking the plaintiff to designate, for the deposition, a person who is prepared to testify about who decided on what parts to purchase. But, conducting a deposition for this purpose alone would be more expensive than posing an interrogatory on the same subject. When, however, the corporation or organization having this information is a non-party, a deposition is the only discovery method available.

While interrogatories are generally useful in preparing for depositions, drawbacks do exist. First, interrogatories may alert your opponent to the areas on which you will be questioning in a later deposition. As a result, at the later deposition you will be interrogating a better prepared witness. Interrogatories submitted pursuant to Rule 33 asking about a party's opinions and contentions are particularly troublesome because of their tendency to inform opponents of possible lines of defense to be taken at later depositions.

Using interrogatories may also delay you from taking depositions, thereby allowing your opponent to gain the initiative. Under the amended rules, interrogatories cannot be sent until after the planning meeting required by Rule 26(f) unless by stipulation, authorization under the local rules, or leave of court.[9] In those jurisdictions that have not adopted the amended rules, a plaintiff may serve a defendant interrogatories along with a summons and complaint in an action, but the defendant will have up to forty-five days in which to respond.[10] The defendant may serve interrogatories on the plaintiff at any time after the commencement of the action but the plaintiff will have thirty days in which to answer. Courts often grant extensions of time for answering interrogatories, particularly early in an action, thereby further delaying the discovery process. If one side delays taking depositions until interrogatories have been answered, the other side will often gain a valuable psychological momentum by proceeding with its own depositions. Where speed and initiative are important you may well forgo interrogatories until a later stage of the litigation and commence taking depositions at the earliest possible moment.

---

8. Fed.R.Civ.P. 30(b)(6). See § 5.1.2.
9. Fed.R.Civ.P. 26(d) and 33(a) (amended 1993).
10. Fed.R.Civ.P. 33(a).

Amended Rule 33(a) limits the number of interrogatories, including subparts, to twenty-five unless modified by a court order or stipulation. Local court rules, which under amended Rule 26(b)(2) override the limitations of amended Rule 33(a), may have higher or lower limits. In addition, absent special considerations, many courts permit you to serve only one set of interrogatories on an opponent. As a result, you may want to defer asking any interrogatories until after all or a majority of the depositions have been taken so that the interrogatories can be used to tie up any loose ends.

Like all else in litigation, no absolute rules apply to coordinating depositions with interrogatories. You must consider and decide each situation individually regarding whether you need any information before taking depositions. If so, the next question will be whether interrogatories are the best method of obtaining that information.

4.2.3 Document requests.

Lawyers frequently use depositions to question witnesses about documents. When documents are in the hands of an uncooperative non-party, taking a deposition in conjunction with a subpoena *duces tecum* was once the only method of forcing pretrial production of the documents. Now, under Rule 45(a), documents may be subpoenaed from a non-party without a deposition.[11] For a party, the Federal Rules of Civil Procedure seem to suggest that the only permissible method of obtaining documents is by a notice to produce,[12] but as a practical matter many party-witnesses respond to a subpoena *duces tecum* without objection. The advantage of using a subpoena *duces tecum* is the shorter response time provided under Rule 45 than under Rule 34.

When you can do so without unduly delaying the taking of the deposition, you should obtain documents in advance rather than having them produced at the deposition. Advance production allows you time to study the documents, check with other sources about information contained in the documents, and more carefully formulate your questions for the deposition. Producing documents at the deposition causes delays while you study the documents and creates the risk that you may not recognize a potential area of questioning until after the deposition has concluded. Since an opponent has thirty days in which to respond to a notice to produce, document production has to occur at an early stage of the litigation if it is not to delay depositions.

When taking the deposition of a non-party witness, it never hurts for you to call the witness and ask them to produce documents

---

11. Fed.R.Civ.P. 45(a).
12. Fed.R.Civ.P. 30(b)(5).

voluntarily in advance of the deposition. If you explain that this will help shorten the deposition, such a tactic is often successful.

4.2.4 Requests for admissions.

Requests for admissions, if admitted, may help to eliminate the need to prove essential facts and may reduce discovery costs by rendering unnecessary those depositions you would otherwise need to establish the disputed fact. Requests for admissions are particularly useful to authenticate documents in the hands of non-parties of whom you would otherwise have to take a deposition to obtain the necessary proof. For instance, in a personal injury case you may have copies of the medical records but in order to authenticate them, you must either depose the hospital records custodian or call her as a witness at trial. If you ask the opposing party to admit the record's authenticity, you can avoid the need for the deposition or, if still necessary, you may be able to impose its cost on the party.[13]

The drawback of requests for admission is that they are time consuming. The opposing party has thirty days in which to respond, and courts readily grant extensions of time if the requests are made early in the litigation.

Also, before expending the time to draft requests for admissions, it makes sense for you to call the opposing counsel to see if a stipulation to the same topics is agreeable. A telephone call is often better received than a discovery request and more likely to achieve what you are seeking.

4.3 COORDINATING DEPOSITIONS WITH EACH OTHER

Deciding on the order in which you should take depositions depends on the facts of the particular case. However, we can identify the factors that you should consider when making this decision.

Is it necessary to obtain evidence from one witness before deposing another witness? Often litigation is similar to building a house; you must lay the foundation before you can erect the walls. Similarly, in litigation you may need to obtain evidence from one witness as a prerequisite to questioning another witness. For instance, the defendant in a personal injury case who is challenging the extent and permanency of the plaintiff's injuries will probably want to depose the plaintiff about the injuries before deposing the plaintiff's medical expert about the prognosis for the plaintiff's recovery. Likewise, in our

---

13. Fed.R.Civ.P. 37(c).

breach-of-contract action, the defendant would generally want to find out from the purchasing agent what parts were necessary to manufacture the signs before questioning the bookkeeper/accountant about the manufacturing cost.

Should key or minor witnesses be deposed first? Sometimes you and your client will be unfamiliar with the facts giving rise to the dispute, the structure of the industry, or the general background to the lawsuit. For instance, in the breach-of-contract action neither you nor the defendant may know much about the sign market or the plaintiff's opportunities to mitigate damages. When you need background information, often you should obtain facts from minor witnesses before proceeding to interrogate key witnesses.

When background information is not necessary or is already available, the general rule is that you should depose key witnesses before minor ones. The reason for this general rule is that deposing the key witnesses first affords less time for them to prepare to testify. Also, as a matter of human nature, if the key witnesses have an opportunity to review the deposition testimony of minor witnesses or to familiarize themselves with what the minor witnesses are going to say, the key witnesses are more likely to adapt their own stories to those of the minor witnesses. Minor witnesses, because they usually have less at stake, are less likely to conform their stories to the expected stories of the key witnesses. However, where a case has more than one key witness with similar knowledge, it may be wise to leave the deposition of one of them until close to the end of discovery. In that way, if after completing discovery of the other witnesses you still have some unanswered questions, you have a key actor available to question.

When should expert witnesses be deposed? Under amended Rule 26(a)(2), most expert witnesses must provide a report of their opinions and the reasons for them as well as any exhibits in support of the opinions or summarizing them. The report must also contain the expert's qualifications, compensation, and previous experience testifying. You cannot depose an expert, nor would you want to, until after they provide this report.[14] The report will provide you important assistance in preparing for the expert's deposition. Even with those experts who need not provide a report or in those jurisdictions where it is not required, it makes sense to wait until the end of discovery so that the expert will have fully developed the opinions to be given at trial and until you have had a chance to fully understand the facts in the case.

---

14. Fed.R.Civ.P. 26(b)(4)(A).

4.4 SCHEDULING THE DEPOSITION

Should you schedule depositions early or late in the discovery process? Again, this depends on the facts of the case. Early scheduling of depositions permits you to: freeze the witnesses' stories before memories fade more than they already have; put pressure on your opponent by requiring them to go on the defensive; discover gaps in your case while there is still time to rectify them; and develop evidence early in the litigation that may allow you to obtain a summary judgment or a quick settlement of the case.

On the other hand, if your opponent's key witnesses are likely to disappear or become unavailable for trial, the deposition may only serve to preserve harmful testimony which will benefit your opponent. Early depositions may also force your opponent to be better prepared for trial than if you had held off until the last minute when it is too late to correct any defects in your opponent's case that were revealed by the deposition. Finally, the deposition of the plaintiff's medical expert in a personal injury case often is delayed until as late in the litigation as possible to take advantage of any improvement in the plaintiff's injuries.

Amended Rule 30(a)(2)(A) limits the number of depositions, absent a stipulation, court order, or local rule to the contrary, to ten per side. Caution dictates you not use up all ten early in the discovery process in the event you discover additional important witnesses later in the case. Hold at least one or two in reserve.

4.5 DURATION AND INTERVALS

The obvious answer to the question of how long a deposition should last is: as long as necessary. Depositions have no magic length;[15] some last for only a few minutes, while others last days or weeks. But, depositions are an expensive form of discovery and the longer they last the greater the burden on your client. When, however, the testimony is complex or comes as a surprise, it sometimes makes sense to slow down the process. When a deposition continues overnight or on to a later date, you have an additional opportunity to analyze what the witness has said. Be aware that the longer the break, the more likely it is that the witness will also have time to reflect on the previous testimony and to correct any errors or misstatements.

The interval between depositions is often as much a function of the lawyers' and witnesses' schedules as it is of strategic planning. Where

---

15. Except that length may be limited by stipulation, local rule, or court order. See Fed.R.Civ.P. 26(b)(2), 29 and 30(d)(2).

you have the freedom to control the schedule, the time between depositions should be sufficiently long to permit review of the prior deposition testimony and to prepare for the next deposition, but no longer. The longer the break, the more complete and thorough your opponent's preparation of the next witness will likely be. Not only will the opposing counsel have briefed the witness about what has occurred in the prior deposition, but the witness may even have read the prior deposition transcripts. Short intervals—even taking several depositions on the same day—are more likely to result in unrehearsed testimony and pressure the opposing attorney.

One problem that occurs time and again is lack of agreement with the notice statement of the duration of the deposition. Typically, the notice for the deposition will recite, "To appear at 9:30 A.M. on the 24th day of June, 1994, for the purpose of providing deposition testimony in the above-captioned matter." Then, at 4:30 or 5:00 P.M. on that day, after seven hours of questioning, the deposing attorney says, "Well, let's recess for today, and we will continue tomorrow morning," and the defending attorney says, "No. You noticed this deposition for today, and it will be concluded today. We've had a full workday, so your time with this witness is over."

No rule clearly governs here and no magic language can avoid all disputes. Certainly, the deposing attorney should have been more explicit about duration at the outset because it may result in an incomplete deposition. A simple recommendation may help: be specific in the notice—don't try to hide the ball. State in the notice: "To appear at 9:30 A.M. on the 24th day of June, 1994; this deposition may take more than one day," or "to continue from day to day." If the defending attorney then wants to try to obtain a protective order before the deposition because she believes this duration to be oppressive, burdensome, or harassing, she is on notice and has the opportunity to object.

Chapter Five

PREPARING TO TAKE THE DEPOSITION

"Speak without emphasizing your words.
Leave other people to discover what it is
that you have said; and as their minds are slow,
you can make your escape in time."
— Schopenhauer

5.1 YOUR FRAME OF MIND

In considering the attitude or approach to be used in taking the deposition, you should review your purpose in taking the deposition. If your primary purpose is to discover new information, then to the extent that you are only reviewing things already known, confirming preconceptions, or displaying your own knowledge of the facts, you are not discovering new information and you may be wasting valuable opportunities to gain knowledge of what your opponent will present at trial or to gain evidence that you may use yourself. Consider the following two approaches to questioning a witness in a product liability case:

Q. Mr. Mikionis, isn't it true that you should have used harder wood for the header in the garage that held the torsion spring assembly?

A. No.

Q. Don't you agree that the wood was just not hard enough, or dense enough, to hold that spring assembly, given the short screws that were used?

A. No.

Q. With the wallboard installed over the wood header, the screws just didn't have enough penetration into the wood to safely hold that spring assembly, did they?

A. I don't agree.

Q. Well, why don't you tell me why you don't agree?

A. The primary cause of the failure of this spring assembly system was the use by the installer of an impact wrench to drive the screws into the header, through the wallboard. That wrench drove the screws past snug and stripped the wood, so that there was really no way that they could be relied upon to hold anything, much less a powerful spring assembly like this one.

Compare that "cross-examination" style of questioning (ending with the frustrated, "open" question), with this style:

Q. Mr. Mikionis, you have studied the causes of the failure of the garage door spring assembly, right?

A. Yes, that's right.

Q. Tell me what caused the failure?

A. The primary cause of the failure of this spring assembly system was. . . .

Q. What other causes of the failure did you find?

A. A secondary cause was. . . .

In the first example, the attorney had the mind-set that he knew the causes and merely wanted the deponent to confirm that he was correct. In the second, while the attorney may have believed that he knew the causes, his goal was not to demonstrate what he knew, but to find out what the witness knew. Obviously, open questions are more appropriate for that purpose, but the distinction to be made here is not just in the form of the question, but also in the attitude of the deposing attorney. Perhaps because of their superior (read "longer") education, many attorneys have come to believe they are omniscient: there are no causes, there are no effects, there are no logical arguments they have not already thought of. That kind of thinking can be fatal on cross-examination; it is equally harmful in taking depositions.

In a deposition, every witness is an "expert" in some area, however small, because they actually know more about that area—their health, their job, their state of mind, etc., than anyone else involved in the litigation. They may actually be "experts" under the rules of evidence, hired by the opposing side to provide opinion testimony based upon education and analysis and carbon dating; or they may be "experts" because they know more about their business affairs or pain and suffering or fraudulent intent than anyone else; or they may be "experts" because they know better than anyone else what they saw at the intersection when the cars collided. With that thought in mind, you should adopt a mind-set that takes advantage of that expertise. This mind-set is that of an interested student, with the witness being the teacher. You can easily see how this changes the attorney's relationship to an actual expert witness: from adversary to be bested, to the student to be taught. The same change can occur with fact witnesses, where your interest and open style of questioning encourages the witness to satisfy their desire to be understood and believed.

5.2 CREATING THE DEPOSITION OUTLINE

Most attorneys conduct depositions using an outline of topics from which to ask questions. The outline serves as a detailed guide to the areas they need to inquire about during the deposition and a method of checking before concluding the deposition that they have covered all of the important areas of questioning and that nothing has been forgotten. The deposition outline is a necessary and important tool for conducting depositions, but preparing such an outline requires careful thought on your part.

No perfect method or formula exists for creating the deposition outline. Most lawyers use more than one method and will change the combination of methods to fit the type of case for which they are creating the outline. The objective of all the techniques is to identify every useful topic on which they should ask questions. The best way to accomplish this will vary with whether you represent the plaintiff or defendant, whether you or your opponent has control over most of the important information in the case, the size and complexity of the case, the role of the witness in the sequence of events, and a myriad of other considerations. Below we list and discuss some steps you should follow in every case regardless of all other factors.

5.3 RESEARCH THE LAW

To state the obvious, you cannot know what questions to ask unless you know what you must prove or disprove in order to win the case, and you cannot know what you need to prove unless you know the legal elements of each claim and defense. Therefore, your first step in preparing the deposition outline is to thoroughly research every legal issue in the case. Only when you have a fix on the law can you know what facts you must establish to prove your claim or defense and to disprove your opponent's claim or defense.

Many lawyers will have done the necessary legal research as part of drafting the pleadings, but a surprising number wait until just before trial to find out what they or the other side must prove. It is usually too late by that point to generate the evidence needed to establish a party's case or to refute the opponent's evidence. Finding out what you need to prove or disprove while you still have the opportunity to generate these facts through discovery is the much better approach.

Discovery and preparation for trial require flexibility. Do not lock into only one legal theory at an early point in the case (unless after careful research you can think of only one). Keep as many options available as possible and identify all potentially applicable legal theories. Once discovery is completed, you can then review and evaluate each legal theory to determine whether it has any viability. You can always abandon a theory late in the case, but adding theories can be difficult. The lesson is to keep an open mind and remain flexible by pursuing all potential legal theories until you establish that a theory has no merit.

5.4 IDENTIFY ALL AVAILABLE FACTS

Once you have identified all of the potentially applicable legal theories, the next step is to take inventory of all the facts currently available. What have your client and friendly witnesses told you? what does the documentary evidence reveal? what does your own expert tell you? what information is available in government records? and what other information is available? Information gathering usually continues up to the day of trial, but the ideal is to gather as much information before conducting discovery as is possible. This means carefully interviewing the client, talking with every witness who is willing to do so, visiting the scene of the accident, consulting with your expert, reviewing every relevant document, finding out as much as you can about the opposing party and the witnesses who will be supporting the opposition's case, and so on.

By learning as much as possible before discovery, you will be in a better position to challenge any lies or discrepancies in the witness's answers. But more importantly, you may find out information that will suggest new legal or factual theories, give you new leads to explore, and help you better to prepare the case for trial. Nearly every lawyer has had the unpleasant experience of having their own client tell them on the eve of trial about some key fact that changes the entire strategy of the case. If only a particular fact had been known earlier in the case, discovery could have been conducted regarding related facts and it would have been possible to develop new evidence supporting or refuting the particular fact. Careful advance factual investigation will help you reduce these situations to a minimum.

5.5 CONSTRUCT YOUR THEORY OF THE CASE

After completing your legal and factual research, the next step is to construct your theory of the case. The theory of the case is the application of the law to the facts of the case so as to justify a verdict in your party's favor. While simple to define, it is much more difficult to create.

Constructing a theory of the case starts with a factual theory of what happened. A successful factual theory explains as many of the facts as possible in a way favorable to your client; in other words, a story of what occurred. A successful factual theory need not contain every available fact, but focuses on those facts which are of significance to the legal theory being advanced.

The story should comprehend all of the characteristics of good storytelling.[1] A good story must:

1) Account for or explain all of the known or undeniable facts. Common sense tells us that a story which contradicts the known facts will be unbelievable to a judge or jury. No more than we would believe a story premised on the world being flat will a jury accept a story which conflicts with other facts they believe to be true.

2) Be supported by the details. Judges and juries are persuaded not only by the major facts in the case, but also by all of the supporting details. For instance, you enhance credibility if the witness can recount not just that a key meeting was held, but also where it was held, who was there, when it occurred, what was said, etc. Detail on every fact is overwhelming; detail on contested key facts enhances the believability of the story.

3) Explain why people acted in the way they did. Why was the defendant driving too fast just before the accident? Why didn't the plaintiff order substitute parts as soon as it learned the defendant was not going to deliver as promised? Why would the defendants want to fix prices? A good story must have the actors behaving consistently with motivations that a judge or jury can understand or else provide a good explanation for why they did not behave in that way.

4) Be consistent with common sense and be plausible. A story may be logical and even true, but if it does not square with the way we believe the world operates, our reaction will be one of skepticism. A story must make sense if it is to be believable.

---

1. Steven Lubet, *Modern Trial Advocacy,* 2d ed., chapter 1 (NITA, 1997).

You should continually revise the factual theory during the course of the litigation as new facts—both positive and negative—come to light. It is not a static product created at the beginning of the case that remains unchanged until trial. In fact, as trial approaches you will revise the story to make it more persuasive. For instance, an effective story also requires that it be told by credible witnesses, be supported by admissible evidence, and be organized in a logical and understandable manner. During the discovery stage you should always be considering these concerns as you examine witnesses. Listening to a witness's answer you should be asking yourself, "Will this evidence be admissible, will this person make a good witness," and so on.

Since this is the discovery stage, you will not yet know many facts. Therefore, it will be necessary to not only continually revise the story as new facts come to light, but it may also be necessary to have several different stories, each incorporating different possible event scenarios. As you acquire more facts through discovery, you will discard some scenarios as unsupported by the evidence while you will expand and refine others. By the time of trial only one story should remain—the one that you will present to the judge and jury. However, do not be too hasty in getting to that point. Keep an open mind involving what happened, and explore all possible scenarios before discarding any of them.

An important warning: The factual theory is not a product of your imagination, but must be a truthful and honest presentation of the available evidence. Lawyers must never manufacture evidence nor urge perjurious facts. What we are talking about in constructing a factual theory is that you work with the facts as you perceive them to construct as persuasive a story as possible, not manufacture facts to fit your needs.

5.6   IDENTIFYING THE OPPONENT'S FACTUAL AND LEGAL THEORIES

A trial is not just proving your party's claim or defense, but also consists of attacking your opponent's position as well. However, you cannot attack something unless you know what it is. Much of your opponent's theory can be gleaned from the pleadings, and certainly your understanding of what the opposition is trying to prove will improve as the case progresses. You should devote the same attention to researching the opposing party's legal theories as your own and to gathering information about their factual theories with similar diligence.

5.7 GENERATING QUESTIONS

You can generate the topics for your deposition outline in a number of ways. As previously mentioned, most good attorneys do not rely on one particular method for thinking of topics, but will use a combination of approaches. The following is a discussion of some of those approaches.

5.7.1 Brainstorming.

Of all of the methods of preparing for a deposition, brainstorming is the best way to identify areas where you need new information. In the large case, assemble the whole team for a day; in the small case, impose on a partner for one hour of her time. If no partner or other lawyer is available, consider using a secretary or spouse. In desperation, brainstorm with yourself. In any event, establish the ground rules that there will be no judgmental responses to suggestions for questions, and that no question is too basic or too stupid to suggest.

After describing the case briefly, begin with a three-minute description of the witness or witnesses and their roles in the case. Then open the floor to questions: What do people want to know from this witness that will help them understand the entire case better? Someone in the room, or several someones, should be responsible for taking down all of the questions proposed, without editorializing or omitting.

The key to successful brainstorming is to get everyone involved and talking; a silly question may provoke an insightful one; an irrelevant remark may lead people to question the bounds of relevance for that witness. Anyone who has participated in a brainstorming session in any context has seen the tremendous synergies that arise as several minds come at a problem or topic from different directions.

If the process hits a slow spot, try to revive the energy by raising a new topic and posing particular questions: "Okay, let's try this: We want to show that the manufacturer knew the product was unsafe in cold weather. How do we show that state of mind?" A white board, on which the main topics are displayed as they arise, helps to recall those topics. Some members of the group will dwell on particular topics while the group moves on, and often the first group will interrupt later with a series of useful questions. Any structure that promotes the free flow of ideas is useful. Books are available on brainstorming, and the procedures are completely applicable to the process of deriving deposition questions (as well as on choosing counts to include in a complaint, or ways to attack an expert on cross-examination, or the choice of graphics for trial).

5.7.2   Relating the factual theory to the legal theory.

A good factual theory is not enough if it does not also establish the elements of a legal claim or defense. You are not constructing a story for entertainment value, but to win a case. Therefore, to be successful, your story must make out a claim or defense. Here, you must tie the theory of the case into the deposition outline.

Once you have established the factual theory to the extent possible and also constructed the legal theory, the next step is to identify those facts that are missing from the factual theory. In developing the story, you can ask yourself a number of questions as a way of generating topics for the deposition outline.

- What happened?
- Who did what?
- Who said what?
- How did it happen?
- Where did it happen?
- Who was involved?
- Who witnessed it?
- Why did it happen?
- What documents would record what happened?
- Who normally would be told about it happening?
- Who can verify it happening?
- What documents can verify it happening?
- What inferences or conclusions can you draw from it happening?
- What facts are missing from the story?
- What are the different ways this story could have occurred? What are all the possible plot variations that could occur in this story?
- If a particular fact is true, what other facts must also be true? If a particular fact is true, what would a normal person do in this situation?
- What evidence do you need to prove the elements of the claim?
- What do you need to refute the opponent's story?

Illustrating how you can use just one of these techniques to generate topics for the deposition outline, assume a breach of contract case. The plaintiff claims that the defendant's sales manager assured the plaintiff's president during a telephone conversation that the plaintiff would replace a missing shipment of expensive computer parts without cost even though there was no legal obligation on the part of the defendant to do so. The plaintiff is now suing because the plaintiff claims the defendant is refusing to live up to its promise. In preparing for the plaintiff president's deposition, the defendant's attorney might want to think about what else would likely have happened if the defendant had promised to replace the parts. Would the president have told anyone about this good news; would a phone log record have been prepared; would the plaintiff's purchasing or parts departments have been notified of the replacement parts; would the plaintiff send a confirming letter of the telephone conversation, etc. All of these may be useful areas on which to question the witness and should be included in the deposition outline.

One way for you to keep track of what facts are available and what facts you need is to make a proof chart. Such a chart is nothing more than a large piece of paper with the elements of the claims and defenses listed along one side. In its simplest form, the proof chart has only four columns across the top: Supporting Facts, Supporting Facts to Be Discovered, Opposing Facts, and Opposing Facts to Be Discovered. By thinking carefully about the facts already known and what additional facts are needed to prove or disprove each element, the four columns are filled in. You keep updating the proof chart as you uncover new information. Facts contained in the To Be Discovered columns are moved to the Facts columns as discovery progresses. A sample proof chart for the above example follows:

	Supporting Facts	Supporting Facts to be Discovered	Opposing Facts	Opposing Facts to be Discovered
Representation				
Reliance in Good Faith				
Action Based on Representation				

The only magical thing about the chart is that it helps you to focus on what information is needed to prove the case or disprove the opponent's case. The chart helps organize this thinking and also is a method of recording the ideas generated.

By having columns for the opponent's case as well as your own, the proof chart also forces you to think about what your opponent will be proving and what evidence you need to meet that proof. The information in the columns labeled Supporting Facts to Be Discovered and Opposing Facts to Be Discovered serve as the basis for the deposition outline. You can keep the chart (which normally will have many more rows and columns) on the computer or on a large piece of butcher paper taped to the wall where it is available for ready reference. The form does not matter; the concentrated thinking about what you need to prove does.

5.7.3 Reviewing the pleadings.

If the deponent is a party, or closely identified with a party, the party's pleadings may raise numerous questions. The questions that ask, "What is your evidence for the allegation in Complaint Paragraph 4?" are not usually profitable. The answers often result in quibbling about what constitutes evidence, or whether this deposition is the appropriate time for a disclosure of exhibits, and so on and so forth.

A better question is to ask, "Do you believe that this allegation or response about control of the other car is accurate?" (or, even better, "Do you believe that the driver of the other car was not paying sufficient attention to controlling his car?"), and then to ask, "Why?" Therefore, when you prepare to take a deposition, review the pleadings, highlight or clip those portions that might provoke discussion, and incorporate them into the deposition outline.

5.7.4 Documents.

Reviewing the documents in the case may suggest topics for you to include in the deposition outline, but the documents may themselves be a topic on which to question. How to question about documents is discussed in chapter 9, but you should decide when putting together the deposition outline what questions you want to ask about the documents.

Do not view the use of the documents at the deposition as a goal in and of itself. But documents can generate questions about phrases or discussions in the documents that need interpretation, why the document was written, who wrote the document, what happened to a document, who has seen a document, or what effect a document had on events. You gain nothing, however, by asking, "Doesn't this document say that the loan was discussed at the meeting?" since the document establishes the content, once authenticated, as well as the deposition testimony would.

Chapter 9, "Using Documents at the Deposition," discusses how some attorneys pile up the "relevant" documents at the start of the deposition, and conclude the deposition after showing each document to the witness and authenticating it in some way. Because you can accomplish authentication in many other much less expensive ways (for example, by asking in the request for production for "documents prepared in the normal course of business which relate to. . .," thereby obtaining not only the documents but an admission that they are authentic business documents of the company) this practice wastes deposition time. Similarly, in preparing to take a deposition you should focus on themes, theories, and occurrences, regardless of whether they are recorded in some document. The documents should be useful; they should not be controlling.

5.7.5 Reviewing depositions.

You can use prior depositions in a case in a number of ways to help you prepare. First, reviewing the depositions of witnesses who have already been deposed may also help you generate topics for the deposition outline. Not only will a witness's answers suggest questions, but the types of questions your opponent is asking will also suggest areas for you to pursue. Next, your opponent's questions will strongly suggest the legal and factual theories being pursued. This will give you ideas on how to counter those theories with your own theories. Finally, spending some time periodically reviewing your own deposition transcripts will improve your questioning for the remaining depositions (and for depositions in other cases).

5.7.6 Working with the client and the expert.

Obviously, the client is one of the best sources of information in preparing any portion of a lawsuit, and the deposition of opposing witnesses is no exception. The client has a recollection of the relevant incidents which she obtained by living through the episode, not from documents. In advance of all of the depositions, therefore, you should meet with the client, perhaps with the main responsive pleading in hand, to discuss the other side's position and the facts which would have to be true to support that position. If the other side claims contributory negligence as a defense, assume, with the client, that the claim is made in good faith. What then must the opposition believe happened? Are there other facts that they must believe? Are there witnesses that have not been considered? Can the client's memory of the episode be faulty, by omitting incidents or conversations, or by accidentally misremembering the sequence of events? Having such a conversation with the client enables you to pursue exactly those types of questions with the deponent. Will the opposition present additional witnesses at trial? Will they claim that the screws went in first, before the bracket was attached, instead of the other way around? Will they try to show that the client reviewed the competitor's pricing sheet before submitting her own bid, and not after?

In other words, you should spend enough time with the client to understand the potential weaknesses in the case and possible holes in the client's version of the facts. Then you can explore the opposition's reliance on those possible weaknesses at the deposition. Using questions such as, "Exactly what was the sequence of events leading to the injury?" you can identify differences between the positions of the two sides and can follow up with additional questions, such as, "What is the significance of the screws being put in after the bracket is attached?" or "If you assume that the board did not receive the appraisal until after it approved the loan, how does that change your conclusion on the adequacy of underwriting for this loan?"

Just as the client can help identify areas for discussion at the deposition, so can the expert. Contrary to common practice, do not use the expert to help prepare only for the opposing expert's deposition; they can be used to help identify questions about facts for the non-expert depositions as well. Indeed, the success or credibility of your expert's testimony at trial probably depends much more upon his ability to deal with contrary factual arguments than upon his ability to refute contrary theories. (If the expert's testimony does not make sense to the jury, they have little choice but to reject the expert's opinions and conclusions; if it is instead a contest between the theories proposed by two experts, the jury is likely to choose that expert whose theory deals with all of the facts more logically.)

Now let's turn our attention back to how you should prepare for depositions by using your experts. You should ask the expert to: identify all of the factual assumptions made; identify the facts which you need to prove to support his conclusions; and identify all of the facts which, if proven, would weaken these conclusions. For example, in an antitrust case challenging a merger between two alleged competitors, the question of relevant market definition will almost always come up. One expert may assume that consumers will be sensitive to a price change of 5 percent in one product, and switch to the other, tending to indicate that the two products are in the same market. Therefore, at the deposition of the sales manager for the first product, ask questions about the consumer's buying habits and price sensitivity. By these answers, you learn not only what that sales manager has to say, but also whether the opposing expert has ready access to facts which are favorable to that side. Thus, preparing with the expert enables you to conduct a more useful deposition of the fact witnesses.

5.8 ORGANIZING THE DEPOSITION OUTLINE

You should organize the deposition outline in a logical way so that topics flow naturally from one to the other. As discussed in § 8.4, with the exception of a few planned traps, you gain little from a hopscotch approach to questioning witnesses. A systematic progression through materials and events, usually chronologically, but also by subject matter, allows you to remain in control of the material.

Triple spacing the outline allows you to easily pick up on the outline as you progress through the questions. The extra space also allows you to add topics at the last moment as you think of new ideas.

5.9 USING THE OUTLINE AT THE DEPOSITION

You should not slavishly follow the outline during the deposition. Any good deposition attorney listens carefully to the questions and goes where the questions lead. If the witness's answers suggest new topics you should explore these as well, even though they are not on the outline.

Most lawyers follow the outline as long as doing so is generating needed information. But when a witness's answer suggests a new topic or because the topic just occurred to you, mark the outline, explore the new topic, and then return to the outline. Sometimes you will also abandon topics if the witness's answers show you have nothing to gain by exploring certain areas. Most attorneys also check off topics on the outline as they complete the questioning on that topic. Then, before concluding the deposition, they take a few moments to review the outline to make sure they have left no topics uncovered.

Notice that we suggest that you outline topics, not write out questions. If your outline is a list of questions, it will not be long before the witness's answers and the outline questions soon part company. Using an outline of topics allows you to shape the questions to react to the witness's prior answers. Using written questions does not permit you this flexibility.

5.10 A FINAL WORD ABOUT PREPARATION

No one is ever prepared for every question or every topic at a deposition: not the witness, not the witness's counsel, and certainly not the deposing attorney. If the progress and twists and turns could be accurately forecast, the amount of actual "discovery" would clearly decline markedly. Therefore, instead of expending your energy on anxiety about inadequate preparation, listen closely to the witness, following up on interesting or incomplete answers, and try to understand the witness's answers and identify subjects the witness wants to avoid.

No one has ever taken a perfect deposition. Fortunately, the service of justice does not depend upon perfection from lawyers or witnesses. From a full day of deposition testimony, perhaps twenty answers will have been worth extracting for possible use at trial; of those twenty, perhaps you will actually use five; and, experience shows those five are most likely to have come in response to questions that you thought up on the spot at the deposition in response to some stimulus in an answer, and not through careful planning the night or week before.

The lesson? To prepare, ready yourself to listen to the answers and to follow up on those answers until you understand what the witness is saying and why she is saying that. If you achieve that understanding, you have assisted your client more than you could through 300 documents.

Chapter Six

BEGINNING THE DEPOSITION

"A few strong instincts and a few plain rules."
— Wordsworth

Some decisions regarding formalities and approach apply to every deposition, regardless of the issues in the case, the personality of the witnesses, or the substance of the information to be discovered. Once you think these matters through you can adopt an approach for most, if not all, of the depositions conducted in your career. Let's review these common areas and evaluate the options.

6.1 STIPULATIONS

Under the Federal Rules of Civil Procedure, you have the power to stipulate to changes in literally all of the rules governing depositions absent a contrary court order. Probably intoxicated with this power, it seems that at least seven out of ten depositions begin with one attorney, usually the deposing attorney saying, "Usual stipulations, counsel?" as though these usual stipulations will change the procedures under the rules. In two of ten depositions it is the reporter who says, "Usual stipulations, counsel?" In the remaining one, no mention of stipulations is made at all. In fact, the seven attorneys and the two reporters are behaving nonsensically because there are no "usual stipulations." There may be stipulations that have been found especially useful by some attorney, or those more commonly used than others in some county or courthouse, but there are no stipulations that are in such widely accepted use that they could meaningfully be called "usual."[1]

When asked to join in the "usual stipulations" at the start of a deposition, your best response is, "We can stipulate that this deposition is being taken pursuant to the Federal (or state) Rules of Civil Procedure. Beyond that, what stipulations do you want to propose?" Quite often, the attorney proposing the "usual stipulations" will have only a vague idea of what she really wanted—something about reading

---

1. In a few jurisdictions the term "usual stipulations" refers to a specific set of stipulations that the court reporter prepares and shows to the parties at the beginning of the deposition. These jurisdictions are a distinct minority.

and signing, and something about documents, and, oh yes, something about objections not being waived. In fact, each of these subjects is important and should be considered separately and carefully. Just as you should not order the "blue-plate special" in a gourmet restaurant, you should not, by vaguely understood attempts at some general and usual stipulations, select the rules that will govern the deposition.[2]

In fact, most depositions will proceed quite smoothly without any stipulations being adopted in advance. You can best handle matters which require stipulation as they arise and when you understand their specifics. For example:

Q. Counsel, will you stipulate that this xerographic copy of the last will and testament can be substituted for the original, which we'll put back in the safe in our office?

A. Yes, I have no problem with that.[3]

The most common of deposition stipulations and the one with the best claim to being "usual" is, "Objections to matters other than form [or 'form and foundation'] are reserved, right, counsel?" And yet this stipulation, which should be more accurately stated, "Objections to matters other than those which can be cured are reserved, right, counsel?" adds nothing to the requirements of Rule 32(b) and (d)(2 and 3). The parallel provisions of most states' rules of procedure will automatically apply unless their application is affirmatively stipulated away.

Another common stipulation which also vies for the title of "usual" is one waiving the reading, signing and notice of filing of the deposition. Amended Rule 30(e) makes superfluous the reading and signing portions of this stipulation since now the witness or one of the parties must specifically request reading, and the witness must sign only when she makes changes to the deposition. The party taking the deposition, however, must still give notice of its filing to all other parties.[4]

If you are taking depositions under a pre-1993 version of the Federal Rules of Civil Procedure, you should consider whether it is wise to stipulate to waiving the reading and signing of the deposition.[5] If you

---

2. Imagine the consternation of the attorney who, having stipulated that the deposition could be taken before any of the five persons on a list provided by opposing counsel, without first investigating who those people were, discovered that she had agreed that it could be taken before the opposing attorney's secretary-stenographer. A subsequent motion to suppress the deposition was denied. *Laverett v. Continental Briar Pipe Co.* 25 F. Supp. 790 (E.D.N.Y. 1939).

3. This stipulation is consistent with Fed.R.Civ.P. 30(f)(1)(A)and with Fed.R.Evid. 1002.

4. Fed.R.Civ.P. 30(f)(3) (amended 1993).

5. The pre-amendment version of Fed.R.Civ.P. 30(e) required that when the deposition was transcribed, it "shall be submitted to the witness for examination and shall be read to or by the witness, unless such examination and reading are waived by the witness and by the parties. . . . The deposition shall then be signed by the witness, unless the parties by stipulation waive the signing. . . ."

are the attorney taking the deposition, you can highlight for the jury the facts that the witness read and signed the deposition if the witness tries at trial to disavow the answers ("Isn't it true that you also read your deposition after it was completed? And isn't it also true that you then signed the deposition on the last page? And this is your signature right here on the last page?"). The only time it makes sense for you to waive reading and signing is when you believe the witness will change a key answer if given the opportunity to review it in the less heated atmosphere following the deposition. If you are defending the deposition, signing provides you with little benefit unless the witness is a non-party over whom you also wish to exert some control. Reading, on the other hand, is very important. Witnesses do make mistakes and misspeak in the deposition. Usually attentive counsel will catch and correct these errors at the deposition, but not always. Reading over the deposition in the more relaxed atmosphere following the deposition allows you and the witness to correct these mistakes. Court reporters also make mistakes, perhaps mishearing a question or answer, and reading the deposition allows you to have these transcription errors corrected. Correcting an answer does not cause the original answer to disappear; both the original and changed testimony are admissible at trial. But where the witness has made an honest mistake, it is foolish to waive the right to correct it by stipulating to waiving reading and signing. If you do decide to waive reading, do so at the end of the deposition when you have had an opportunity to listen to the questions and answers and can make an informed decision as to whether the stipulation is wise.

Waiving notice of filing is very much a matter of local practice. If you can trust the court reporter to promptly provide you with a copy of the deposition, there is little reason to insist on being notified of filing. In fact, few courts still require filing. Instead, most have the taking attorney preserve the deposition until it is needed.

In certain situations, you should establish a clear understanding on the record—a stipulation—in advance, but these are not handled well by an off-handed agreement to the "usual stipulations." Where an expert is also a percipient witness (the treating physician), the parties may decide that the deposition on eyewitness information should be separate from his expert opinions. If so, you should stipulate at the outset of the first deposition that it is being taken without compromise of the right to take the expert deposition, and that no expert opinions shall be elicited during the first deposition.

However, the fact that we can identify some special circumstances in which the parties may explicitly want to preserve certain rights and obligations obviously does not demonstrate that there is any use for a request for the "usual stipulations." Indeed, you should identify important concerns which are not adequately covered by the rules of procedure and deal with them through explicit agreement and stipulation, not catch-all phrases such as "usual stipulations." As an example, in those jurisdictions following the pre-1993 version of the Federal Rules of Civil Procedure, there is one stipulation that is often useful and poses little danger. In place of requiring the deponent to return with his corrections and signature to the same court reporter who recorded the deposition, parties commonly stipulate that the signing may be before "any notary." The oath and its significance will be the same, so you need not worry about this stipulation.

6.2   SET-UP AND COMMITMENTS

At the beginning of the deposition you should make it clear, on the record, that the witness understands the deposition process and his rights and obligations. Here is a typical deposition introduction:

Q. Mr. Landsbergis, my name is Joanne Backus, and I will be taking your deposition. Have you ever been deposed before?

A. No, I haven't.

Q. Well, in the deposition I will ask you questions, and my questions and your answers will be recorded by Mr. Emanuel, the court reporter at the end of the table. You understand that you need to speak up, to answer orally in giving your answers, so that Mr. Emanuel can hear you clearly? He won't be able to record a nod or shake of your head.

A. Yes, I understand.

Q. Now, on occasion, I may ask a question that I don't state very well, or that for some other reason you don't understand. If you don't understand my question for any reason, don't answer it. It is my job to ask understandable questions, so if you say you don't understand, I'll try to ask a better question. Okay?

A. Yes, that's fine.

Q. I also want you to understand that if you need a break at any time, or for any reason, you should tell me or tell your attorney, and we will finish your answer if we are in the middle of it, and then see what we can do about a break. Do you understand that?

A. Yes, thank you, that sounds fine.

Q. And you see that we have water and coffee here for you if you want. Feel free to get up and get whatever you need during the deposition, okay?

A. Yes, thank you.

Q. I am sure that your attorney has told you this, but let me reinforce it: if you want to talk to your attorney, that's fine; I just ask that you finish your answer if we are in the middle of an answer, and then you can talk to your lawyer. Okay?

A. Yes.

Q. Sometimes it happens that you will give an answer as completely as you can, and then later on, maybe five minutes later or maybe two hours later, you remember some additional information in response to that earlier question, or perhaps some clarification. If that happens to you, please just tell us that you would like to add something to the earlier answer, and we can do that right then while it's on your mind. Is that all right with you?

A. Yes, I think I know what you are saying.

Q. Sometimes, when you are answering, you may think of some documents that might help you remember the answer, or might help you give a more accurate answer. If you do, tell us, and we may have those documents here, or we may be able to get them to help you answer completely and accurately. Is that okay?

A. Yes.

Q. Are you taking any medication or drugs of any kind which might make it difficult for you to understand and answer my questions today?

A. No.

Q. Have you had anything alcoholic to drink in the last eight hours?

A. No.

Q. Are you sick at all today?

A. No.

Q. Are you currently under a doctor's care for any illness?

A. No.

Q. Is there any reason you can think of why you will not be able to answer my questions fully and truthfully?

A. Nothing comes to mind.

The primary purpose for this set of instructions, at least for the witness represented by counsel,[6] is not to ensure fair treatment of the witness, but to discourage attempts at trial to avoid the effect of deposition answers[7] and to begin the process of attempting to develop rapport with the witness. Let's go through this introduction, comment by comment, and analyze what is actually going on:

"Have you ever been deposed before?"

This sounds innocent enough, but if the witness answers that he has been deposed it can be used later to undermine the witness's claims in front of the jury that he was confused or uncertain about the deposition procedure. For example, in closing argument:

> "Members of the jury, you heard Mr. Landsbergis admit in his deposition that he attended that pricing meeting in Chicago, and then try to deny it here on the stand in front of you. He claimed he was confused about the deposition procedures, that he was very nervous. But you also heard him testify that he had been in a deposition three earlier times. He was a veteran at depositions. He was not nervous; he was not confused. He was telling the truth at the deposition; he was at the meeting in Chicago; and his attempts to deny it here in front of you show that he is not very credible."

"You need to speak up, to answer orally."

This does indeed help the reporter, but it may also help the attorney taking the deposition, because it keeps the witness from letting his voice trail off toward the end of an answer that may embarrass him, and it reminds the witness of the special process of recording his answers. Some attorneys believe, however, that the attorney taking the deposition should do as little as possible to remind the witness of the fact that his answers are being recorded, so that the witness is more spontaneous and less guarded. If that approach is taken, the deposing attorney should watch for nods or shakes and merely confirm their meaning with, "You are shaking your head to mean, 'No'?"

---

6. For the witness unrepresented by counsel, such as the non-party witness, it is all the more important that you demonstrate to the jury later on that you were more than fair in your treatment and questioning techniques. Furthermore, without getting too deeply into the ethical obligations involved, deposing counsel may well have a duty of fair treatment toward an unrepresented person, and a duty not to take unfair advantage of their lack of counsel.

Where the dependent is unrepresented, the instructions concerning discussions with counsel should be amended, to remind the witness that he could obtain counsel if he choses.

7. "Unfairness" to the witness, of course, is not an option, and the lawyer should always be fair in dealing with witnesses. The question here, however, is whether the introductory instructions have that as their primary objective, and they do not. In dealing with the unrepresented witness, general obligations of good faith and fair dealing would seem to impose an affirmative duty to inform the deponent of the nature of the process, what is expected of him, and what he is permitted to do.

"If I ask a question that you don't understand. . . ."

When trapped at the trial between his trial testimony and his prior answers at the deposition, the embarrassed or desperate witness often claims, "I didn't understand the question; I was confused." If the jury can see that the deposition question was in fact understandable, it may contribute further to the witness's loss of credibility. On the other hand, failing to understand and recognizing that you fail to understand are really two separate events. Of all the preliminary instructions, this is probably the least useful.

Some attorneys prefer this instruction with a twist:

> "Tell me if you don't understand one of my questions. If you answer a question, I am going to assume that you understood it."

This does not avoid the problem of the witness who fails to recognize that he does not understand, and the fact that the deposing attorney is going to make an assumption is really irrelevant. Her decision to make an assumption does not constitute any sort of admission by the witness or the opposing party.[8] Quite often, this "assumption" instruction merely impels opposing counsel to interject that the deposing attorney must ask understandable questions, that to make the witness monitor the quality of the questions is unfair, and that the deposing attorney can "assume" anything she wants, but that will not change whether or not the witness understood a question. The opposing counsel probably has the best of this debate.

"If you need a break at any time. . . . We have water and coffee here. . . ."

If the witness needs a break, the witness is going to take a break whether the deposing attorney gives this instruction or not. The instruction's purpose, however, is to show the jury that this deposition was not a "third degree" interrogation in which the witness was questioned in the basement until exhaustion under bright lights without a smoke or a cup o' java. In depositions where this instruction is given, and those where it is not, there is no detectable difference in the number of breaks taken by the witnesses.

"If you need to talk with your attorney. . . ."

This instruction actually may have some effect at the deposition, as well as at trial. When the questioning gets intense and the witness gets anxious, many witnesses will want to check with their attorney before

---

8. Furthermore, even if the deposing attorney did not mention this assumption, the normal human response is to assume that someone who answers a question has understood the question; thus, this stated "assumption" seems to add nothing but more legal verbiage to the task of gaining information.

answering the tough question. This instruction gives the questioner a bit of a lever:

> "Now, Mr. Stralkus, when we started, you agreed that you would answer my question before you talked with your attorney. Could you please give me your answer, and then we can take some time for you to talk with your attorney?"

Although not a guaranteed remedy for dealing with constant discussion between question and answer, the instruction does help. You can later show the jury that the witness had time to talk with counsel and yet he made these incredible admissions. This instruction is worth giving.

"If you remember some additional information or clarification. . . ."

This instruction may actually help at the deposition. You cannot expect witnesses to know the proper procedures at depositions or what they are allowed to do. This instruction provides concrete direction on how to correct or supplement an answer. Since as the deposing attorney you are trying to discover all of the witness's pertinent knowledge, you should encourage such clarifications and corrections. At trial, you can repeat this instruction to the witness to discourage any thought of saying, "Well, I remembered this explanation later, but I didn't know if I was allowed to go back and correct my answer." In addition, if the witness read, corrected, and signed the transcript of the deposition, those are additional facts which support its accuracy and completeness.[9]

"If you think of some documents that might help. . . ."

Consistent with the goal of maximum discovery, this instruction encourages the witness to mention documents that occur to him. Without the instruction, the witness may not know whether he is supposed to mention those documents. At trial, the fact that he received this instruction logically precludes the witness from saying, "Well, if I had the documents in front of me then, I might have remembered this other bank account."

"If you need a break. . . ."

The witness and his counsel will decide when he is too tired to go on, no matter what instruction you give. But this instruction sounds considerate to the jury later at trial, and makes it more difficult for the witness to say, "I did give that answer about stealing from the poor box,

---

9. With respect to "after-remembered" information and documents which are responsive to deposition questions, those will often be included as part of the deponent's corrections to the deposition transcript. The duty of a party to supplement responses given in a deposition is controlled by Rule 26(e), and is discussed in § 15.2.

but I was very tired and you just kept pressing me without giving me a chance to breathe."

"Are you taking any medications? . . ."

This question and the following questions about alcohol, feeling ill, and doctor's care allow you to cut off excuses that a witness might give at trial to avoid an unfavorable deposition answer. You foreclose excuses about being sick the day of the deposition, taking medication that caused sleepiness, etc.

The question about alcohol is worth asking again following the lunch break to forestall the excuse of "I was so upset by your questions in the morning that I went and had a couple of drinks over lunch."

Of course, a witness may actually be feeling ill or a personal injury plaintiff may be on pain medication that affects his memory and so on. When this happens, you should question how much of a problem actually exists.

Q. Are you taking any medications or drugs of any kind which might make it difficult for you to understand or answer my questions today?

A. Well, I had my wisdom teeth out two days ago and I am taking something for the pain.

Q. Do you know what medication it is that you are taking?

A. I have the bottle here. Let's see. The label says it is Hydrocodone. I think 500 mg.

Q. When did you last take one of these?

A. At 8:00 this morning.

Q. How many did you take?

A. Just one.

Q. Have you taken any of these before?

A. About five or six since I had the operation.

Q. What effect do they have on you?

A. They make my mouth quit hurting and I get a little sleepy.

Q. Do they affect your memory at all?

A. Not that I can tell.

Q. You don't have any problem remembering things?

A. No.

Q. How about understanding or answering questions—does the medication cause you any problems with doing that?

A. No.

Q. How about having your wisdom teeth out. Is that causing you any pain or difficulties now?

A. Not since I took the pill.

Q. Feeling fine now?

A. Yes.

Q. Will you be sure to tell me if you feel that your teeth or the medication are causing you any problems in understanding or answering my questions?

A. Yes.

If after questioning it appears the problem will cause difficulties with the deposition, for instance medications are making the witness sleepy to the point that he is having difficulty staying awake, your best response is to reschedule the deposition.

6.3 SPECULATING OR GUESSING

Some attorneys like to ask the witness not to speculate or guess about answers. They argue that by putting this request on the record, it is harder for the witness later to try to avoid an unfavorable answer by claiming it was a guess or speculation. These attorneys also argue that the witness can be asked to disregard the instruction and guess and speculate if that is what is wanted.

Other attorneys recommend against an instruction not to speculate because it seems counterproductive and most jurisdictions have no rule that guessing is not permitted at depositions. Indeed, the speculation of a knowledgeable witness may be much more valuable than the limited actual information possessed by other witnesses. For example, consider these questions to the executive secretary in an office about his boss's activities:

Q. Mr. Smalkus, how much time did your boss spend on the Century account in May?

A. Well, I'm not exactly sure. You know, I don't keep track of his every minute.

Q. Yes, I understand that. Give me your estimate of how much of his time he spent.

A. Well, it would be more of a guess, I suppose.

Q. All right, give me your guess.

OPPOSING COUNSEL:

> I'm going to object here. This isn't worth anything at all. I mean, all we're getting is guesses. He has already told you he's not sure.

Q. Mr. Smalkus, tell us what you know of your boss's time on the Century matter in May?

A. I don't know how much time he spent.

Q. Fine. Now, give me your speculation or guess?

OPPOSING COUNSEL:

> Same objection. We've been through this.

Q. Answer the question, please, Mr. Smalkus. Give us your best estimate or guess as to how much time she spent on the account in May?

A. I guess it was about half her time. I can't be sure, but we only had one other big account in the office then, and she seemed to be working on Century almost all the time. It could have been more than half.

While this testimony might not be admissible at trial, since it is a "guess" or "speculation," there is no question that it is clearly useful to know what the witness believes is the fact, because this witness presumably observed "the boss" daily. Once again, you should keep in mind that the scope of allowable discovery is broader than the scope of admissible evidence.

Chapter Seven

QUESTIONING TECHNIQUES

"It is not every question that deserves an answer."
— Publilius Syrus

The types of questions asked in a deposition can take many different forms. Speaking broadly, however, all of the questions being asked can be broken down into two different types: information-gathering questions and questions seeking admissions. Many attorneys err by asking only one or the other type of question. Effective attorneys know how and when to ask both types of questions.

7.1 INFORMATION-GATHERING QUESTIONING

In the information-gathering phase of a deposition, you are attempting to learn as much as possible about the witness's relevant knowledge. In this phase you should focus on encouraging the witness to talk—to lecture, to reminisce, to discuss, to evaluate—generally, to speak as freely as possible, without the constant intrusion of narrow questions that invite narrow answers. Your focus should not be upon displaying your own knowledge and how well you already understand the facts of the case, but in learning new facts from the witness.

For ease of analysis, consider the questioning during a discovery deposition as having three phases: the open phase, the clarification phase, and the closing-off and pinning-down phase. You can often weave back and forth in these three phases or approaches, so that you examine one topic first with open questions, then ask clarifying questions on that topic, and finally pin down the witness on details or particularly helpful information with more controlling questions.

7.1.1 The Open Phase

In the open phase your questioning should be as wide open as the direct examination questioning of a trusted and competent witness at trial. Picture this aspect of the deposition like the wide mouth of a funnel, gathering up everything that might be useful to understanding and winning the case.

The reporter's questions—who, what, when, where, why, and how, and "describe that for me" and "tell me about that"—accomplish the goal of encouraging the deponent to talk. Open questions cause the deponent to provide the information, making it much more difficult for him to "hide the ball" or drag the process out, hoping to exhaust you before substantial disclosures are made.

Imagine a personal injury automobile collision case where the defendant is being deposed. Examples of open questions are:

Q. Tell me what you were doing just before the accident.

Q. What were you looking at?

Q. What did you see?

Q. What was the traffic like?

Q. Describe the intersection for me.

Q. When did you first see the plaintiff?

Q. Tell me everything that happened after you saw the plaintiff.

7.1.2 The Clarification Phase

Nevertheless, open-ended questions will not entirely suffice. You also need to know the details of the broad outline provided by the witness's answers to these broad questions. During the clarification phase your job is to flesh out the details of the information provided by the witness. In other words, your questions are now moving down to a narrower part of the funnel. Let's take the answer to one of the previous open questions and see how it can be narrowed down.

Q. When did you first see the plaintiff?

A. I saw him about 200 yards away approaching in the oncoming traffic lane.

Q. How fast were you going when you first saw him?

A. About thirty-five miles per hour.

Q. How do you know that was your speed?

A. I had looked at my speedometer about a half block before.

Q. Had your speed changed between the time when you looked at your speedometer and when you saw the plaintiff?

A. I don't think so.

Q. When you first saw the plaintiff, how long did you watch him?

A. Just for a second.

Q. Where did you look next?

Many of the questions are still open, but now they are becoming more focused on the particular topic. As the questioning on the topic progresses, your questions should become increasingly more narrow and closed.

Q. Did you look at your speedometer again between the time you first saw the plaintiff and the collision?

A. No.

Q. Did you see any other cars approaching in the plaintiff's lane?

A. I think he was the only one.

Q. Did the plaintiff have his lights on?

A. You know, I can't really remember.

As the funnel narrows, more of your questions should start with words such as "did" and "do" and require yes or no answers. However, it is not a neat or uniform progression from open to closed questions. Often an answer to a closed question will cause you to back up and ask more open questions before moving on.

Q. Did the plaintiff have his lights on?

A. You know, I can't really remember.

Q. How light was it at the time?

A. It was starting to get dark.

7.1.3 Closing Off.

One of your goals at a discovery deposition is to prevent the deponent from reserving information for surprise use at trial. You want to obtain all of his information on all relevant points on which he might testify. But three constraints hamper this: first, your questioning abilities; second, the witness's possible lack of candor; and third, time. As a partial cure to these problems, you can use "closing off" questions to limit the witness to particular facts.

The usual method of closing off a topic is by asking "What else?" or "Anything else?" until the witness answers "No." Depending on the topic being closed off, your question can take any number of forms: "Were there any other meetings?" "Have you now told me everyone who was present at the party?" "Did you do anything else to mitigate your damages?" and so on.

An important technique to remember is if you want a witness to recall additional information, ask "What else?" but if the goal is to limit recall, it is better to ask "Is that it?" The first phrasing invites the witness to remember more, the second offers the witness an easy way of saying there is no more.

More and more often you will encounter witnesses who have been instructed in the strategic use of the phrase, "That is all I can remember at this time." Many clever attorneys believe by arming their witnesses with such a shield, the attorneys will be able to rehabilitate the witnesses more easily with "refreshed recollections" at trial. First, you should recognize that if a witness is intent on concealing the truth, whether it is the truth as to the extent of his knowledge or the truth as to the identity of the murderer, you will often have only the jury's perceptiveness to count on. Nevertheless, you should try to limit the witness's ability to claim later refreshment by cutting him off from some of the sources. Assume a construction site accident:

Q. Have you now told me the names of everyone who was on the site on the day of the accident?

A. That is all I can remember at this time.

Q. Mr. Summers, did you make any notes about who was on the site on the day of the accident?

A. No.

Q. Do you know if anyone else made such notes?

A. Nobody that I know about.

Q. Have you talked with your co-workers about this accident?

A. Yes, but it's just the people I've told you about that know anything about it.

Q. Are there labor sheets you could check to see who was working that day?

A. Sure, but I already did that for the company's lawyer. It's just the people we've talked about.

Q. Is there anything that might help you remember who was there at the site on that day?

A. Not that I can think of.

7.2 EXHAUSTION

When questioning a witness on a topic, you want to make sure that you have extracted every important item of information from the witness before moving on to a new topic. In short, you want to exhaust each topic completely and thoroughly. Doing so requires attention to the types of questions you are asking.

7.2.1 Breadth.

Exhaustion of a topic means covering the full scope of the topic as well as engaging in detailed questioning on every aspect of the topic. In other words, you want to cover the breadth *and* depth of the topic. The usual approach is to stake out the breadth of the topic before exploring the depth.

Let's assume that you are questioning a shipping manager at a machine parts supplier about the procedures for filling orders.

Q. What are your responsibilities as shipping manager?

A. I am in charge of all shipments going out of the company.

Q. What other responsibilities do you have?

A. If insurance is required on a shipment, I also arrange that.

Q. What else?

A. I have to arrange the type of shipping used.

Q. Any other responsibilities?

A. I have to make sure that the amount of the shipping charges are passed on to billing.

Q. What else?

A. That's everything.

Notice that in addition to getting the full breadth of the witness's responsibilities, you are also closing off the topic by asking what else. You repeat this until the witness says that is everything. In this way, you push the witness's memory to recall additional responsibilities. Consequently, the witness will find it difficult later at trial to add new responsibilities.

7.2.2 Depth.

Once you have determined the full breadth of a subject, the next step in effective questioning is to explore in depth the answers given. In other words, you now exhaust each topic within the subject. Assume again that the shipping manager is being deposed.

Q. You said that it is your responsibility to arrange the type of shipping used. How do you go about doing that?

A. Well, I usually get a quote from the rate books each of the shippers provides.

Q. What happens next?

A. I then draw up a shipping invoice for the cheapest shipper with service to that destination and contact them for a pickup.

Q. What else?

A. I will also fill out the insurance forms if insurance was requested.

Q. What else?

A. That's it. The shipper picks up the shipment and I am done.

Notice again that the questioner is closing off the topic, this time by asking "What else?" until the witness says that's it.

You can continue the exhaustion by turning to the next topic, sending the shipping charges to billing, or if you want to learn more about shipping, by further exploring this topic. For example, the next line of questioning might be about how the rate books are kept current or how the witness knows when to order insurance. The important lesson is not to move on to a new topic until you know everything about a topic that you want to know.

After a witness has given all of the information he can remember, you may help trigger his memory by suggesting other information. For example, in the shipping agent example, after the witness answers that he has given all of his responsibilities, you may want to ask some follow up questions:

Q. Are you also responsible for making sure the shipments are properly addressed?

A. Yes, we have to do that too.

Q. How about packing the shipments?

A. No, that's done in packaging.

Only suggest a topic that you want the witness to remember. On the other hand, if your goal is to limit the witness's recall or knowledge, then once the witness has said that is everything, move on to a new topic.

Use your intelligence and judgment in deciding how far to explore a topic. You should use the exhaustion technique only on those topics which you need to know about. Too often you will have the experience of defending depositions where the questioning lawyer spends endless hours exhausting the witnesses' knowledge about topics which have not the slightest relevance to any issue in the case. Such an approach is expensive to the client and also runs the risk of losing sight of the forest for the trees. Exhaust where the issue is important, and move on where it isn't.

7.3 ELICITING CONVERSATIONS

Often the trial court will rule that some out-of-court conversations are admissible as non-hearsay under Fed.R.Evid. 801(c) or (d), or within an exception to the rule excluding hearsay. If the witness at deposition has given only the "substance" or "gist" of the conversation, paraphrasing or summarizing what was said, the court may reject the evidence of the conversation because of the danger that it contains too much interpretation by the witness, and not enough evidence of what the speaker said. Therefore, at deposition, you should ask a witness testifying about a conversation to state, in as close to the actual words as possible, what each speaker said and what the response was.

Another reason for you to insist on learning what the speaker actually said rather than the witness's summary of the words is that often the speaker's words will reveal more than a summary suggests. Consider this segment of deposition testimony concerning a conversation after an accident, as reported by a non-party witness:

Q. Mr. Richkus, did anyone say anything at the scene of the accident?

A. Well, when the owner got there, he was really upset. You know, it sounded like the driver was trying to explain what happened, but the boss just wouldn't listen. I thought he was going to fire him. He, the boss, I mean, kept yelling and screaming about the brakes and he was getting madder and madder. The driver finally sat down on the running board of the truck cab and he didn't say anything.

Compare that testimony with the following additional testimony where the attorney takes care to follow up to obtain actual language:

Q. Okay, let's just go through this one piece at a time. Tell me first what the driver said to the owner or boss, what words he used, and what the boss said back to him.

A. Okay. As best I can recall, the driver said, "The brakes went soft; they just didn't grab." And then the owner got really mad and started yelling at the driver.

Q. What words did he yell at the driver?

A. I can't remember everything he said, but I remember him saying, "Don't say that to anybody, don't say anything about the brakes. Just tell them it happened too fast." I don't know, I was kind of embarrassed about hearing this, you know. I mean, obviously, they didn't know I could hear them.

Q. Did the driver say anything back to the owner?

A. No. He just sat down on the running board of the truck and didn't say anything else that I could hear.

Q. Where were you when you heard this conversation?

A. I was standing at the back of the truck, about ten feet from them.

Q. Who else heard this conversation?

A. I'm not sure. Maybe the woman who was driving the Cadillac, because she was standing next to me. Both of us were waiting for the police to come.

Q. Did anyone besides the Cadillac driver overhear this conversation between the boss and the driver?

A. I don't think so.

Q. Is that all that you heard of the conversation between them?

A. Yes, then the police came and I was talking to them.

Q. Do you remember anything else about that conversation between the boss and the driver?

A. No, that's about it.

Q. Did you make any notes about that conversation?

A. Well, no, I didn't make any notes, but I told the police officer about what I had heard, and he was writing while I was telling him.

Q. And that was Officer Davis that you mentioned before?

A. Yes.

With the second example, there are specific statements, free of interpretation, which you can later use as party admissions. The litany for having a witness recount a conversation in which he was involved generally asks the following questions, in one form or another:

- Who was present (speakers and eavesdroppers)?
- Where did the conversation occur?
- What were you doing?
- What were the other people doing?
- What did you say to her and what did she say to you?
  Or, What did she say to him and what did he say to her?
- Was anything else said at that time?
- Is there anything else you can remember about that conversation?
- Did you make any notes about that conversation? Are there any documents that refer to the conversation?

A note of caution is in order here: If the witness starts to talk about the conversation in generalities and impressions, take that answer. You have to avoid intimidating the witness by demanding specificity that may seem too onerous. If you insist, you may only obtain, "I can't remember." If the witness testifies about the substance of the conversation first, you can then prompt the witness, "Well, you said that the boss was angry. What did he say that sounded angry?" More limited questions about actual statements will seem less difficult.

Another technique is to ask first "What was said?" This simple question allows the witness to recount the conversation as it is remembered. After the witness has told you everything she remembers, including responding to prods of "What else was said?" you should then take the witness through the conversation again. The second time through ask the witness what she first remembers being said, what was said in response, and so on until the conversation is concluded. By using this "two-bite" approach the witness is usually able to recall much more than if the conversation is only recounted once.

Whatever the approach used, if the conversation is important, you should exhaust the witness's memory, that is, learn everything that was said. You do this using the same funnel approach as in the rest of the deposition.

7.4 LISTENING

Both information gathering and theory testing require you to use one of the most important but least noted deposition skills: listening to the witness. While preparation is to be applauded, if you have an extensive outline or lengthy checklist of questions for the deposition or if you are trying to take copious notes, you must be careful not to allow those outlines or notes to interfere with your concentration on the witness. Remember, your goal in the deposition is not to complete the outline or take the best notes, but to learn about the witness's knowledge. Armed with lists, outlines, and notepads, counsel too often get caught up in completing those materials, with two unfortunate results: they do not appreciate many of the answers that the witness gives and they do not see the non-verbal communication which is occurring before their eyes.

First, we must distinguish between hearing and listening. If you are reading while the television is on, you hear the voices and sound effects, but you are not listening to them. You do not appreciate the word choices that the dramatist has made, or the subtleties of language that the comedian depends upon. Those things require much more attention. You must listen.

At the deposition, if you are involved in checking outlines, refining notes, or completing a review of a document while the witness speaks, you will miss the subtle changes in meaning which the witness's tone of voice, hesitation, or word choice often provide. As a trivial example, you might not appreciate the message in the answer from the following exchange:

Q. Did you see John again?

A. Not on that day.

However, if you are listening and focusing on the witness you will immediately recognize the need to follow up with:

Q. When did you next see John?

You will also miss other obvious cues, such as eye contact between the deponent and his attorney, silent coaching through head or hand gestures, a glance at a document, shifting in the chair, or any other physical gesture which, while it cannot be accurately translated into a sign of truth or falsity, can often provoke you to probe a little further for information the witness may be screening.

Some attorneys have difficulty reconciling the need to keep track of items that a witness lists with the need to watch and listen to the witness. When asking the witness to name the people who were at the party or to list his bases for an opinion, they then feel compelled to write the names and bases down as the witness recites them. The answer is simple: maintain eye contact with the witness while the answer is being given; probe for more ("Was anyone else there?") while still looking at the witness; and probe again ("Are there notes that might list more bases?") while looking at the witness. Then ask the reporter to read the answer back so you can make a list of the people or bases and review them one at a time, or, if the list is short, go through it with the witness a second time.

Attorneys sometimes rely in this way on an attorney or paralegal who is second-chairing them ("John, did you get those names?"). They should recognize that the reporter, an official note-taker, can be used for the same purpose, and will probably have more accurate notes. Once you obtain the information you can mark your notes with circles, paper clips, or yellow stick-on squares, to remind you to come back and ask about each of those points until you exhaust the witness's useful information.

7.5 RECAPITULATING AND SUMMARIZING

Oftentimes an important fact or piece of information is buried in the middle of an otherwise useless answer. If you ever need to use the answer to read to the jury or to impeach or control the witness, its impact will be lost on the listener. For example, assume the issue in the case is whether the defendant contractor had followed the manufacturer's instructions in assembling a prefabricated building.

Q. Did you have the manufacturer's instructions before you started putting up the building?

A. We have always worked very closely with Chief in putting up their buildings. Several of my crew have attended training sessions at Chief and we have worked with their instructions a number of times, but I don't think we had a set when we started this job. But the crew members were very experienced in this type of work and knew exactly what they were doing.

You could extract the kernel of this answer with a quick summarizing question either right after the answer or at the conclusion of the topic.

Q. Let me see if I got this correctly. You did not have a set of the manufacturer's instructions when you started putting up the building?

A. Correct.

Of course, if opposing counsel has prepared the witness to give the long, rambling answer then any attempt at summarizing will draw more of the same. But most witnesses will respond to a reasonable summarizing question with a fair answer.

In one special situation, the witness must be pinned down and the groundwork must be carefully prepared. It often happens in a deposition that the witness finally concedes some important point, but only after much wrangling by both the witness and the defending attorney. See if the following exchanges ring a bell in a price-fixing case where the deposing attorney wants to establish that the two competitors had the opportunity to set prices at industry meetings:

Q. Mrs. Vasys, as sales manager for Ajax Technology, you went to conventions and industry conferences and meetings, didn't you?

A. Yes, probably once a month or so.

Q. Representatives of your competition also attended those meetings?

MR. ROBERTS:

> I am going to object here unless you take these meetings or whatever one at a time. I don't know what you are talking about, which one, or when.

Q. Mrs. Vasys, can you answer my question, please? At these industry meetings that you attended, there were representatives of your competition, right?

MR. ROBERTS:

> Same objection. Answer it if you can understand it, June.

A. Yes, well, I think that I understand it. There were . . . there are meetings during the year that I attend for the company, and our competition also sends their sales managers or, sometimes, their vice-presidents of sales.

Q. And there were meetings like this in 1989 and 1990, right?

MR. ROBERTS:

> Meetings like what, counsel? That question doesn't make any sense. Ask a better question and we'll get out of here a lot sooner. I object.

Q. Please answer my question, Mrs. Vasys. Do you remember it?

A. Yes, I think so. We did have industry meetings and conferences in 1989 and 1990. Is that your question?

Q. Yes. And at some of those conferences, you met with sales representatives or officers of the World Technology company, didn't you?

MR. ROBERTS:

> Hold on now. I object. You are way beyond anything that the witness has testified to, and I think that you are trying to lead her to say things that she just hasn't testified to. You are just trying to tell your own story here. I object.

Q. Can you answer the question, please?

A. Well, during 1989 and 1990, there were several meetings where I met with the salespeople from World Technology, but. . . .

MR. ROBERTS:

> I object to this line of questioning. You are not being fair to the witness unless you go through these meetings one at a time. This testimony just doesn't mean anything at all.

Q. Mrs. Vasys, you hadn't finished your answer, had you?

A. No, I was just going to say that there were only a couple meetings where I spent any time with the vice-president of sales for World Technology.

The defending attorney saw exactly where this was going and tried, with legitimate and illegitimate objections, to disrupt the deposition. As a result, while the deposing attorney got the desired information, it is in bits and pieces and will not make a coherent transcript if it needs to be read at trial. Even if only used for impeachment at trial, the witness's answers are so chopped up that the point may be lost on the jury, and opposing counsel will be cued to make further objections to the use of the transcript.

The pinning down technique that can help here is for you to leave the line of questioning on meetings at this point, and proceed to other areas. Then, thirty minutes, three hours, or three days later, come back with the following:

Q. Mrs. Vasys, I think that I am almost done here, and we can wrap up in just a few minutes. Let me check on some odds and ends. You finished business school in 1967?

A. Yes, June of 1967.

Q. And I think I have this right—yesterday you told us that you were assistant sales manager before you became sales manager—do I have that right?

A. Yes, I was assistant sales manager for three years.

Q. And as sales manager you met with the vice-president for sales of World Technology approximately twice in 1989 and 1990?

MR. ROBERTS:

I object. We have been over this enough.

A. Yes, that's right.

At trial, for admissions or impeachment, use this recapitulation in place of the earlier, disrupted testimony. Even with the objection, it is much cleaner and clearer than the earlier testimony. The defending attorney could, of course, try to disrupt you at this point in the deposition also, but, because you have said you are almost done and because it may be late in the afternoon when he is too tired to fabricate illegitimate objections, it may all come out as planned.

When you use this transcript at trial the defending attorney has the right, under Rule 32(a)(4), to introduce earlier portions of the transcript which "ought in fairness be considered with the part introduced." Even if he can find the earlier transcript quickly enough, since it may be separated by many pages from your portion, you have now shifted the burden of using the chopped up portions to him, while you can rely on the clean and clear portions.

7.6 GAINING ADMISSIONS

After you complete the information-gathering phase of questioning, either for a subject area or for the entire deposition, you can begin the process of theory testing. Here you can explore the witness's testimony on specific facts which are necessary to support your factual and legal theory of the case or on facts necessary to destroy or weaken the opponent's theory.

For example, in a breach of contract case the plaintiff claims that he lost other business because the defendant did not deliver the parts, and, implicitly, the plaintiff could not "cover" from other sources. Consider the deposition of the plaintiff's purchasing agent:

Q. Now, Mr. Shadis, before you began doing business with the defendant as the supplier of the fasteners, who supplied them to you?

A. Well, several sources. One was Jones' Cabinet Works. Another was Hinges and Hardware, Inc., in Paramus. We did some business with Barkers Builders' Supply.

Q. Were any of those companies still in business in February, when you say you were waiting for the defendant's fasteners?

A. Yes, as far as I know.

Q. Did you ever purchase your piano hinges from one of those companies, before you bought from the defendant's company?

A. Yes, but then the Janis Company, you know, the defendant, gave us a better price, so we switched.

Q. What communications did you have with any of those companies at that time?

A. I believe that I called Barkers.

Q. How many times did you call Barkers?

A. Once, I think.

Q. Did you have any contacts at that time with Jones' Cabinets or Hinges and Hardware?

A. No, I don't think so.

Q. How about anybody else in your company—did they call any of those suppliers at that time?

A. No, I'm in charge of purchasing.

In this simple, factual situation the questions are obvious. Nevertheless, the answers demonstrate that the plaintiff probably had other sources that he did not call to check the availability of parts for cover. Thus, the plaintiff's theory that substantial business was lost because cover was unavailable is weakened.

Notice that extensive use is made of leading questions in this "theory testing" situation, for the simple reason that the questioner has temporarily abandoned the goal of discovering new information and is trying to confirm specific and limited information necessary to the theory being developed. Non-leading questions can also be used, particularly if these are more likely to cause the witness to give you the answers you want.

Chapter Eight

STYLE, ORGANIZATION, AND OTHER MATTERS

"The partisan, when he is engaged in a dispute,
cares nothing about the rights of the question,
but is anxious only to convince his hearers of
his own assertions."
— Socrates

The interrogating attorney can bring many styles to the deposition and many methods of organizing questioning of witnesses. The attorney's techniques vary from witness to witness and from case to case. The common thread, however, is the need for the attorney to find ways to encourage the witness to talk and to tell his story completely, so that no surprises pop up at trial.

8.1 STYLE

At a deposition, you should be assertive, bold, controlling, deferential, effective, fair, generous, hospitable, intelligent, just, kind, lucky, magnanimous, nurturing, original, professional, questioning, retentive, studious, thorough, unexcitable, versatile, wary, xenophobic, yielding, and zealous. *Caveat:* Reading a long list of adjectives will not prepare you to adopt the proper style for taking a deposition. From deposition to deposition, witness to witness, case to case, and from time to time at the same deposition, you may display many of the characteristics from this list; however, you cannot predict in advance the most profitable demeanor.

It is more helpful to set out the goals for the deposition and then to examine the relationship between the attorney's style and the likelihood of achieving these goals using the attorney's traditional style. In general, a primary goal of a deposition is to find out everything the witness knows that can harm or help your client at trial. Therefore, during the open phase of questioning, which may well take up two-thirds of the deposition, you should adopt a demeanor that encourages the witness to talk. Your success will depend upon the degree to which you can display interest in the witness's story, make eye contact while he answers, show reasonableness and poise when his counsel argues and complains, and exhibit a willingness to give the witness a chance to explain whatever he wants to explain. Finally, you should take care to ask open-ended, reporter's questions (who, what, when, where, why, and how) instead of relying exclusively on closed questions.

Specific witnesses will demand using variations on the strategy described above. With a non-party eyewitness, for example, to an accident, an assertive, official demeanor may encourage cooperation. With a nervous deponent, unfamiliar with lawyers and the deposition process, a friendly, helpful demeanor may gain trust. Every witness will present a combination of characteristics and challenges, and you may be adopting several different approaches before you achieve your goal of obtaining complete information. To illustrate, usually you will not make the witness more forthcoming by starting with an aggressive cross-examination style and then moving to a more friendly open style.[1]

Nevertheless, some witnesses react to aggressive questioning and control with what is referred to as the "whipped dog syndrome." These witnesses become meek and malleable, willing to agree to almost anything that you suggest. Sometimes you can bring on this defeated attitude by shocking the witness with difficult or embarrassing questions at the beginning of the deposition; other times by pressing the witness who is unsure of his facts into repeatedly admitting, "I don't remember." Sometimes the witness will react in the opposite manner. Through persistent and aggressive questioning, you can anger the witness until he is tempted to lash out with intemperate responses that can often be quite revealing and helpful.

Even with the extensive caveat that witnesses come in endless varieties requiring varied responses, some generalizations may be helpful. First, honey draws more flies than vinegar; being pleasant and courteous to the witness is more likely to elicit cooperative answers than being rude or nasty. Second, open questions usually are the best way to obtain information because they prompt the witness to talk and may also put the nervous witness at ease by permitting a broader range of acceptable responses. If you can achieve a conversational exchange with a witness, more information is likely to flow. Compare the two questions below:

Q. Was the Cadillac heading south on Kirby when it came through the yellow light at Madison?

---

1. This is true for the same reasons that at trial constructive cross-examination (that does not attack the witness's credibility but rather tries to obtain those portions of the witness's story that are favorable to the cross-examining party) should ordinarily precede destructive cross-examination (that which attempts to diminish the witness's credibility).

Q. Tell us about how the accident happened.

The first question contains at least five factual statements[2] which the witness must analyze and accept or reject before she can answer. Each factual statement involves a test of memory; one involves a test of map skills ("heading south") and one involves judgment ("came through the yellow light"). These complicating factors reduce the witness's comfort in answering, and will naturally tend to make the witness reluctant to fully answer the question in a relaxed manner.

In contrast, the second question asserts no facts except that an accident happened. The question adopts no version of the accident, so no version is implicitly rejected. The question gives full freedom to the witness to tell a story and sets out no "right answers" in advance to intimidate the witness. Clearly, with a witness who is nervous or reluctant to speak in public, the second question is more useful in relieving pressure and encouraging conversation.

8.2 ORGANIZATION: BACKGROUND OF THE WITNESS

Most attorneys generally agree that some preliminary, non-confrontational questioning is useful after the commitments are set up as discussed in § 6.2. In a deposition, you should try to develop a rapport with the witness before you begin the intrusive questioning and are compelled to press for details, and before squabbles with opposing counsel arise. Whether you set the tone through background questioning or through questioning on relatively unimportant introductory matters, your goal in the initial stage of the deposition should be to draw the witness into a conversational mode.

Many attorneys start depositions by extensively questioning about the witness's background. With an expert witness, however, this technique may be counterproductive and a waste of time. Similarly with a percipient witness, this extensive background information may be irrelevant. If you accept the premise that depositions should not go on any longer than necessary because they are expensive for clients and inconvenient for witnesses, then there will be times when you should avoid or postpone questioning the witness on background.[3]

With the percipient witness, you should determine early on what background questioning will be useful. If you feel that a particular

---

2. (1) Was it a Cadillac? (2) Was it heading south? (3) Was it on Kirby? (4) Was the light yellow? and (5) Was that the light at Kirby and Madison?

3. Background questioning of expert witnesses is dealt with separately in chapter 19, "Overview of the Expert Deposition."

witness, normally a non-party witness, may be more forthcoming if relaxed, you may want to extend your background questioning. While the answers may not be substantively useful, they will give the witness an opportunity to become accustomed to the deposition procedure while you ask non-threatening, non-challenging questions.

In addition to relaxing the witness, a second purpose of background questioning is to assist you in assessing the witness's personality, background, intelligence, ability, etc. In short, you can better judge how best to examine the witness if you can assess what type of person this is.

You should consider four factors when deciding how much background questioning to do with a witness.

1. What role does the witness play in the facts of the case? If the witness merely had the bad luck to be standing on the corner and to observe the collision between the plaintiff's and defendant's car, you do not have to do much background questioning. On the other hand, if you allege that the witness is the principal perpetrator of a complicated securities fraud, you will want to know much more about her.

2. How important is the witness's background to the issues in the case? When the witness's background helps to prove some issue in the case, then background questioning takes on a whole new meaning because you are not questioning about "background" but about substantive issues in the case. For instance, in a securities fraud case where the broker is accused of taking advantage of a customer's naivete, the customer's educational history is more than just background; it directly addresses the issue of how sophisticated or naive the customer was.

3. How large is the litigation budget? Intelligent litigators prepare a litigation budget as part of initial preparation and client counseling. You should make an effort to accurately estimate litigation costs and communicate these costs to the client early on. Clients do not appreciate finding out that litigation is costing more than the amount at issue in the case. Attorneys operating on a contingent fee who regularly find at the end of the case that the time invested exceeds their fees will soon be seeking a different line of work. In short, good attorneys budget the amount of time to be invested in a case and try to adhere to that budget as the case progresses.

4. How long will questioning the witness on substantive matters take? The seven-hour, one-day time limit on depositions

effective December 1, 2000,[4] imposes a new deposition limitation with which to contend. Unless the length of the deposition has been extended by stipulation or court order, the deposing attorney must make decisions about what topics must be covered during the available time and what topics can be jettisoned if the deposition begins bumping up against the Rule-imposed time limits. Questioning on the witness's background is a topic often dropped if other topics are likely to take the full seven hours.

Time you spend during a deposition developing the witness's background has a cost, both in dollars and in opportunity cost (it is time that cannot be used in working on other aspects of the case, or even other cases). You must balance the time you spend in background questioning against the expected payoff from this line of questioning. If you are learning important, useful information, then your time is being well spent. If not, then keep the background questioning short or omit it altogether.

As a general rule, it is helpful to know for any witness: (1) some personal background, e.g., how old she is, if she is married, single, or divorced, does she have children and their ages, where she lives; (2) educational background, e.g., how far she went in school, what her college major was, if any; and (3) employment history, e.g., what jobs has she held, her current employment, how long has she held this position, what her duties and responsibilities are.

Begin your background questioning with basic personal information (address, family, years in the town—information which establishes the witness's position in the community) and proceed chronologically through educational background and employment history. By proceeding chronologically, you are less likely to miss periods of time the witness may not want to talk about—like the two months in the mental hospital. After you have established the general chronological pattern, you can then ask the witness to supply specific dates to make sure that he has not omitted any periods of time, which would not be mentioned if you allow him to say, "Well, three years ago I left that job and then I started work at Century."

By asking background questions and responding to the witness's answers in an interested way, you will build rapport with the witness that carries over into the substantive portions of the deposition. While an opponent may be tempted to object that such questioning is beyond the proper scope of the deposition, or is a waste of time, the objecting attorney knows that such objections are useless. Even if the attorney

---

4. Fed.R.Civ.P. 30(d)(2).

objects, just to interrupt, her contentiousness may backfire and further help to build the rapport between you and the witness who had been getting along just fine.

A percipient witness who is a party or who is identified with a party, is less likely to relax and open up to you just because you have asked a few background questions. The witness's counsel will be cautioning the witness throughout the deposition, and any gains you make in building rapport will have evaporated by the time the witness and his counsel return from a break in the hallway. Your efforts to open up this type of witness must therefore be more subtle and persistent. With such a witness, you are best advised to address background questions last, since they are less likely to provide useful information.

The opposing attorney undoubtedly will have cast you as the devil incarnate—ruthless, cool, calculating, conniving, and not to be trusted. After all, you cast her in the same way when you were preparing your witnesses to be deposed. Because of this, the witness is likely at the outset to be wary of you and your motivations. Therefore, aggressive questioning is least profitable at the beginning of the deposition. You should look for some opportunity to engage in apparently harmless discussion: If the witness says that she has been deposed before, take a minute to talk about how long that deposition went and whether the case settled or involved testifying at trial.[5]

8.3 GETTING AN OVERVIEW

When you reach the substantive portion of the deposition, you should develop an immediate understanding of the witness's role in the important events in the case. If this witness is an eyewitness to an accident: "Can you give us a general description of what you saw that afternoon at the intersection of Kirby and Madison?" If this is an executive in a company allegedly engaging in false advertising: "Can we talk for a few minutes about what responsibility you have for the advertising of 'Fatso-Gone' weight reduction tablets?" If the witness is an expert in a construction case: "Tell us what opinions or conclusions

---

5. Before the deposition session begins, usually both counsel and witness stand around the coffee table engaging in our morning ritual for a few minutes. Counsel taking the deposition should look for these moments to show that he is human and not particularly to be feared. Of course, discussions with the opposing party without her counsel or with a witness who is represented at the deposition are not appropriate, but the unrepresented non-party witness, and opposing experts, are not protected in the same way. If you have had the opportunity to chat a bit with the deponent before the formalities began, try to carry that conversational tone over into the deposition. Otherwise, the witness's defenses will be raised even higher when the pleasant and chatty Dr. Jekyll who poured the coffee and talked about the Redskins-Cowboys game becomes the aggressive and insistent Mr. Hyde who slings accusations and argues with opposing counsel.

you have reached on the causes for the collapse of the parking garage ramp." Once you have identified the witness's role or knowledge of the relevant events, or relevant opinions, you can then ask questions to exhaust all of the witness's information without concern that you may have incorrectly limited the scope of the deposition.

8.4 THE LOGICAL (OR ORGANIZED) TOUR OR THE "LEAPFROG" APPROACH

The issue of how to best elicit the witness's knowledge presents two clear alternatives: first, question the deponent in an organized way, moving from one topic to the next related topic until the entire field has been covered; or second, jump from one topic to some other, preferably unrelated topic, and then jump again, until all intended topics have been covered. Those who argue in favor of the second approach, the "leapfrog" approach, contend that it keeps the witness off-guard, prevents the witness from anticipating your goals, and reduces the opportunity for prevarication. Let's analyze each of these arguments.

First, the witness is more likely to relax, and be "off-guard," when she believes that she understands the nature and direction of the questioning. Conversely, her defenses will be up if she is anxious about where your questioning is going. Thus, while increasing anxiety by leapfrogging may affect a witness in a number of ways, it will not lower her guard.

Second, leapfrogging does prevent the witness from anticipating what the next topic will be, but, within each topic, the questions still must be related to one another and build upon the answers given. If not, the deposition would degenerate into a chaotic exchange, and there would be no follow up or progression at all. Therefore, once you ask the first question in the new topic area, the witness can adjust her mind-set to the new topic area and to some degree will be able to anticipate the questions. You must therefore develop more sophisticated questioning techniques than leapfrogging to mask the deposition goals. Probing the witness's answers with follow-up questions, seeking to exhaust the witness's knowledge, coming back to areas to check the consistency of information given, and asking general questions before coming to specific events are the types of techniques that will frustrate the witness's attempts to anticipate your questions and block your goals.

Third, the witness's opportunity to prevaricate depends more on the amount of time between his last answer and the next question—what is sometimes called the "pace" of questioning—than it does on the relationship between the topics. In other words, if the witness is motivated to shade the truth about whether the sales agreement included the tool bench and tools, that motivation exists whether your previous topic was changing the name of the business, the method of financing the sale, or the number of partners in the new operation.

Furthermore, at a deposition no jury can observe the witness's demeanor when, like Perry Mason, you leapfrog to the crucial question: "Isn't it true that you never intended to buy the hammers?" and the witness, taken totally by surprise, stammers, "Why, I . . . I . . . I couldn't . . . I just couldn't; I never liked the hammers; I lied about wanting to buy them; I hated the hammers and everything they stood for." At the deposition, if the witness's jaw drops open, his eyes roll back, and he is momentarily speechless, but then recovers and delivers his version of the truth, you have gained little because the cold record reveals nothing of the witness's demeanor.

Of course, gaining little is not the same as gaining nothing. If there were no negatives to the leapfrogging approach with your particular witness, it is useful because once in a hundred times it will help prove advantageous for the case. In reality, however, a number of negatives are associated with the leapfrogging approach that diminish its value as a questioning style. First, when using the leapfrogging method it is difficult for you to keep track of which topics have been covered. If you are consciously avoiding a logical pattern, no logic dictates what you have done and what remains. Of course, you can mitigate this problem by using a detailed outline and checking areas off as you finish them. However, preparing such a complete outline involves considerable discipline, and its completeness depends upon your "omniscience"—few attorneys can predict in advance all the topics they will cover in a deposition.

You will also find the leapfrog approach makes it difficult to ensure that the witness's knowledge has been exhausted in an area, either because such exploration would be predictable or because the witness would anticipate the follow-up questioning. Thus, when leapfrogging you must also resist the natural inclination to follow the witness's answers with more detailed questions in an area. If you merely leapfrog from one major area to another major area, the questioning will be predictable within the areas, and the leapfrog approach will offer no particular strategy advantage.

Finally, the leapfrog approach reduces the likelihood that you will discover unanticipated areas of knowledge, which is one of the most important goals of a discovery deposition. Because leapfrogging involves moving from one area to another unrelated area, you consciously discard the most important tool in discovering new information: following little clues, chasing small leads, asking about odd words, pursuing hesitations, questioning illogical transitions, and insisting on some adherence to order and chronology.

Because we know that events happen in chronological order, that causes precede effects, and that motivations accompany actions, we try to recreate and understand sequences of human behavior. By asking a deponent why something was done when we learn that it was done, and by inquiring carefully about all of the actions surrounding a result to find the likely cause of that result, you can sometimes uncover the truth about a historical event by employing a form of probing questions.

But leapfrogging as a questioning technique encourages you to work against those logical connections which identify patterns in human behavior in order to gain the limited benefit of surprise. When the witness has the information you are trying to obtain, you should not abandon the logical tools of coherent, exhaustive questioning. Sometimes a question asked "out of the blue" will provide a valuable answer, but many more times leapfrogging will cause you to leave areas undiscovered and connections unseen. In short, leapfrogging depends upon inspiration for its success; ordered questioning depends upon thoroughness. You should therefore plan to be thorough, and then hope to be inspired.

8.5 IMPEACHMENT AT DEPOSITIONS

As a general rule, you should set up impeachments at a deposition, but not execute them until trial. Therefore, if you get the opposing expert to say that a treatise which helps you is considered a reliable authority, put that in your briefcase and save it for cross-examination at trial. If the company manager agrees at deposition that she wrote the series of memoranda on the contract negotiations, do not confront her at deposition with another memorandum she wrote that contradicts the first set of memoranda—save it for trial. Rest assured that if you get the desired effect at the deposition—the witness looking befuddled and caught in a lie—this helpful performance will not be repeated at trial. By the time you repeat the impeachment at trial, the witness will be prepared for the question and will have worked out an appropriate answer and demeanor in response to it.

This general rule is consistent with the recommended goal for all discovery depositions: Your goal is to obtain information, not to disclose how much you already know. Nevertheless, at least two possible exceptions to this general rule bear discussion:

- An impeachment or disclosure which may by itself provoke settlement; and

- An impeachment which may dissuade an expert from testifying.

The first happens almost exclusively when you are deposing the opposing party, and then only when you have somehow obtained material which directly contradicts the party. These are special circumstances, but they do occur and they can result in rapid settlement. Suppose, for example, that the owner of a company is suing for unfair competition, alleging that your client's business practices have cut his sales by half in the past year. Suppose that you discovered, through a private investigator, that the manager suffered from alcoholism which limited his ability to manage. Revelation of that fact at deposition might settle the case; on the other hand, use of it at trial might embarrass him, and it might antagonize the jury, but it would not necessarily guarantee a verdict for your client.

The second exception sometimes occurs with an expert who has not devoted substantial time to the matter. You may have an opportunity at deposition to show the expert some of her prior writings, which are inconsistent with the position she must take in this case and which make it virtually impossible for her to reconcile the conflicting positions. While an expert is no less (and no more) anxious to earn a high fee than any other professional, the expert recognizes that intellectual consistency is an important credential, and that her reputation for integrity must survive each trial even if the expert's client loses. If the expert has already sunk substantial time and resources into trial preparation, perhaps the expert will be withdrawn or will withdraw as a testifying expert; your judgment then may be to preserve your knowledge of the inconsistency for use during cross-examination at trial. But if the expert has not begun serious preparation, confronting the expert during deposition with barriers in her own writings that she must overcome may well dissuade her from continuing on the case.

Beyond these two situations—provoking a party to settle and showing an expert the dangers to reputation from testifying—you gain little from impeaching your deponent. In general, the best advice is—keep your powder dry!

8.6 HANDLING OBJECTIONS AND INSTRUCTIONS NOT TO ANSWER

The most important rule for you in handling objections is to *listen*. Listen to the objection and make a judgment about whether it is valid. Depending on your assessment of the objection—valid or invalid—you can either rephrase the question or ignore the objection.[6]

---

6. This discussion assumes that the opposing party is objecting in good faith. Techniques to deal with the obstructionist opposing counsel are offered in chapter 11, "Obnoxious or Obstructionist Defending Counsel."

Let's look at the first situation where you have listened to the objection and made the decision that the objection is valid.

Q. Mr. Vidinvas, just a moment ago you said that as you approached the intersection, you started to brake. How far away from the intersection were you when you started to brake and how fast were you going when you started to brake?

OBJECTION:

Objection. Compound question.

Q. Please go ahead and answer Mr. Vidinvas.

A. About 150 feet and I was going thirty-five miles per hour.

Q. Okay, let me break that apart. You were about 150 feet away from the intersection when you started braking?

A. That's right.

Q. And you were going thirty-five miles per hour when you first started braking?

A. Yes.

Notice what the interrogating attorney has done. First the attorney listened to the objection and decided, correctly, that it was a valid objection. Second, rather than correcting the question immediately the attorney insisted on an answer to the objectionable question. In this way, the attorney has conveyed to opposing counsel that the attorney is not going to be thrown off track by the objection. Third, when the attorney got an answer to her objectionable question, the attorney went back and rephrased the questions to make them non-objectionable. The attorney should only rephrase the question if the answer to the objectionable question was useful enough to merit rephrasing the question.

There may be times that the objectionable question is so poorly phrased that it cannot be answered without first correcting it.

Q. Mr. Vidinvas, how long did it take you to go from here to there?

OBJECTION:

Objection. Vague. Counsel we have been talking about so many "heres" and "theres" that I don't know which ones you are referring to in your question.

Q. Please answer the question.

A. I'm sorry. I don't know either.

But often you will listen to an objection and decide that the question is proper. The proper response to opposing counsel then is to politely ignore the objection and insist on an answer to your question. Assume the deposition of the opposing party:

> Q. Sir, before you sent Mr. Tiltson Exhibit 1 canceling the contract, you did not telephone him to discuss the problem?

OBJECTION:

> You're leading the witness counsel. I object.[7]

> Q. Your objection is noted. Please, go ahead and answer.

Note the interrogating attorney did not argue with opposing counsel about the objection nor try to convince opposing counsel that the objection was invalid. The only person who can determine whether the objection is valid is the judge or magistrate. They will only rule on the objection if you or your opponent attempts to use the deposition for some purpose such as introducing the answers at trial or for summary judgment. The witness must therefore answer the question subject to the objection[8] so nothing is gained by debating with counsel.

One word of caution is in order. Since the only time objections will be ruled on is if you are using the deposition at trial or to support or oppose a motion, it is critical that the objection not be sustained and important questions and answers thrown out. For example, assume that you have taken the deposition of a key witness and have successfully obtained many critical admissions. Unfortunately, the witness is dead by the time of trial and you must introduce her deposition testimony. If the trial judge now sustains opposing counsel's objections made at the deposition, you are left without a witness and without the witness's deposition testimony. The rule, therefore, is when in doubt, cure the objection. The perils of ignoring a possibly valid objection are too great to do otherwise.

Opposing counsel, under Rule 30(d)(1), may validly instruct a witness not to answer a question only when necessary to preserve a privilege, to enforce a court order limiting discovery, or in order to present a motion to the court under Rule 30(d)(3) seeking to limit or terminate the deposition. If the instruction not to answer is based on a claim of privilege, Rule 26(b)(5) requires opposing counsel to expressly claim the privilege and to describe the documents, communications, or things in such a way that, without revealing the claimed privileged information, the other parties will be able to determine whether the claim of privilege is valid. Therefore, whenever opposing counsel instructs a witness not to answer a question, you should ask for the basis of the instruction. If privilege is claimed, you should also insist on

---

7. Fed.R.Evid. 611(c) permits the use of leading questions when examining an adverse party.
8. Fed.R.Civ.P. 30(c).

having opposing counsel explain the applicability of the privilege to the question being asked.[9] Let's look at an example:

Q. Mr. Valinces, what information did you hear about the plaintiff before you decided to terminate him?

OBJECTION:

I am going to instruct the witness not to answer that question.

Q. Counsel, please state the reason you are instructing the witness not to answer.

MR. JONES:

It calls for information protected by the attorney-client privilege.

Q. Counsel, are you claiming the attorney-client privilege for communications between you and the witness concerning the plaintiff?

MR. JONES:

Yes.

Q. Mr. Valinces, did you learn any information about the plaintiff outside of any communications from your attorney?

A. Yes.

Q. Tell me what you learned.

8.7 THE WITCHING HOUR OF 4:00 P.M.

In preparing the witness for deposition and during the deposition itself, you should caution the witness that by about 4:00 P.M. each day the possibility for making mistakes is the greatest. Indeed, you can confidently tell the witness:

> At about four o'clock, you will make a mistake. I will make a mistake at about that same time, and so will opposing counsel. They may not be important mistakes in terms of the substance of the case, but they will be important because they will remind us that we are tired, that it is harder to concentrate, and that our patience and our listening skills have begun to run down. It probably has to do with blood sugar levels or some such thing, but there is no question that being deposed is hard work, and takes energy, which eventually runs out.

---

9. See § 12.1 which covers the procedure to be followed if the interrogating attorney believes the privilege was incorrectly claimed.

I will point your mistake out to you, and you can point mine out to me, and from that time on we will both be especially careful in our answers and statements. We won't go much longer than that. In a case that, by court order or stipulation, is scheduled to last more than one day, the explanation might continue. If we have to come back the next day, that is better than making mistakes, because the next mistake, or the one after that, may hurt the substance of the case. If, after that time, I state that we are adjourning because it has been a long day, do not argue with me. I am in a better position to determine whether you are answering as well as you were earlier. If you disagree, we can discuss that disagreement back in the hotel lounge.

The "four o'clock mistake syndrome" is so predictable that many deposing attorneys save especially important questions for the four o'clock time period, in the hope that the witness will be less guarded in his response. Knowing that this late afternoon slump is going to occur, the defending attorney should not commit to a specific stopping time much beyond 4:30 or 5:00 P.M., a conventional "target" time. Of course, the beginning time must be adjusted to allow the seven hours for the deposition permitted by Rule 30(d)(2). In fact, it would probably make more sense to agree to go until 4:00 P.M., and to reassess the situation at that point. When you do recess at 4:00 P.M., do not be swayed by deposing counsel's promise that "there are only one or two more areas and then we can wrap this up." Even if that is true, the witness may make mistakes in those areas that his attorney will have to correct. And often those two areas drag on for another hour, lead to other areas, and result in a deposition lasting longer than seven hours.

While we are discussing the effect of the timing of depositions on the witnesses, we should consider the situation of the witness or attorney who has come in from another time zone and has not stayed in the local time zone long enough to become adjusted. For example, if travel has been from west to east, the deposition should probably start later, so that the witness or attorney begins working at about 9:00 A.M. in his home time zone. In that instance, the defending attorney should worry about 4:00 P.M. in the witness's home time zone, which may be 7:00 P.M. at the location of the deposition. If travel has been from east to west, it may be difficult to get the deposing attorney to start at 6:00 A.M.; but the 4:00 P.M. slump will hit the witness a few hours early, and the defending attorney has to caution the witness about it and watch for it.

Chapter Nine

USING DOCUMENTS

"The historian, essentially,
wants more documents
than he can really use. . . ."
— Henry James

In the complex commercial case, where depositions alone can consume far more resources than the entire remainder of preparation and trial, you will commonly see attorneys controlled by the documents—by an apparent need to get through, to handle, and to discuss each and every document—even though the witness's testimony might replace dozens or hundreds of them. You should not let documents control depositions; use documents to refresh, to direct, to encourage, but you should prefer direct testimony from the witness.

In general, documents come into play for the deposing attorney in three ways: first, the lawyer uses the documents she already has to prepare for and to organize the deposition; second, she uses them to prod the witness's memory or candor; and third, she uses them to identify documents that she does not have so that she can request them. In each of these areas, inexperienced counsel make mistakes that unnecessarily prolong and complicate depositions. These mistakes are not the kind discussed in court of appeals decisions; instead, they are the kind discussed at coffee breaks at bar association meetings when attorneys exchange stories about "depositions I have known and hated."

9.1 USING THE DOCUMENTS TO PREPARE

In the large, well-financed corporate case, it is routine for one of the assigned paralegals to receive a notice of deposition and immediately begin to gather all the "appropriate" documents. "Appropriate" is used with some caution here because what the paralegal actually does is gather the documents called for on some generic list. Typically, that list will direct the collection of documents which the deponent wrote, received as the addressee or "copyee," or in which the deponent is mentioned. The paralegal consults the computerized database, calls up a list of those documents, and has the imaging system print them out automatically, or has a file clerk pull them from hard copy files and make copies manually. The paralegal then provides these documents in chronological order to the attorney. Next, the attorney reviews them, noting questions to ask at the deposition. Even in the smaller document case someone in the office, perhaps the attorney, normally conducts a "search and arrange" mission like this to find "all the witness's documents" for a deposition.

This apparently logical system for preparation contains a few holes. First, the witness's name will not appear on some relevant documents. For example, the blueprints or plan drawings in a construction case will not have the name or initials of the "clerk of the works" or the subcontractors, but are certainly important at their depositions. Second, subject matter of the documents is probably a more compelling and useful arrangement than straight chronological order from first to last. Therefore, you should rearrange the documents by topic, and then chronologically within each topic, to support questioning to exhaust the witness's knowledge in each area. Third, arranging the documents in subject matter and chronological order helps you to identify what the witness knows. Something else must be done to identify what she does not know, a most important goal in preparing to take a discovery deposition.

If you adjust this process a bit, however, it provides good support. First, you should review those documents which the witness has written or received, covering the relevant period of time, to get some understanding of where the witness fits into the case. Next, you should consider the issues in the case which logically could have been affected by the witness's activities. Thus, if the witness was involved in sales during the relevant five-year period and the issues involve mislabeling and adulteration, you might easily think to ask about complaints from customers, contacts with irate competitors, differences in price levels and sales volumes. These topics come to mind because they involve the witness's position and the issues in the case and not because they are specifically mentioned in documents. The documents may or may not mention the topics, but you should ask about them nevertheless.

After you have given some thought to issues about which you could ask this witness, search the documents for memoranda and letters and the like which deal with these topics, regardless of whether the witness's name is mentioned. Finally, within each topic, arrange the documents selected chronologically, so that they are available in an efficient way to help prod the witness's memory or honesty. If you then place the documents for each topic into a labeled manila folder, you will be able to move through those topics in any order that seems most productive at the deposition.

Many attorneys note questions on the face of their working copies of the documents, which seems efficient. Once again, however, you must remember that confirming the information already learned from the documents is only one objective; obtaining new information is usually a more important goal. You should have a topic outline, independent from the documents, which helps direct the examination, and then the questions on documents become one part of the plan. Following this method of preparation, the documents support the deposition but do not control it.

9.2 COMPELLING PRODUCTION OF DOCUMENTS FOR USE AT DEPOSITIONS

Frequently, you will want to obtain documents and depose some knowledgeable witness about those documents. You can handle this in two ways. First, a subpoena or request to produce can direct the production of the documents before a deposition, so you have an opportunity to analyze the documents and determine appropriate lines of questioning in order to understand the documents. Second, if there are only a few documents involved, you can schedule the deposition and the document production for the same time (or thirty minutes or so apart, if the document custodian and the substantive deponent are not the same person).[1]

If your request for production or subpoena called for "all documents relating to," as opposed to listing specifically identified documents, you may need to depose the custodian on the scope of the search for responsive documents to ensure a reasonable effort was made to discover and produce all appropriate documents. In such a deposition, use the typical "open-to-close" or "funnel" technique of questioning, so document locations are not missed inadvertently.

Q. Ms. Arrowsmith, as secretary of the corporation, what responsibilities do you have for record keeping?

A. I supervise all of the record-keeping procedures in the company, and all of the people involved in creating important records report to me.

Q. What do you mean by important records?

---

1. Fed.R.Civ.P. 30(b)(5) states that a notice of deposition directed to a party witness can be accompanied by a request to produce made pursuant to Rule 34. Non-parties can be made to produce documents at a deposition by a subpoena *duces tecum* issued pursuant to Rules 30(b)(1) and 45(a). Of course, parties can also be required to produce documents prior to the deposition by a request to produce under Rule 34. Non-parties can be made to do the same by a subpoena issued under Rule 45(a).

A. Well, the records that the company needs to operate, like sales orders, invoices in and out, bills of lading, inventory records, disbursements, receipts, everything that goes into compiling balance sheets, and other records.

Q. You are talking primarily about financial records. What are the procedures for collecting and maintaining non-financial records, like correspondence and memoranda?

A. Well, those are not quite so rigorous. We do have a document retention policy that requires each office to keep files of all correspondence and memoranda for one year, at least; then we move the files to an inactive file area, unless there has been activity within the past year. After three years in the inactive file storage, those types of documents are destroyed. Our financial records, of course, we keep much longer; some of them we keep forever.

9.3 MARKING AND HANDLING DOCUMENTS AT THE DEPOSITION

Just like at trial, documents you use at the deposition need unique names—exhibit numbers—so documents can be specifically identified. Not only do the people at the deposition need to know what piece of paper is being referred to at any particular time, but people using the deposition later (at a summary judgment motion, at another deposition, or at trial) also need to know that the piece of paper they are looking at is the piece of paper the witness was talking about.

The great majority of courts today require, by pretrial order or otherwise, that you pre-mark documents for trial. In such a case, try to mark them with their trial exhibit numbers before the depositions begin. Put all of the documents in chronological order and number them consecutively.[2] In most "big document" cases, the bulk of documentary discovery occurs before substantive depositions begin. If for some reason that is not the case, you should postpone chronological numbering of the exhibits until after you have received most of the documents.

Of course, this system will leave blanks in the sequence at trial where documents are not offered, but that is not a problem except to the most compulsive record keepers. Some judges, however, want the documents numbered at trial in the order in which they are offered. The

---

2. One excellent advantage of the chronological numbering of all documents is that, if the attorney is wondering what else was happening at the time that PX-679 was written, she can take a look at PX-670 through PX-689. If she is looking for responses to a document, she reviews only those with higher numbers; in fact, only those with slightly higher numbers.

reason for this preference is not clear. No instruction reminds the jury that "the numerical order of the documents provides you with a means of recalling the order of events at trial." Furthermore, the order of events in the "historical" scene that the trial is examining—the actions between the parties which gave rise to the dispute—is the important order. Therefore, you should arrange documents chronologically, and number them consecutively, if you desire to give meaning to the numbering system. Of course, you will still offer documents in the order that suits the story being told by the witnesses, whose appearance one at a time normally prevents a straight chronological retelling.

Even if the court requires you to renumber exhibits to follow the order of their use at trial, chronologically ordering and numbering documents for the depositions is useful to the attorneys because it provides a reference between the documents and gives them unique names. However, other systems are used.

Some attorneys like to number the documents anew for each deposition: Jonas Deposition Exhibit 1, Jonas Deposition Exhibit 2, Sugis Deposition Exhibit 1, etc. However, this approach can cause some confusion if you are not careful. Often, a document is used at several depositions. Thus, Jonas Deposition Exhibit 7 is also Sugis Deposition Exhibit 43. The attorneys on both sides must keep a meticulous "table of concordance," which, before computers, often provided a paralegal or secretary with many wearisome hours of work.

TABLE OF CONCORDANCE
SUGIS-JONAS DEPOSITION EXHIBITS

Sugis 1	Jonas 17
Sugis 2	Jonas 4
Sugis 3	Jonas 39
Sugis 4	Jonas 1

* * * * *

JONAS-SUGIS DEPOSITION EXHIBITS

Jonas 1	Sugis 4
Jonas 2	Sugis 9
Jonas 3	Sugis 42
Jonas 4	Sugis 2

If there are only two deponents, only two lists have to be prepared, with two columns. With the big document case, and the client who can support such extensive pretrial preparation, more record keeping is necessary. If there are three deponents, you need three lists with three columns, and so forth. With the current easy access to computers, a database program can take care of this record keeping rather easily, although the burden of putting the information into the database still exists.

After each deposition, someone must determine what exhibits were used and what numbers they were given. If you are using an imaging system for the documents, and all the transcripts are put on the system, then when you entered the exhibit number into the system as associated with a particular document, the concordances can be produced automatically. If you are using a manual hard-copy system for the documents, the pages of the deposition transcripts at which documents are used are often included in the document control database or in a special exhibit control database. Then, once you have assigned trial numbers and you have put that information into the imaging system or the database you are using, the concordance has another column that shows the trial numbers. The final pretrial product, after all depositions are complete and all trial numbers have been assigned, looks like this:

FINAL CONCORDANCE

Exhibit Number	Sugis No./Used Tr.	Jonas No./Used Tr.
DX-1	73 / 153–157	14 / 43–44
DX-2	74 / 168, 179	3 / 10
DX-3	5 / 23	72 / 198–199
DX-4	15 / 68	31 / 97, 201
DX-5	46 / 109	62 / 153

If you seek to present a witness with his prior testimony about an exhibit at trial, you should add an additional foundational step to relate the deposition document to the trial document.

Q. Ms. Vardas, you then wrote a letter to the president of the Shadis Company, didn't you?

A. I'm not sure what you are referring to. I don't think I ever wrote to him.

Q. In the same deposition we have talked about, Ms. Vardas, I asked you this question, didn't I? Page 73, counsel. "Isn't Vardas Deposition Exhibit 15 a letter from you to the president of the

Shadis Company?" And you answered, "Yes, I wrote that to him." Wasn't that your answer?

A. Yes, I said that.

Q. Ms. Vardas, let me show you what has been marked as Defendant's Exhibit 142. That's the Deposition Exhibit 15 we've been talking about, isn't it?

A. Yes, it looks like the same letter.

Obviously, it makes a much cleaner trial examination if only one set of numbers is involved; therefore, this is another reason you should assign trial numbers before the depositions of significant witnesses.[3]

Once you have chosen a numbering plan and arranged the working copies of documents chronologically within subject-matter categories, you should copy the documents at least twice: one copy for the witness to use and the other for the defending attorney to use.[4] Some attorneys resist providing a copy to opposing counsel, thinking there is no reason to make the deposition easier for her. But in fact, it makes the deposition easier for the deposing attorney, too. If defending counsel has to ask for time to find her copy, or insists on examining the witness's copy before the witness can see it, the deposition is slowed and fewer answers will be obtained. In the worst case, the defending attorney will review the document with the witness, pointing out various things as they go through it, thereby affecting the witness's testimony.

For the few extra cents it costs, you should have a second copy for the defending attorney. If you establish this practice, you will likely benefit from receiving copies when you defend your witnesses. The only advantage you lose is the unfair advantage of making it mechanically difficult for the other attorney to participate in the deposition.

Many attorneys put their pile of documents right up on the conference table, shifting them from the "to be asked about" pile to the "already asked about" pile as the deposition wears on.[5] Again, this two-pile arrangement has the tendency to allow the documents to control the course and content of the deposition. This also may signal the defending attorney and the witness as to how much of the deposition

---

3. Once trial begins, you can supplement the computerized concordance to track rulings on admissibility of exhibits and transcript pages where witnesses testify about exhibits. In the 100-document cases, this may sound trivial. In the 30,000-document cases, it is not.

4. If feasible, have a third copy for the reporter to attach to the deposition so that later users of the transcripts will not have to conduct a file search to figure out what exhibits were being referred to, and of equal importance, so that there will be little chance of dispute at trial about which document the witness was being asked.

5. Obviously, if you follow the advice given earlier, and have arranged the documents by topic in manila folders so you can move to a topic out of order if the witness's testimony takes you there, this "two-pile system" would not be used.

is left, since they can watch the "to be asked about" pile dwindle. One simple solution is to put the "already asked about" documents back under the "to be asked about" pile whenever there is a break and opposing counsel and the witness are out of the room. Another is to keep the documents in a file box below table level, so that only you know how many documents are left to ask about.

When you use a document, if it has not been prenumbered, you should hand it to the reporter and ask him to mark it with a specific number:

> Mr. Reporter, would you please mark this next four page document as Jonas Deposition Exhibit Number 17A through D?

The reporter will then affix a label to the document (often one color for plaintiff's exhibits and another color for defendant's) and write in the number and the date. Some reporters use a stamp and then fill in the blanks. The label or stamp affixed by the reporter has no evidentiary value; nothing is "received in evidence," that is, admitted into the trial record at a deposition. The label or stamp merely serves to identify the document so there is no confusion about what is being discussed.

After the document is marked by the reporter or the pre-marked number is given aloud so it appears in the record, you should refer to the document number often enough so the record is clear. You can do this without any particular formality or cumbersome phrasing:

Q. Ms. Vardas, let me hand you what has now been marked as Vardas Deposition Exhibit 43. Counsel, here's another copy you may use. Would you look at that, please, Ms. Vardas?

A. Yes, this is the letter we were talking about.

Q. And is Exhibit 43 the same letter that you say you wrote after rejecting the Shadis Company offer?

A. No, there's another letter that I was thinking of.

Q. Let me show you another letter. Mr. Emmanuel, would you please mark this document as Vardas Deposition Exhibit 44? Now, Ms. Vardas, take a look at Exhibit 44. Counsel, here's an extra copy for you. Is this the letter you wrote after receiving the Shadis offer?

A. Yes, that's the one.

Q. Exhibit 44 is dated March 25, isn't it?

A. Yes.

Q. Now, could you tell us how this letter, Exhibit 44, relates to your rejection of the Shadis offer?

A. Yes, I can explain.

Q. Please do.

Later, perhaps at trial or when the parties are presenting their summary judgment motions, this care in keeping documents straight by using their "proper names" will allow all counsel and the court to know exactly to what document the attorney and the witness were referring.[6] Of course, if you attach copies of the exhibits to the deposition itself, there will be little chance of dispute at trial about which document was being examined at deposition.

If you have a multi-page document, it is important that each page have some unique identification. Otherwise, the witness may come back later and claim that she was referring to a different page. If, in order to save time, you ask the reporter to mark the front page only and then you use the document's internal pagination, make sure you use the document number along with the page number when you refer to a portion of it. Also, take care to ensure the witness is looking at the same page:

Q. Ms. Vardas, would you please look at the fifth page of Vardas Deposition Exhibit 57. That's the page which begins with the language, ". . . and to tour the plant with Jonas and his employees." Do you have that page in front of you?

A. Yes, I have it.

Sometimes, although trial numbers have not yet been assigned, the documents will have unique "Bates numbers"[7] on them, and many attorneys use those unique identifiers to refer to internal pages of voluminous documents.

All of these decisions on how to handle documents at a deposition are intended to reduce the possibility of confusion in the record. As with so many other areas of depositions there are virtually no "rules" about how to mark exhibits; your common sense is quite enough, once you understand the goal.

---

6. The availability of transcripts on computer disks has created another reason for proper reference to documents by their numbers: when the transcript database is being searched for references to the document, you will pick up more occurrences if the number has been used instead of "this document," "that letter," or "the first memo."

7. These are called "Bates numbers" because Bates is the manufacturer of a popular handheld number stamping machine, which is often used in manual document control systems to stamp sequential numbers, identical numbers, or "duplicate sequential," that is, two documents in a row with the same number, and then the next two with the next sequential number. Computer imaging systems can number documents automatically and print the documents with or without the assigned number. Even when done by computer, these are often called Bates numbers.

9.4 LAYING FOUNDATION FOR DOCUMENTS AT THE DEPOSITION

If the deponent later becomes unavailable for trial, you may need to rely on the deposition transcript to lay foundation for documents which you wish to put in evidence. Under the Federal Rules of Civil Procedure, lack of foundation may be a problem which the deposing attorney could cure. Therefore, opposing counsel should object if she is concerned about the foundation for the document.[8] If such an objection arises, and the deposing attorney sees that he may need some additional information to lay the foundation for admission at trial, he should do that examination at the deposition.

The easiest way to think about foundation in the deposition context is to confine it to four essential elements: (1) competence of the witness;[9] (2) relevance of the documents;[10] (3) identification of the document (the witness has some basis for knowing what the exhibit is, and thus "identifying" it);[11] and (4) authenticity of the document (the document in fact is what it appears or is claimed to be).[12] At a deposition, the same facts will supply these foundational elements as at trial, and no extended discussion of them is needed here.[13]

We can note, however, that the second of these elements, relevance, while "foundational" in the sense that it must exist for any evidence to be received at trial, is specifically excluded by Rule 32(d)(3)(A) from those matters which are waived, if not raised. This means that silence from the defending attorney is not a waiver of this "foundation" objection to an asserted lack of relevance, and the objection can be raised for the first time at the trial stage.

With regard to the fourth element, authenticity, that is, that the "matter in question is what the proponent claims" it to be under Fed.R.Evid. 901, you can frequently save a great deal of time by discussing categories of documents:

> Q. Mr. Shadis, this form of document with "Shadis Co." in the upper right hand corner, and "Invoice No." with a blank in the left corner, and then spaces for entering items and amounts, is that your standard form of invoice for bulk purchases of Shadis construction materials?

---

8. Fed.R.Civ.P. 32(d)(3)(B). See § 14.5.1.

9. Fed.R.Evid. 601 (lay witnesses), 702 (expert witnesses).

10. Fed.R.Evid. 401.

11. Fed.R.Evid. 602, 901.

12. Fed.R.Evid. 901, 902, 903.

13. For those interested in pursuing the topic, see Deanne Siemer, *Tangible Evidence: Using Exhibits at Deposition and at Trial,* 3d ed. (NITA, 1996) and Steven Lubet, *Modern Trial Advocacy,* 2d ed., chapter 10 (NITA, 1997).

A. Yes, that's the form we use.

After obtaining that answer, you need not ask about the form every time one of them occurs as a deposition exhibit. Similarly, you could identify the form for internal memoranda generically, so the question, "Was this an internal memorandum?" need not be asked over and over.

Finally, if a foundation objection is made and you are in doubt as to what your opponent believes is missing, ask. If the opponent refuses to reveal the basis for the objection, it will be harder later, under Rule 37(d)(3)(B), to make the argument that the objection was made. It is hard to cure a lack of foundation if the objector refuses to identify what is lacking in that foundation.

If you are successful in laying a proper foundation, your opponent has three types of objections to a document: (1) hearsay objections;[14] (2) best evidence objections;[15] and (3) policy objections.[16] Your opponent may request a stipulation at the outset of the deposition that these objections are not waived if they are not raised at the deposition. This type of stipulation is discussed at § 5.6.1. If the witness may not appear at trial, and the objection is either made or preserved if not made, you will need to elicit the testimony at deposition that provides the basis, if one is available, for overcoming these objections. Lawyers who make an objection to an exhibit at a deposition may use the term "foundation" to cover both the foundation itself (competence, relevance, identification, and trustworthiness) as well as specific objections (hearsay, best evidence, and policy grounds). If an objection is made, you need to be sure you understand whether your opponent thinks the foundation is not complete, that is, one of the four elements is missing, or whether she concedes that the four elements are present but is basing the objection on the hearsay, best evidence, or policy rules.

9.5 INQUIRING ABOUT DOCUMENTS USED TO PREPARE FOR THE DEPOSITION

A favorite question of deposing attorneys is, "What documents have you reviewed in preparation for this deposition?" The witness typically will then disgorge a list of various types of documents ("The letters from the government about the spill site, internal memoranda concerning the clean-up efforts, diagrams and maps of the area. . . .") and defending counsel will make no objection. The attorneys in such an instance believe they are applying the provisions of Fed.R.Evid. 612, which

---

14. Fed.R.Evid. 801–806.
15. Fed.R.Evid. 1001–1008.
16. Fed.R.Evid. 403.

states, "if a witness uses a writing to refresh his memory for the purpose of testifying . . . before testifying [at trial]" the adverse party is entitled to see the document "if the court in its discretion determines it is necessary in the interests of justice." Indeed, if the documents have not already been produced, defending counsel will often agree to produce them without regard to whether they were required to be disclosed under the mandatory disclosure requirements of Rule 26(a)(1)(B) or were called for by any subpoena or document production request.

Inquiring about documents used by a witness to prepare for the deposition raises two separate evidentiary concerns. If the documents were selected by counsel for the purpose of preparing the witness to testify, regardless of whether counsel was present when the documents were actually reviewed, the identity of the documents is within the work product privilege. Neither the documents nor the fact that the witness reviewed them are privileged, but "the selection process itself represents . . . counsel's mental impressions and legal opinions as to how the evidence in the documents relates to the issues and defenses in the litigation."[17] If the witness's testimony establishes that the document actually refreshed his memory, many courts have held that Fed.R.Evid. 612 requires the witness to identify the document regardless of the work product privilege.[18] Other courts hold that Fed.R.Evid. 612 cannot displace the work product privilege.[19]

An approach that would be approved of by most courts is set forth in *Sporck v. Peil*:[20] Counsel should first ask the witness about a specific area and then ask the witness what "documents informed that testimony."[21] Thus, the question, "On what documents do you rely in making that statement?" or "What documents refer to the meeting you just testified about?" or even "Have you seen this document before?" must be answered, while the question, "Is this one of the documents shown to you by plaintiff's counsel?" need not. Of course, except as discussed in the next paragraph, documents selected by the witness for review without any input from counsel are not subject to any privilege.

The other evidentiary issue raised by the question of what documents a party witness has reviewed in preparation for the deposition concerns documents subject to the attorney-client privilege. Imagine that a party witness has reviewed copies of letters she had sent her counsel concerning key facts in the case before the deposition, and

---

17. *Sporck v. Peil*, 759 F.2d 312, 315 (3rd Cir. 1985).

18. See, e.g., *In re Joint Eastern and Southern District Asbestos Litigation*, 119 F.R.D. 4 (S.D.N.Y. 1988).

19. See, e.g., *Omaha Public Power District v. Foster Wheeler Corp.*, 109 F.R.D. 615 (D. Neb. 1986).

20. 759 F.2d 312 (3rd Cir. 1985).

21. *Id.* at 318.

the letters refreshed her recollection about what occurred. Many courts have held that this may, pursuant to Fed.R.Evid. 612, justify production of documents that would otherwise be protected under the attorney-client privilege.[22] This should serve as cautionary warning that you should never refresh a client's memory with privileged documents that you wish to shield from discovery.

In conclusion, inquiries about documents selected by counsel and used by the witness in preparing to testify can be easily parried.

Q. What documents did you review in preparation for this deposition?

BY COUNSEL:

Counsel, Mr. Shadis reviewed a number of documents with me as we prepared for this deposition. That review, and the identity of the documents we reviewed, is privileged. You may of course ask about whether he has seen particular documents before, and he will answer you as fully as he can without waiving the privilege.

Of course, the deposing attorney could also ask about documents which the deponent reviewed *of his own accord*, that is, without having been directed to do so by his counsel, and about documents used to refresh recollection on particular topics. However, the rules do not require the defending attorney to educate the deposing attorney on what questions might be helpful and allowed.

9.6 REQUESTING DOCUMENTS IDENTIFIED DURING THE DEPOSITION

Often during depositions, witnesses will refer to documents which have not yet been obtained by the opposing party, and deposing counsel then turns to defending counsel:

DEPOSING COUNSEL:

Vito, will you provide us with these documents we've been talking about?

DEFENDING COUNSEL:

Well, I don't think they were on any of your requests to produce, Ann, and they certainly weren't among the documents subject to mandatory disclosure under Rule 26(a)(1)(B).

---

22. See, e.g., *Derderian v. Polaroid Corp.*, 1121 F.R.D. 13 (D. Mass. 1988).

DEPOSING COUNSEL:

> I'm not saying they were. I'm just asking whether you will agree to provide us with the file of letters and the other materials, the memoranda, Mr. Shadis has referred to in the last hour or so.

DEFENDING COUNSEL:

> We don't have them here.

DEPOSING COUNSEL:

> When can you produce them?

DEFENDING COUNSEL:

> I don't know. I'll have to get back to you.

DEPOSING COUNSEL:

> Well, it's going to have to be soon, because you can see that we're probably going to have to have some more time with Mr. Shadis after we get the documents.

DEFENDING COUNSEL:

> I'm not going to agree to that. You should have asked for the documents before you scheduled this deposition. We're not going to just hold it open and let you keep coming back again and again.

DEPOSING COUNSEL:

> Well, we scheduled the deposition to fit your witness's schedule, and you know that. If you've held back some documents we have to ask him about, then we'll get an order for him to return.

DEFENDING COUNSEL:

> Ann, we'll look at the transcript when we get it and do the best we can, consistent with our need to represent our client's best interests and to avoid subjecting him to harassment through repetitive depositions.

In fact, this unproductive colloquy occurs so frequently we ought to just give it a number, or a nickname, and whenever this situation arises we could just announce, "Document production argument number three," and it would be understood that all of the above worthless verbiage was intended.

Why is it worthless verbiage? Because it neither created nor waived any legal obligations. Defending counsel has merely agreed to look at the transcript and make a decision. If, after two months, he then decides not to produce the documents, he has not violated any agreement, stipulation, or order, and no motion to compel discovery is appropriate. In fact, all that is appropriate is a request to produce documents (or a subpoena, if it is a non-party deponent)—the same request to produce which would have been appropriate immediately after the deposition if none of this discussion had occurred.

Many times less contentious counsel does agree to produce the requested documents, but often the record is not crystal clear on what documents must be provided, nor within what time period. If, a month later, a few memoranda have been produced, the record supporting a request to the court for an order compelling further production is not as clear as it ought to be. A more likely scenario is that following the agreement to produce the documents, the deposition proceeds and both sides promptly forget about the matter. Only months or even years later, when reviewing the deposition transcript in preparation for trial, do both sides recall that they had made an agreement.[23]

How should the attorneys have handled the situation?

DEPOSING COUNSEL:

> Counsel, I don't think that document has been produced to us. Will you provide it without a formal request for discovery?

If defending counsel knows the document and is comfortable agreeing to release it without further review for privilege, he can agree at that time, since the scope of his obligation is clear. It eases his burden, however, if he agrees to produce the document only if deposing counsel will write a letter requesting it, because then defending counsel does not have to keep track of these informal production obligations. Therefore, his best response is:

DEFENDING COUNSEL:

> Ann, I don't think we'll have any problem producing this memo. Write me a letter to remind me of exactly which document you want, we'll review it, and give it to you if there's no privilege.

This places the burden of following up and identifying the precise document to be produced on the party seeking discovery, where it logically ought to be. As other documents are identified and requested, defending counsel can merely respond by saying, "Why don't you put that in your letter?"

Some attorneys insist upon a request for production in place of a letter after the deposition, although the advantage is not clear. We can hope an attorney's agreement to treat a letter as though it were a formal request for production would be sufficient, without any need for judicial intervention to determine the mutual obligations. Nevertheless, it is possible that attorneys find it easier to gain clients' attention if they can tell them, "These documents are subject to a request for production,"

---

23. Such an agreement is an enforceable stipulation under Fed.R.Civ.P. 29.

than if they have to say, "Well, they wrote me a letter asking for them." Even if counsel does insist upon the request for production, deposing counsel should not debate the point. If the documents need not have been produced in response to earlier discovery requests, another request is appropriate; if the documents should have been produced earlier, then a motion to compel may be appropriate. In either event, arguing about the matter at the deposition achieves nothing.

One final note is in order. Threats to force the witness to come back for further deposition because of the need for additional documents are counterproductive and should be ignored. As discussed in § 10.3, your right to call the witness back for further deposition does not depend upon what counsel says, but upon whether you have had a fair opportunity for a complete deposition. Only the court reporter who gets to transcribe additional pages of deathless attorney-prose benefits from the debate on this point.

9.7 REFRESHING RECOLLECTION

In order to be certain that you have exhausted a witness's knowledge at the deposition, you should sometimes try to refresh the witness's recollection. When you do this with a document, however, do so with care, because once you show a witness a document, it becomes the extent of the witness's knowledge. In other words, if a deponent testifies that he remembers only three subjects discussed at a meeting, and is then shown a memorandum which lists four subjects, the witness will adopt those four as the complete meeting agenda, regardless of how many subjects were really discussed. The key to avoiding this premature closure is to keep the document in reserve for as long as possible. Use the information in the document to probe the witness's memory, but bring the document out only at the end of that portion of the examination. Here is an example, based upon a document which shows that the prime contractor met with the roofing subcontractor at least three times about the change order on the roofing material. The subcontractor is being deposed for discovery:

Q. Now, Mr. Strongis, when did you discuss the materials with the prime contractor, Mary Jonas?

A. Well, we had one meeting on the site, and that would have been around the first of April, I suppose.

Q. Who was at that meeting?

A. Just me and Mary; oh, and maybe the clerk of the works, Harry Barker.

Q. What did Mary say about the roofing material at that meeting?

A. Well, I remember we discussed using a rubberized membrane covered with gravel, instead of the roofing felt shown in the drawings.

Q. Do you remember anything else about that meeting?

A. No.

Q. Do you remember any other meetings about the roofing material?

A. Yes, I think there was one in the middle of May, because the membrane we wanted to use was not available.

Q. Who was that meeting with?

A. Someone from Mary's office, probably John Forsythe and me.

Q. Who said what?

A. Well, I told John that the membrane from the Harrelson Company wasn't available when we needed it to dry in the building [seal the roof], so we really should plan on some substitute.

Q. What did John say?

A. He told me to write up the proposed change and submit it as soon as possible, and I gave it to him that day, or maybe the next day.

Q. Was there more to that conversation?

A. No, that was about it.

Q. Can you remember any more meetings about the roofing material?

A. Yes, I remember we talked once more about it, after we laid the roofing membrane. The question came up whether we needed to use more gravel, and we decided that we didn't.

Q. Who talked about that?

A. I think that this time it was Mary and John Forsythe and me. That was near the end of the entire outside job, so it would have been in August sometime.

Q. Can you tell us who said what at that meeting?

A. Well, not really; just that I said that I thought that the gravel in the plans was sufficient, and they asked about the lighter weight of the new membrane, and I told them that really wasn't a problem because we were putting down a lot of gravel anyhow. That was about it.

Q. Can you remember any other conversations or meetings about the roofing material?

A. You mean, before this lawsuit came up?

Q. Right.

A. No, I think you've got them.

Q. Do you recall that there was a meeting at the end of July, about ordering more gravel?

A. Oh, yeah, but that . . . well, that wasn't more gravel so that we'd have more per square foot; that was more to cover a projection that had been added, over the front entrance. We kept the per square foot number the same.

Q. Who was present at that meeting?

A. That was just me and John, I think, because it was no big deal.

Q. Who said what?

A. Well, just what I told you. I told John that we needed more gravel to cover the area that wasn't in the original plan, and he said go ahead and order and submit a change order right away. So we did.

Q. Do you remember any other meetings on the roofing material?

A. No.

Q. Let me show you what has been marked as Strongis Deposition Exhibit 15. Is this a letter that your office sent to the general contractor at the end of the job?

A. Yes. Oh, yeah, I looked at this last night.

Q. This letter lists one more meeting about the roofing materials, doesn't it?

A. Yeah, its got two meetings that I mentioned, and then there's a meeting mentioned in here where the owner actually came down, in early July.

Q. Who else was at that meeting?

A. Well, Pierson, the owner, and me, Mary Jonas, and I think the architect, Penn Sharp, was there, too.

Q. And who said what at that meeting?

A. Well, of course, the owner, all he wanted to talk about was when we'd be finished, you know, when the building would be dried in. Sharp and Mary were looking at the weight limits for the roof. All I wanted to know was whether they would sign off on the subroof so that we could finish up, since the new membrane had come in and we were ready to go.

Q. What happened as a result of that meeting?

A. Oh, it all got worked out. The weight was good, and the subroof passed, so we could start.

By using the document in this way, we have made the whole equal more than the sum of the parts: the deponent remembered three meetings; the document had two of those meetings and another. If we had started with the document, we would have heard only about the three meetings in the document. If we didn't use the document, we would have learned only about the three that the witness initially remembered. By holding back on the document until the witness's recollection was exhausted, we learned about all four meetings.

Chapter Ten

CONCLUDING THE DEPOSITION

"It ain't over, til it's over."
— *Yogi Berra*

10.1 MAKING SURE YOU HAVE IT ALL

Before you conclude the deposition, take a recess. Normally you have only one opportunity to depose the witness; once you let the witness go, it is difficult to bring him back.[1] Therefore, take a moment or several to think carefully about any areas of examination or particular questions that you may have overlooked. If your client is there or a co-counsel, check with them as well. Don't rush to conclude the examination, which is probably what opposing counsel is encouraging you to do.

Attorneys often ask a set series of questions at the end of the deposition:

Q. Now Mr. Tilts, are there any answers to my questions that you wish to change before we close this deposition?

A. Not that I can think of.

Q. Is there any information I asked about that you remember now but you didn't recall when I asked the question about it?

A. No.

Q. Thank you.

A witness rarely remembers anything new or changes an earlier answer. The value of these questions occurs when impeachment is necessary. If a witness attempts to avoid the sting of your impeachment, you can then come back and show that you gave him a chance to correct and change his answers during the deposition.

---

1. Fed.R.Civ.P. 30(a)(2)(B) prohibits more than one deposition of a witness unless leave of court is obtained or the parties otherwise stipulate.

10.2 ARRESTS AND CONVICTIONS

Under appropriate circumstances, you may use prior convictions to impeach a witness.[2] The court also has discretion to allow you, when cross-examining a character witness, to inquire about arrests of the person whose character is being attested to.[3] For some strange reason, however, most witnesses become quite resentful when asked if they have ever been arrested or convicted of a crime. You may reasonably assume that the witness will cease any cooperation with you once you have asked these questions. Therefore, while you should always ask the witness about arrests and convictions, save these questions until the end of the deposition when cooperation no longer matters. But ask. You may find yourself surprised by the answer. Even if you decide the information is not worth bringing out at trial, the mere prospect that you may reveal a prior secret conviction may be enough to induce the opposing party to settle the case.

10.3 COMPLETING, ADJOURNING, RECESSING, TERMINATING, ENDING, CONTINUING THE DEPOSITION: HOW DO YOU KNOW IF YOU ARE DONE WHEN IT'S DONE?

In those jurisdictions that have not adopted the 2000 Amendment to the Federal Rules limiting depositions to seven hours on one day[4] or some similar limitation, the deposing attorney at the end of the deposition normally selects "appropriate" language from this shopping list of stock phrases:

1. The deposition is adjourned until next month;

2. It is suspended until a time to be identified in the future;

3. It is adjourned until such time as the court rules upon certain outstanding motions;

4. It is terminated pending further discussions between the parties on the production of documents;

5. It is suspended to permit her to move for an order to compel discovery;

6. It is concluded, subject to her right to recall the witness for further questioning should that be required; or,

7. It is over.

---

2. Fed.R.Evid. 609.
3. Fed.R.Evid. 608(b).
4. Fed.R.Civ.P. 30(d)(2).

What is the legal effect of using phrase four as opposed to phrase two? Young attorneys, or attorneys inexperienced at deposition, have probably spent collective centuries worrying over this question. In fact, none of these phrases have any effect at all. Unless you have agreed to continue the deposition or have obtained a court order permitting you to do so, Rule 30(b)(4) requires the officer to state on the record that the deposition is complete and to give any stipulations made by the lawyers.

All of these phrases, and any other similar phrases that regional creativity has brought into local practice, accomplish the same thing: the witness is excused to go home with no obligation to return unless ordered by the court or requested by agreement of counsel. In this matter, there is no arcane ritual to be followed to achieve a certain effect; no magic language to preserve one's rights and opportunities.[5]

But how about the situation where the deposing attorney has done all that she can, but she knows that new documents are on the way? Or that later witnesses may provide information justifying further questioning of this witness? Or that rulings from the court on claims of privilege may open new areas? What should she do to protect her right to come back later for further deposition questioning? And what about the defending attorney who believes that the deposing attorney is trying to "hold open" the witness's deposition just to irritate or discomfort the witness with the threat of having to return? How can he protect the witness without exposing either the witness or himself to paying costs for a motion to compel discovery?

The entitlement to have a witness return to answer more questions is governed not by whether the deposing attorney selected the proper phrase at the end of the day, but by whether there is some justification for the return. In other words, if the court is later persuaded that it should deny the witness's privilege claims and orders the deposition to resume, the witness will have to come back regardless of the language used at the "end" of the last deposition session. Conversely, if the deposing attorney cannot demonstrate a sufficient reason for resuming the deposition, then the witness does not have to come back, no matter how careful the attorney was to say at the deposition, "Adjourned, subject to my right to recall."

---

5. In fact, Fed.R.Civ.P. 30(d) is the only section of the Rules which touches upon the procedure for concluding a deposition: on the grounds of bad faith, annoyance, embarrassment, or oppression of the deponent or a party, the court in which the action is pending or where the deposition is held may terminate the deposition (or may place limitations upon its continuation). If a party to the deposition demands suspension so that a motion for such an order may be made, the deposition "shall be suspended." Under Rule 37(a)(4), the court may impose costs of making or defending the motion upon the unsuccessful party or witness.

Rule 30(a)(2)(B) requires court permission or a stipulation before you can depose a witness a second time. If attorneys disagree on whether the deposition was completed, the simple and safe approach is to seek an order permitting the witness to be deposed again. A slightly more risky approach is simply for the deposing attorney to notice the deposition again, thereby putting the defending party in the position of either appearing for further deposition, applying for a protective order, or failing to appear. If she fails to appear, you can bring the matter to the court on a motion to compel discovery. In any event, this process will resolve the question; arguing about the particular litany used at the "end" of the deposition does not.

Chapter Eleven

OBNOXIOUS OR OBSTRUCTIONIST DEFENDING COUNSEL

"[The enemy] must be hounded and
annihilated at every step and all
their measures frustrated."
— Joseph Stalin

Some attorneys believe it is their job in defending a deposition to prevent the discovery of information at virtually any cost. At least three reasons account for such behavior: first, the attorney is unprepared to defend the deposition and is desperate to avoid the substance of the case where he is ignorant; second, the attorney is inexperienced in depositions and trial, and therefore lacks the confidence to allow the facts to come out; and third, the attorney does not accept the premise of the Federal Rules of Civil Procedure that pretrial discovery of the opponent's information is favored[1] and trial by ambush, obfuscation, and surprise is disfavored.[2]

The obstructionist attorney is more likely to prey upon young or apparently inexperienced counsel, whom he believes he can intimidate, but he may try his tactics on any attorney in any deposition, from the small tort case to the multi-district commercial contract and RICO matter. A few, simple techniques will help you to control the obstructionist attorney; if they do not control him, at least the techniques will help you to complete the deposition despite the interference.

---

1. The goal of the discovery rules is to promote "free and open" exchange of information between the parties and to prevent surprise and delay. See, e.g., *Davis v. Romney*, 55 F.R.D. 337 (D. Pa. 1972); U.S. v. I.B.M., 68 F.R.D. 315 (D.N.Y. 1974); *Wiener King, Inc. v. Wiener King Corp.*, 615 F.2d 512 (3d Cir. 1980).

2. From time to time, it seems that a "fourth category" attorney is discovered —the absolute jerk—but, like the "new" dinosaur that turns out to be the scrambled bones of previously known dinosaurs, the "jerk" usually turns out to be an energetic combination of two or all three of the previously known categories.

11.1 IRRITATING OR OBSTRUCTING BEHAVIOR

Your first step in dealing with the obstructionist defending counsel is to ask yourself if she is merely being irritating and making the deposition more difficult or actually obstructing and frustrating your ability to obtain information from the witness. In one situation, opposing counsel may make long speaking objections which do not have the effect of coaching the witness, or she may ask for clarifications of questions but not instruct the witness not to answer. In the second situation, opposing counsel may whisper in the witness's ear while a question is pending or instruct the witness to refuse to answer merely because she does not like the way you phrased the question. The effects on the deposition from the two types of behavior—irritating and obstructing—are different and your responses to the two should also be different.

11.2 THE IRRITATING OPPOSING COUNSEL

First, let us examine the first situation described above—the irritating opposing counsel. The following are a few steps you can take to deal with this type of interference.

11.2.1 Size up your opponent.

Some lawyers are naturally "jerks" while others sometimes behave that way as a calculated strategy. Never forget, however, that every time opposing counsel asks for a question to be clarified or confers with the witness while a question is pending, it does not mean that the lawyer is being a jerk and is engaging in obstructionist tactics. Some lawyers ask for clarification because your question has genuinely confused them and they do not want the witness to be similarly confused. Some lawyers confer with the witness while a question is pending because a legitimate issue of privilege must be cleared up before the witness can answer. Some objections are made because they are valid and legitimate.

Unless you have had previous bad experiences with the opposing counsel or have learned through your intelligence system that this lawyer is one of the hated breed of obstructionists, you should assume, until proven otherwise, that he is dealing with you in good faith. Responding with nuclear weapons to a polite request for clarification of a question is guaranteed to turn the deposition into an unpleasant experience for all involved. More importantly, it is also likely to interfere with your ability to obtain the maximum amount of information from the witness.

Treating opposing counsel as the enemy every time he opens his mouth may also cause you to ignore a proper objection. If it later becomes necessary to offer the deposition at trial and the court sustains the objection, important evidence in support of your case may end up being excluded. It may be that opposing counsel is being a jerk, or it may be that legitimate objections are being made (or perhaps both are true). Make this decision on an objection-by-objection basis.

In short, if opposing counsel is behaving reasonably and is not disrupting the deposition, respond accordingly. A pleasant, courteous response on your part may engender the same sort of behavior from opposing counsel when you are defending his deposition of one of your witnesses.

11.2.2 Keep your goals in mind.

In all discovery depositions your primary goal is to obtain information, helpful or harmful, in order to prepare better for trial. To state this goal more succinctly, it is to ask questions and receive answers. As we have said before, you want to exhaust the witness's information about the case.

In order to accomplish this goal, especially when the time for deposition is limited, you must operate efficiently. By engaging in obstructionist behavior, the opposing attorney is trying to get you to act inefficiently by inviting you to argue about objections, by encouraging debate on procedural points, or by calling on you to refine and further refine questions.[3]

Therefore, whenever you find yourself doing something at a deposition other than asking questions and taking answers, you should pause and ask yourself whether you have abandoned your primary goal for a good reason. Unless the "extracurricular activity" is more important than discovering your opponent's case from this witness, you should go back to asking questions. Your "cue" for this kind of reflection is very clear: To whom are you talking? If you are talking to the opposing attorney, rather than to the witness, your primary goal of obtaining information has been abandoned.

11.2.3 Do not play his game: act, do not react.

This point is closely related to keeping the primary goal in mind. For whatever of the reasons that motivate his behavior, the obstructionist defending attorney does not want the flow of information at the deposition to go forward. In other words, his primary goal is directly opposed to your primary goal. If you respond to his objections; if you

---

3. The Advisory Committee Notes to Fed.R.Civ.P. 30(d)(2), limiting depositions to seven hours and one day, states that "if the deponent or another person [opposing counsel] impedes or delays the examination, the court must authorize extra time."

begin to debate points with counsel and the witness; if, as often happens, you unconsciously switch from open questions to closed, cross-examination style questions; if you begin to become formalistic, objecting to routine and legitimate conferences between the witness and defense counsel which are not actually interfering with the deposition; then you have begun to play his game, and that is a victory for him.

If, instead, you merely ignore him and literally do not look at him while he is making his outrageous objections and do not so much as acknowledge that he has made a statement or objection, the odds are he will tire of the game and become much more docile. In short, behave as if opposing counsel were dead and no longer involved in the deposition. This approach requires discipline and patience, however, and it undoubtedly will throw the deposition off track somewhat, because the witness may well be confused about what is happening. Nevertheless, if you can discourage the obstructionist counsel, the remainder of the deposition may be much more profitable.

Let's look at an example of this tactic of ignoring opposing, obstructionist counsel:

Q. Now, Mrs. Adomaitis, what makes you believe that your broker was not handling your stock account properly?

OBJECTION:

Well, wait, let's just get our time periods straightened out here before we all get confused. What are you talking about? When she first believed that he was churning, or what?

Q. Mrs. Adomaitis, please answer the question.

OBJECTION:

Counsel, now, you haven't answered my question. I don't know when we are talking about here, and I'm sure that the witness doesn't either. That's just not the way to take an intelligent deposition, and I'm surprised your senior partners didn't tell you that, because maybe you just don't know. But you've got to have a time period for all these things.

Q. Mrs. Adomaitis, do you remember the question?

A. Well, no, I'm not sure that I do.

Q. All right, let me ask it again. What makes you believe that your broker was not handling your stock account properly?

OBJECTION:

Counsel, you are just trying to confuse the witness now, by not telling her when you are asking about her knowledge. Clearly, she knows a lot of things today that she didn't know back when this guy was handling her account, and it's not fair for you to just ask about what she knows or what she knew without saying "when." So, why don't you ask a better question?[4]

Q. Mrs. Adomaitis, will you answer the question, please?

A. Yes. I think that I was first, you know, a little suspicious when I saw some interest charges on my monthly statements, and he wasn't very direct when I asked him about them.

The important things to notice here are that the attorney taking the deposition never responded to the challenge by the defending attorney and that she continually pressed the witness for an answer. If we were watching this little drama, we would have seen that the taking attorney kept her eyes on the witness at all times, never looking at defending counsel. No attention at all was paid to his spurious comments; she did not even say, "Your objection is noted," or "The question is proper," or make any other comment indicating she even heard him. The objection will be in the record whether she says it will be or not; the question is proper, or it is not; there is no need for comment. So she ignores him and takes almost all of the fun out of his game.

By watching the witness throughout defending counsel's comments and then immediately coming back to the witness with, "Can you answer the question?" you clearly send the message that those interruptions will not deter you from obtaining the information and that the witness should not gain any courage from them.

If you were to put this message into words, it would be: "I will stay here until next Tuesday if it's necessary because of the jerk sitting alongside of you; so you decide—do we do this the easy way, or do we do this the hard way, because we are going to do it." Where the witness cannot really understand why the objection is important, or even understand it at all, this appeal has some chance of success.

Having said this, sometimes merely acknowledging that opposing counsel has made an objection will cause the deposition to move forward. Opposing counsel feels it necessary for reasons of ego to receive some sort of recognition that he has made a statement and he will continue to be disruptive until you give that recognition. Your response

---

4. "Why don't you ask a better question?" or "Why don't you ask the witness? . . ." are apparently among the most potent needles a defending attorney can jab into a deposing attorney. There are reported instances of attorneys getting into physical wrestling matches in the deposition room, spilling out into the hallway, over who has the right to suggest questions at a deposition; and there is one instance, transcribed in what has become a famous page of transcript in Washington, D.C., where the attorneys end a series of bitter exchanges about "suggested" questions with the taking attorney shouting at the defending attorney, "___ you, I'll ask whatever questions I want to!" This is probably not the most efficient way to obtain information from the witness.

is quite simple: Without looking at counsel merely state, "Your objection is noted. Now, Mrs. Adomaitis, please answer my question." Remember, the objective of the game is to get answers to your questions, not to fight with opposing counsel.

11.2.4 Ask good questions.

One of the most effective ways to frustrate opposing counsel, who is waiting to pounce upon every minor flaw in questioning, is to ask good questions to begin with. While you certainly cannot plan every question that you are going to ask at a deposition taken for discovery purposes, you can think in advance about matters like form of questions and the proper handling of documents.

If opposing counsel has the opportunity to object that your questions are compound, and they are, you would be foolish to try to argue in their defense; all you should do is correct them by asking two questions instead of one. But there is no doubt that this type of success encourages the obstructionist opposing counsel. Therefore, you have to beat him by avoiding those kinds of problems with your questions by thinking them through in advance. Do not put yourself, with poor questions, in the position of letting him be right in his obnoxious objections.

11.3 THE OBSTRUCTING OPPOSING COUNSEL

While the approach for dealing with the merely irritating opposing counsel is to ignore him, this tactic does not work with the obstructionist who actually prevents you from obtaining necessary information. Ignoring opposing counsel when he is coaching the witness about what answer to give to your question or improperly instructing the witness not to answer only rewards what is clearly improper behavior. The question is how to control such behavior.

11.3.1 Relate to the witness.

The first tactic for controlling such behavior is to relate to the witness. Even when the witness is the chief executive officer of the opposing company, you may well be able to develop a relationship with her that helps when her counsel gets too obnoxious and unreasonable. For example, when you ask a simple question and opposing counsel claims it is actually as complicated as the Theory of Relativity, the witness may be too honest or too embarrassed to agree. Consider the following exchange, which is rather common:

> Q. Mrs. Lemontas, how long have you been in charge of sales for the Crabtree Company?

OBJECTION:

> Counsel, you have got to be more specific than that. I mean, what are we talking about, in terms of "in charge" of sales? That could mean, "How long has she been involved in selling any products for them?" or "How long has she supervised anyone in sales?" or any number of things. You have to ask a better question.

Q. Mrs. Lemontas, do you understand my question, "How long have you been in charge of sales for Crabtree?"

A. Well, yes, I think that I do.

Q. Could you answer the question, please?

You may think the responsible executive, as well as the lowly corporate employee, would carefully follow the defending attorney's lead in such a situation, but in fact the relationship is just not that simple. First, at the human level, the witness may feel a bit offended that she is being told by a lawyer that she does not understand something, especially when that something seems perfectly clear and understandable. Second, while she may be willing to sit quietly while the lawyer makes his speech about simple things being complicated, it is quite another thing to be called on herself to agree. That direct question, "Do you understand?" calls on her to lie or tell the truth, on the record, and that requires more deliberation than just sitting and letting the lawyer make his lawyer noises. Third, as she may already have learned in this deposition, the net effect of these kinds of arguments is that the information is eventually obtained, but it just takes longer. It wastes her time (and the company's money). This last consideration is especially persuasive with executives and professionals who have a healthy estimate of the value of their own time. Sometimes this fact can be brought rather forcibly home to the witness:

Q. Doctor, I am sure your time is worth more than mine, but it appears that at the pace we are moving it will not be possible to finish up your deposition today. I will do my best, however, to tie it up by five o'clock. So let me ask you again the question I just asked and to which your counsel objected.

11.3.2 Making your record and escalating the response.

Every once in a while it is useful to demonstrate to opposing counsel that you are aware of his tactics and you are keeping track of them for later discussions with the court. Obviously, if his objections about "ambiguous" or "compound" or "confusing" are having little effect upon the witness's answers and your opportunity to gain information, there is no sense at all in having any discussion with opposing counsel. In such a situation stick with rule number one, which is to ignore him.

Sometimes, however, such obstructionist tactics cause some trouble; they do not bring the flow of information to a halt, but they slow it down so the effect is felt. You may be concerned the witness's answers are being affected. You can clearly note each obstruction on the record for later reference by saying something such as, "Let the record reflect that Mr. Barkauskas is again conferring with the witness before the witness has answered the question."

If the interruptions are becoming more serious and your low-grade noting-for-the-record approach does not discourage them, the next approach is to escalate the response and draw a line, a tactic that did not work particularly well in Vietnam, but often performs better in depositions. A typical series of escalating responses is to:

1. Note for the record the improper conduct in which counsel is engaging. "Let the record reflect that counsel is conferring with the witness while the question is pending."

2. Have the court reporter mark the point in the record where the offending conduct is occurring. "Counsel, this is the third time in a row that you have conferred with the witness while a question is pending. You know that is improper and I am asking the court reporter to mark the deposition."[5]

3. Threaten to seek the assistance of the court. "Let the record reflect again that counsel is conferring with the witness while a question is pending. Counsel, if this conduct persists, you will leave me little choice but to ask the court for assistance. Of course, if I do that I will also ask that your client be held responsible for expenses [or the lawyer if you think that will be more persuasive]."

4. Take a break and talk with opposing counsel away from the witness. Counsel cannot afford to back down in front of his client; that is not the way to maintain good client relationships. Sometimes a reasonable request made in the hallway apart from the client will have better prospects for success. "Bill, this is getting out of hand. I don't want to break this off and see Magistrate Jones—you're busy and so am I—but you are putting me in a corner. If you don't stop the conferring, I am going to have to call him."

5. Display anger. Use this tactic with caution. Depending on your ability to display outrage and to intimidate opponents, you may cause opposing counsel to back down or to become angry himself and even more outrageous in his behavior. Opposing counsel will never back down immediately—that would be

---

5. Most court reporting machines have a key that places a mark in the margin of the tape. The purpose of this is so the reporter can quickly locate a particular question or answer.

conceding defeat in the eyes of his client—but it may cause a change in behavior later in the deposition. "[Slamming down the hand on the table] This has got to stop. What you are doing is outrageous and a complete violation of the rules. Either you stop it or I am going to get the judge to stop it!"

6. Note on the record the time consumed by breaks, conferring while a question is pending and other disruptive contact. "Let the record reflect that counsel and the witness took a break while a question was pending and were gone for seventeen minutes." The Advisory Committee Notes to 31(d)(2), the rule limiting depositions to seven hours on one day, states the court must grant additional time if the witness or counsel engage in inappropriate, time-consuming conduct.

7. Draw a line in the sand. Remember, however, if that line is crossed you have little choice but to follow through with what you threatened. "Counsel, if you confer one more time I am adjourning the deposition while I seek a protective order and expenses. It's your choice."

8. Go to the magistrate or judge. See § 12.2.1.

11.3.3   Use the discipline of the rules.

While it may not always be evident, many lawyers feel somewhat constrained by a clear statement in the law that certain kinds of conduct are prohibited. Bringing to the offending lawyer's attention the prohibitions of Rule 30(d)(1) may control the improper conduct.

> "Counsel, that last objection was argumentative and suggestive and clearly designed to coach the witness. I hardly need to point out to you that Rule 30(d)(1) of the Federal Rules of Civil Procedure states that 'Any objection during a deposition must be stated concisely and in a non-argumentative and non-suggestive manner.' Please do not violate that rule again."

11.3.4   Use a videotape deposition.

Where opposing counsel has a reputation for obstructionist behavior or previous experience with this lawyer has convinced you that improper behavior is likely to occur, recording the deposition by videotape may stop the behavior before it starts. For whatever reasons, lawyers who engage in the most outrageous conduct when only a court reporter is present, will be on their best behavior when their actions are being recorded on videotape. Perhaps their knowledge that the tape can be shown to the judge or magistrate accounts for this, but it works. Rule 30(b)(2) gives the noticing attorney the option of recording the deposition by videotape, audiotape or stenographically. Use videotape if you expect problems.[6]

11.3.5 The special problem of instructions not to answer.

Instructing a witness not to answer can be a perfectly proper response by opposing counsel to one of your questions. If your question calls for privileged information, you are inquiring into an area that the court has previously ordered off limits, or opposing counsel is adjourning the deposition to seek an order terminating the deposition because of your own improper conduct, instructing the witness not to answer is the correct approach. A problem arises, however, when opposing counsel gives the instruction, not because of a legitimate reason, but because he does not like the answer that will be given.

An instruction not to answer is a complete frustration of your ability to obtain information, at least on the topic covered by the question. The first step in dealing with such an instruction is to request opposing counsel to state the reasons for the instruction.

Q. Mr. Glietus, when did you first learn about the problems with the computer design?

OBJECTION:

Hold on. I have no idea of what you mean by first learning about the problems. You make it sound like all of sudden he learned this. He could have gradually learned about it.

Q. Please answer the question.

OBJECTION:

No way. I am not going to let him answer that question the way you are asking it.

Q. Again, please answer the question.

OBJECTION:

Are you deaf? I am instructing the witness not to answer.

Q. Are you following your lawyer's instruction and refusing to answer?

A. Yes.

Q. Counsel, I am asking you to state the reason for your instruction not to answer.

OPPOSING COUNSEL:

Because your question stinks.

---

6. See § 1.11.2.

Q. Rule 31(d)(1) states you may only instruct a witness not to answer in order to preserve a privilege, to prevent me from violating a protective order, or if you are adjourning the deposition to seek an order limiting or terminating the deposition. Which one of these are you relying on?

OPPOSING COUNSEL:

I don't have to tell you that.

Q. Are you refusing to give the basis for your instruction?

OPPOSING COUNSEL:

Yes.

Q. Counsel, I am sure you are aware that Rule 26(b)(5) requires that if you are claiming privilege as the basis for your instruction, you must expressly claim the privilege and describe the nature of the documents, communications, or things in a manner which will allow me to determine the applicability of the privilege. Rule 37(a)(2)(B) also requires that we confer to see if I can obtain the information called for by my question without seeking court action. Do you see any way for me to get that information or to get around this problem?

OPPOSING COUNSEL:

You guys who sit there and spout off statutes make me sick. If you don't have any more questions, I suggest we end this deposition now.

Once opposing counsel has given the instruction not to answer, it is difficult for him then to change his mind without losing face. The attempt is worth making, however, but you are more likely to be successful if you do so out in the hallway away from the witness. If unsuccessful, be sure to place your efforts on the record when you return to the deposition room.

If opposing counsel will not bend, it makes sense to finish the deposition before seeking the assistance of the court. If you adjourn the deposition to seek an order compelling an answer and the court refuses to grant the order, opposing counsel may oppose resuming the deposition. Finishing the deposition also allows you to think calmly about the legal merits of the instruction outside the heated atmosphere of the deposition room

Finally, earlier instruction not to answer may be completely forgotten if you ask the same question several hours or, in a longer deposition, even days later. The additional time may also give you some ideas of how to work around the instruction and get the information you need.

11.4 OBSTRUCTING BEHAVIOR THAT ISN'T

There are several common deposition tactics that, at first glance, appear to interfere with your ability to obtain information, but with experience are easy to avoid. Let's look at several of these.

11.4.1 Objection, vague.

You can ignore objections that do not coach the witness, unless of course, they are valid—in which case you should rephrase the questions. Sometimes, however, opposing counsel and the witness have worked out a routine, particularly for questions that have been objected to as vague, which effectively stops the flow of information. Here is an example:

Q. Mrs. Lemontas, how large is the sales department at the Crabtree Company?

OBJECTION:

Objection, vague.

Q. Mrs. Lemontas, do you understand the question?

A. No, I don't.

These responses are repeated every time opposing counsel makes a vagueness objection and are obviously rehearsed.

The easiest method of dealing with this tactic is to ask the witness what it is that she does not understand about the question.

Q. Mrs. Lemontas, what is it that you do not understand about the question?

OPPOSING COUNSEL:

She doesn't know whether you are talking about the number of employees in the sales department or how big is that physical area of the company.

A. That's right.

Q. I am asking about how many employees. How big is the sales department?

A variation of the vagueness game is when, as above, opposing counsel argues that the question can mean one of two or more things. A quick way of punishing this behavior is always to ask for all of the alternatives.

Q. Mrs. Lemontas, what is it that you do not understand about the question?

OPPOSING COUNSEL:

> She doesn't know whether you are talking about the number of employees of the sales department or how big is that physical area of the company.

A. That's right.

Q. Well, let's take both of them. First, tell me the physical size of the sales department.

A. About 2,000 square feet.

Q. And how many employees does the sales department have?

A. About thirty-six.

This tactic ends when opposing counsel realizes that every time all of the proposed interpretations are addressed and the questioning attorney is learning even more information.

11.4.2 Dictionary.

Sometimes witnesses play this game without any help from opposing counsel. Sometimes counsel alone plays it. Here is an example:

Q. What procedures does the purchasing department follow in placing orders for computer parts?

A. What do you mean by procedures?

Q. Well, I mean what does purchasing routinely do when it buys computer parts?

A. What do you mean by routinely?

Q. I mean regularly. Do you have a regular practice for ordering parts?

A. I am not sure what you mean by regular practice.

The witness may well be genuinely confused by the meaning of the questions. Or it may be that this is a sharp witness who is attempting to lure you into playing the game of dictionary and diverting you from your original question. The way to respond to this game is to turn it back on the witness.

Q. Mr. Vitar, what precautions did you take when you learned that the boiler was overheating?

OBJECTION:

> Objection, vague. What do you mean by precautions?

Q. Mr. Vitar, are you familiar with the word "precautions"?

A. Yes.

Q. What does that word mean to you?

A. Well, I guess it means what you do to prevent problems.

Q. Okay, using that definition, what precautions did you take when you learned that the boiler was overheating?

Chapter Twelve

PROTECTIVE ORDERS AND APPLICATIONS TO THE COURT

*"They say that the first inclination
which an animal has is to protect itself."*
— *Diogenes Laertius*

12.1 PROTECTIVE ORDERS

Sometimes you can anticipate that problems will occur before a deposition. Perhaps the deposition has been noticed for an inconvenient time or place, you anticipate difficulties with issues of privilege or the proper scope of discovery, the opposing attorney's past behavior in the case makes you fear that improper behavior will occur at this deposition, or you are concerned that trade secrets will be revealed during the course of the deposition. When these occur, one of the parties or the witness should seek a protective order resolving the problem before convening the deposition with its attendant costs and inconvenience for all involved.[1]

Rule 26(c) gives an indication of the wide variety of problems that may be subject to a protective order. Under this rule, a court may make "any order which justice requires to protect a party or person from annoyance, embarrassment, oppression, or undue burden or expense," including one or more of the following:

1. that the . . . discovery not be had;

2. that the . . . discovery may be had only on specified terms and conditions, including a designation of the time or place;

3. that the discovery may be had only by a method of discovery other than that selected by the party seeking discovery;

4. that certain matters not be inquired into, or that the scope of the . . . discovery be limited to certain matters;

5. that discovery be conducted with no one present except persons designated by the court;

---

1. In fact, if you fail to obtain a protective order in advance, you may not be allowed to object to the discovery during the deposition. *Mitsui and Co. (U.S.A.) Inc. v. Puerto Rico Water Resources Authority*, 93 F.R.D. 62 (D.C. P.R. 1981).

6. that a deposition, after being sealed, be opened only by order of the court;

7. that a trade secret or other confidential research, development, or commercial information not be revealed or be revealed only in a designated way; and

8. that the parties simultaneously file specified documents or information enclosed in sealed envelopes to be opened as directed by the court.

You can move for a protective order either to the court in which the action is pending or the court where the deposition is to be taken. Under Rule 26(c), however, you must file with the motion a certification that you have in good faith conferred or attempted to confer with other affected parties in an effort to resolve the dispute without court action. Many of the jurisdictions following the pre-1993 version of the Federal Rules of Civil Procedure also have rules imposing a similar requirement. The risk of bringing a motion for a protective order is that, if unsuccessful, the court may order the moving party or lawyer to pay the opposing party's reasonable expenses, including attorney's fees for opposing the motion. Conversely, if the motion is granted, the opposing party may be required to pay the reasonable expenses, including attorney's fees for bringing the motion.

While protective orders have traditionally been used defensively, you can also use them offensively. In advance of the deposition you may also seek a protective order that supports inquiry into a certain area if you believe that this inquiry should be permitted and that opposing counsel is likely to refuse to permit questioning in the area.

A written request for a protective order can be simple in form and ordinarily does not require the support of lengthy case authority. Rule 26(b)(1) provides the primary authority for a motion for a protective order granting permission to inquire into an area. This rule allows discovery into all matters, not privileged, which are relevant or which may lead to the discovery of admissible evidence. Thus, the best support for a protective order motion seeking permission to inquire into an area is a strong factual argument that the area is relevant to your case or may reasonably lead to admissible evidence. A motion for a protective order seeking to preclude inquiry into an area should, conversely, demonstrate that the material sought to be protected is either privileged or is so clearly irrelevant that it could not reasonably lead to admissible evidence. If you seek a protective order because of previous improper treatment of deposition witnesses by the deposing attorney, you should attach relevant transcript excerpts from previous depositions to the motion, or remind the court of its prior rulings in the case, prohibiting such abuses.

Whether topics are open to discovery is essentially a question of fact whose answer is determined by comparing the issues in the case to the materials sought to be discovered or protected, except when it comes to defining or recognizing a privilege. Because the determination of whether to issue a protective order is primarily fact-driven, extensive legal argument is not helpful in winning the motion. If you are seeking discovery, you are better advised to argue why the information sought is relevant to the claims or defenses in the case or is likely to uncover other admissible evidence, such as the names of additional witnesses or the existence and location of potentially relevant documents, than to string out a series of case citations. As a matter of logic, the more relevant the material you seek, the more likely it is that the court will allow or compel the inquiry.[2] If you are opposing the discovery you must demonstrate that the information sought is substantially unrelated to the claims or defenses in the case. Further, if you can demonstrate that the questions also invade the privacy of the deponent, it is even more likely that the court will grant a protective order.

In a case where the application for a protective order depends upon a factual determination by the court, the court may examine relevant material *in camera*, so that a finding can be made on privilege or trade secrecy (Rule 26(c)(7)), relevance, harassment, invasion of privacy, and so forth. Sometimes the court will permit counsel seeking discovery to participate in such *in camera* inspections. This inspection is governed by rules of confidentiality which counsel must obey. The counsel producing the documents for *in camera* review should be on guard in this circumstance because inspection by opposing counsel may provide leads for other discovery, and therefore confer an advantage, even if discovering counsel does not violate confidentiality rules.

12.2 APPLICATIONS TO THE COURT

Modern discovery is intended to function largely without judicial intervention. Occasionally, however, either substantive problems or an attorney's posturing interfere with the appropriate flow of information. In such instances, the only recourse may be requesting relief from the court.

Born of necessity, the oral application to the court provides a vehicle for quick resolution of discovery disputes. Although "Let's get the judge

---

2. This balancing test is analogous to the test under Fed.R.Evid. 403, where the court must weigh relevance against unfair prejudice. In the discovery context, the court is weighing relevance against the burden of production.

on the phone!" may actually be wielded more often as a threat than as a real suggestion, it is generally an efficient way to resolve discovery problems where magistrates or even judges are willing to listen to disputes over the telephone. If the courthouse is relatively close, the attorneys may appear in person, but obviously that takes more time.

While protective orders are used if a problem arises before the deposition is convened, the procedure for obtaining relief once the deposition has commenced or is scheduled to commence is to move for relief under several provisions of the rules. The type of problem determines what rule should be relied upon.

12.2.1   Rule 30(d).

Under Rule 30(d)(3) or Rule 30(d) of the pre-1993 version of the Federal Rules of Civil Procedure, a party or the witness may suspend the deposition and request a court order to terminate or limit the deposition as provided in Rule 26(c) because the deposition is being conducted in bad faith or in such an unreasonable manner as to annoy, embarrass, or oppress the witness or party. You can make the motion either to the court in which the action is pending or the court in the district where the deposition is being taken. If either court terminates the deposition, only the court in which the action is pending may permit it to resume. Under the provisions of Rule 37(a)(4), the court can award expenses for either bringing or defending the motion.

12.2.2   Rule 30(d)(2).

This rule permits the district court by an order in the particular case to alter the time limits for conducting a deposition, which otherwise is one day of seven hours. The rule also permits the court to extend the time, if needed, for a fair examination or because the witness or another party has impeded or delayed the examination. The motion is made to the court in which the action is pending and if the court finds that one of the parties has impeded, delayed, or frustrated the fair conduct of the deposition, it may impose sanctions on that party.

12.2.3   Rule 30(g).

If the party noticing the deposition fails to attend and proceed with the deposition or if the party fails to subpoena a witness who then fails to attend the deposition, the other parties attending the deposition may ask the court in which the action is pending to award them their reasonable expenses, including reasonable attorney's fees.

12.2.4   Rule 32(d)(4).

Errors and irregularities in the transcribing, preparing, signing, certifying, sealing, endorsing, transmitting, filing, or in the way the officer is otherwise dealing with the deposition must be raised by a motion to suppress the deposition or some part of it. The motion must be made with reasonable promptness after the defect is, or with due diligence might have been, ascertained.

12.2.5 Rule 37(a)(2).

If a witness refuses to answer a question at a deposition or if a party fails to make a designation under Rule 30(b)(6), the questioning party or, in the case of a failure to designate under Rule 30(b)(6), the noticing party may move for an order compelling an answer or designation. Rule 37(a)(3) treats an evasive or incomplete answer as a failure to answer. Under Rule 37(a)(1), any motion concerning a party is made to the court in which the action is pending, while motions concerning the witness are made to the court in the district where the deposition is being taken. Under the pre-1993 version of the Rule, motions concerning parties could also be made to the court in the district where the deposition was being taken. Rule 37(a)(2)(B) requires that you file with the motion a certification that you have in good faith conferred or attempted to confer with the witness or party failing to answer or designate in an effort to resolve the dispute without court action. The court may award expenses for bringing or opposing the motion pursuant to Rule 37(a)(4).

12.2.6 Rule 37(b).

If the court issues an order under Rule 37(a) compelling a witness to answer a question at the deposition or compelling a party to designate a witness pursuant to Rule 30(b)(6), and there is a refusal to obey the order, the court may impose a variety of sanctions against the witness or party. The court in the district where the deposition is being taken may hold in contempt a witness who refuses to obey an order to answer. The witness may also be held in contempt for refusing to be sworn. A party who refuses to answer a question or to designate after being ordered to do so is subject to the sanctions listed in Rule 37(b)(2). A party failing to abide by the order and the attorney advising the party or both can be required to pay the reasonable expenses, including attorney's fees, caused by the failure.

12.2.7 Rule 37(d).

If a party or an officer, director, or managing agent of a party or a person designated to testify pursuant to Rule 30(b)(6) fails to appear at the deposition after being served with notice, the court in which the action is pending may make whatever orders are just, including imposing any of the sanctions listed in Rule 37(b)(2)(A), (B), and (C). The court can also require the party and the attorney advising the party or both to pay the reasonable expenses, including attorney's fees, caused by the failure to appear. That the discovery is objectionable is no defense to the motion unless the party has a pending motion for a protective order.

12.2.8 An Example.

Let's see how one kind of these disputes actually arises during a deposition and review the process for obtaining a hearing over the telephone:

Q. Mr. Steponkis, let me ask you a few questions about the early days of your corporation. Who were the original shareholders?

BY OPPOSING COUNSEL:

Objection. That was ten years ago. It has nothing at all to do with this case. Let's try to stick to relevant questions here, Adrian.

Q. Mr. Steponkis, will you answer the question, please? Who were the original shareholders?

BY OPPOSING COUNSEL:

Adrian, I just objected to that question. Now, you're not going to try to play hardball here, are you? Why don't you move on?

Q. Are you going to answer the question, Mr. Steponkis?

BY OPPOSING COUNSEL:

I'm sorry, you are being so unreasonable, Adrian. I'm going to instruct the witness not to answer.

Q. Mr. Steponkis, will you answer the question, please?

A. No, I am going to follow the instructions of my lawyer.

Q. Well, let me ask this, then. Were the shares originally held by more than ten people?

BY OPPOSING COUNSEL:

Again, this just has nothing to do with the issues here, and I instruct Mr. Steponkis that he need not answer this question.

Q. Mr. Steponkis, how many people held the shares originally?

A. I'm not going to answer the question, on the advice of my attorney.

Q. Counsel, are you claiming some sort of privilege here? You realize, of course, that under Rule 30(d)(1) a witness may be instructed not to answer only to preserve a privilege, because I am violating a protective order, or you are adjourning the deposition so you can seek an order terminating or limiting the deposition. Which one of these reasons are you relying on?

BY OPPOSING COUNSEL:

> I'm claiming that these questions have nothing to do with the claims or defenses in the case, or with discovering admissible evidence in the case, and are far beyond the scope permitted by Rule 26. So, the witness does not have to answer them.

Q. Mr. Steponkis, let me see if I can get at the information in another way. There is some question whether the owners on the certificate of incorporation were all of the original owners. Let me show you that certificate, which is Steponkis Deposition Exhibit 13. Are those all of the original owners?

BY OPPOSING COUNSEL:

> Same objection. You are way out of line here, Adrian. Just ask relevant questions and we will have no problems, but you're just not going to snoop around on some fishing expedition.

Q. Mr. Steponkis, will you answer my last question about the certificate?

A. No, I am going to follow my lawyer's advice and decline to answer the question.

Q. Counsel, this is important to me, so before I call the magistrate let me confer with you, as required by the rules,[3] to see if there is anything further I can do or if there is some agreement or arrangement we can make so that I can get the information I need.

BY OPPOSING COUNSEL:

> I think I have made my position very clear. I am not budging.

Q. Well, since this is the last area I need to question the witness about, I might as well see if we can get the magistrate on the phone right now rather than waiting until the deposition is concluded.

> [Since the deposing attorney has now asked about the same subject matter in three different ways, he has created a solid record demonstrating that discovery in that area is being precluded by directions to the witness not to answer. He also has specifically asked whether the instructions not to answer were premised upon a claim of privilege, and the defending attorney refused to claim privilege or any of the grounds permitted under Rule 30(d)(1), relying instead upon a "beyond the scope of Rule 26 discovery" argument. Let's return to the deposition room:]

---

3. Fed.R.Civ.P. 37(a)(2)(B).

BY COUNSEL:

Mr. Reporter, would you please mark those last few pages, where I am asking about the original owners of the corporation and the certificate of incorporation? Then, let's just go off the record until I can get the magistrate on the telephone.

[Then, after the magistrate is on the telephone:]

Your Honor, we have a problem here in the *Smith* case, Docket Number C-93-1443. Plaintiff is taking the deposition of Mr. Julius Steponkis, the vice-president of the defendant corporation, and we have asked who the original shareholders were and how many there were. The defendant has instructed the witness not to answer on the grounds that the information being sought is beyond the scope of discovery under Rule 26. Let me now orally certify, as required by Rule 37(a)(2)(B) that I have in good faith conferred with opposing counsel in an attempt to avoid the need for court action. We have the reporter here, prepared to read the questions and objections, if you would like.

MAGISTRATE:

No, counsel, not at this point. Let me talk to defendant's counsel.

DEFENSE:

Your Honor, what plaintiff's counsel has been doing here is egregious. These questions about original ownership have nothing to do with the issues in this case, and he knows it. He is just trying to fish around to see if he can bring other people into this controversy, people who have nothing to do with the problems that his client has experienced, so that he can inconvenience and embarrass them. Besides that, I know that he is working with other counsel in a different case against my client, and he may very well be intending to share the answers in this deposition with that other lawyer to give her an advantage in that other lawsuit. That's why I had no choice but to direct the witness not to answer these improper questions.

MAGISTRATE:

Okay, let me hear the questions from the reporter.

[The questions are read back from the paper tape by the reporter.]

Counsel, put me on the speaker phone, so you and the witness can all hear my ruling. The witness is directed to answer these questions, and other questions reasonably related to them. There is nothing privileged here and, as I understand it, defense counsel is not arguing privilege. These questions may not be on matters directly part of the claims or defenses in the case, but they are reasonably intended to lead to the discovery of admissible evidence, such as the identity of witnesses with knowledge of the initial purposes and profit-sharing structure of the company. If counsel in some other lawsuit can take advantage of these answers, that has nothing to do with whether the answers should be given in this case. Their use in the other case depends upon a determination of the judge in that matter on the relevance of the information to that other case.[4] I find that these questions present a legitimate area for discovery, and, counsel for the defendant, you will not interfere by directing this witness, or other witnesses who may be asked about these topics, not to answer. Are there any other problems now, counsel?

BOTH COUNSEL:

No, Your Honor.

After closing the telephone conference with the magistrate, counsel can return to the deposition table and resume questioning. Deposing counsel should, of course, start right back into the deposition with the questions that were the subject of the application to the magistrate and to which he did not get answers. He may also want to "push the envelope" a bit, i.e., press into areas he thinks the defendant has something to hide or may claim privilege, under the assumption that the defendant's counsel is unlikely to provoke another hearing before the magistrate so soon after a loss. On the other hand, the magistrate may not be prepared to rule in favor of the plaintiff if another dispute arises immediately after the first ruling, either because the magistrate thinks that the plaintiff is pressing his luck, or because she is trying to alternate the parties receiving favorable rulings in order to give the appearance of evenhandedness. The best approach is to ask the questions that you had intended to ask and not get caught up in the "gamesmanship" of discovery.

---

4. However, the magistrate or judge ruling on this application has the discretionary power to order deposing counsel not to release the information obtained during the deposition to anyone, including counsel in another case. See, *Scott v. Monsanto Co.*, 868 F.2d 786, 792 (5th Cir. 1989). Generally, courts find this "gag-order" power relates only to matters obtained through discovery, and may not be used by courts to restrict the dissemination of material that counsel has obtained during pretrial from sources other than discovery under the rules. See, *Seattle Times v. Rhinehart*, 467 U.S. 20 (1984); *Rodgers v. United States Steel Corp.*, 536 F.2d 1001 (3d. Cir. 1976); and *International Products Corp. v. Koons*, 325 F.2d 403 (2d. Cir. 1963).

PART THREE:

DEFENDING DEPOSITIONS

Chapter Thirteen

PREPARING THE WITNESS TO BE DEPOSED

"Oh the nerves, the nerves;
the mysteries of this machine called Man!
Oh the little that unhinges it:
poor creature that we are!"
— *Charles Dickens*

About 40 percent of attorneys prepare witnesses for deposition by extensively reviewing the substantive facts of the case; another 40 percent do so by reciting an inordinately long list of "do's" and "don'ts" that even attorneys cannot remember (and therefore they are presented in writing, or on videotape, for the witness "to take home" after the last preparation session). Only the remaining 20 percent of attorneys realize that neither of these approaches deals with the primary factor affecting the witness's performance at the deposition, which is his level of confidence about his ability to perform in the deposition environment.

No matter how well you prepare the witness on the substance of his testimony, he will not present clear and persuasive testimony unless he remains calm enough to understand the questions and to respond appropriately and cautiously; by his demeanor he must demonstrate his confidence in the truth of his testimony. Your primary goal in the preparation sessions should therefore be to take burdens off of the witness's shoulders so that he can focus only on the substance of his answers.

As a general rule, the witness interview and preparation for a deposition should be separate and distinct events. Sometimes, however, the witness's role is so minor or the witness is located at such a distance that it makes good economic sense for you to combine the two sessions. Separating the two sessions permits you to be better prepared for the witness preparation session and also to have some idea of the witness's personality, intelligence, etc., when you start getting the witness ready for the deposition. Finally, having separate sessions also allows you to do any follow up investigation that might prove necessary before the deposition.

Your first task in preparing a witness for a deposition is reducing the witness's anxiety. Most witnesses dread the prospect of giving testimony at a deposition or trial. Anxiety and worry can overwhelm the witness as she conjures up scenes from *Perry Mason* and *L. A. Law* and what happens to witnesses in those shows. If the witness is a party or has her job on the line, her worries and concerns become even more heightened. In short, testifying at a deposition is not often a pleasant experience and anticipating the experience can be even more unpleasant.

Anxiety prevents witnesses from focusing on those things you want them to remember. When a witness is thinking about the types of embarrassing questions that might be asked instead of concentrating on what you are saying, the preparation session has gone far astray. Anxiety, because it is distracting, interferes with the witness's ability to understand and remember what you are saying. Therefore, if the session is going to serve its purpose—preparing the witness to testify—you must first lessen the witness's nervousness and worries about what is going to happen.

The following discussion of witness preparation assumes the attorney interviewed the witness sometime before the witness preparation session. As a result, the attorney can focus on how the witness will answer at the deposition rather than finding out what will be said.

13.1 THE WRONG WAY

We start with a portion of a "conventional" preparation session.

Q. So, John, how do you feel about this deposition coming up? You're not nervous about it, are you?

A. Well, I guess I am, a little. I'm not sure exactly what to expect, you know, I don't want to make any mistakes.

Q. Well, that's right, it's important that you don't make any mistakes, so I thought that we would go over your testimony, what you know about the facts in this case. All right?

A. Sure, that seems like a good idea. But, you know, I was just wondering, are they going to try to make me look stupid or forgetful or anything? I'm just not sure what to do if I get confused about what they're asking.

Q. Well, it is very important that you be sure about what they are asking. Don't answer any question that's unclear to you, or that is ambiguous. They may try to make you look forgetful, so watch out for that.

A. Well, you'll be there, right?

Q. Yes, of course, I'll be right there, and I can object if they try to take advantage of you. Make sure that you pause, maybe take a deep breath, before every answer, so that I have time to object if I think it's necessary. Then, pay attention to what I say in my objection, because there may be something in the question that I think is unfair or improper, and you should be aware of that when you answer.

A. Are they allowed to ask unfair or improper questions?

Q. Lawyers do it all the time. They ask questions that have a double meaning, or they try to get the witness to admit things that he really doesn't mean, or they only put in part of the story; those kinds of things. So, we have to watch out for them, and only answer fair questions. Now, another thing for you to remember is not to volunteer information. By "volunteer," I mean answering with more than you were asked for. If the other attorney asks you, "Where do you work?" your answer should be "Strongis Ironworks," not "I've worked as a foreman at Strongis for the past seventeen years." You see, he didn't ask, "What is your position?" or "How long have you worked there?" So, just answer what is asked; those lengthy answers just cause trouble.

Let's just pause here and take a moment to examine whether the attorney is actually helping her witness. The attorney asked whether the witness was nervous in a way that suggested that it is wrong to be nervous. This caused the witness to feel he is not doing the right thing. When the witness answered that he was nervous because he did not want to make any mistakes, the attorney emphasized that it is important not to make mistakes. That certainly did not reduce the witness's anxiety level. Instead, the witness might be comforted to hear the following:

> "I know that you don't want to make any mistakes, but you should not worry too much about that. You know, you will have a chance to read this deposition over once it is typed up, and I'll read it with you. If we see any mistakes, we can correct them. You really shouldn't feel that you need to be perfect. You'll make some mistakes, I'll make some mistakes, and the attorney on the other side will make some mistakes, but they just won't matter when we get to trial. Besides that, I'll be there, and if I think that anything is important enough to need correction right at the

deposition, I'll make a note of it, and I can ask you questions after the other attorney is finished."

The whole idea here is to reduce the witness's nervousness. No one has ever given a mistake-free deposition, no matter how much he was cautioned not to make mistakes, so we might as well tell the witness that there are procedures for fixing mistakes, and that we, the attorneys, will worry about identifying mistakes that need to be fixed.

Next, the witness expressed concern that the other side would try to make him look stupid or forgetful, and he said he did not know what to do if he got confused. Instead of providing reassurance, the attorney said, "Watch out for that." In other words, "You are right, that may happen, and it's your job to avoid it." The attorney could have said:

> "I'm going to be there to deal with any unfair questions, so you don't have to worry about them. I don't think they will try to be unfair, because they just want to know what you know about this case. But if I think that a question is unfair, I will deal with it, and I will tell you what to do at that time."

Further, you should tell the witness directly what to do if he feels confused by a question. "Don't answer" is not sufficient because, absent an instruction from you not to answer, the witness will be pressed for an answer and will likely become more confused. In preparing the witness, you should tell her that if a question is confusing she should say, "I don't understand the question," and not feel embarrassed by doing so.

Next, the witness asked, "You'll be there, right?" Clearly, this question signaled the witness's lack of comfort with the proceedings. By responding that she will be there to object "if they try to take advantage of you," the attorney caused more problems than she solved. "Take advantage of you" is an ominous phrase that raises the specter of more problems than the witness has yet thought of. The attorney then burdened the witness further by telling the witness to "take a breath" before every answer. Now, besides worrying about the content of his answers, and losing some undefined "advantages," the attorney has put the witness in charge of timing, also. Then, the attorney told the witness to interpret her objections before giving his answer. This did not lift burdens from the witness's shoulders, but added more.

Furthermore, the attorney reminded the witness that lawyers ask unfair and improper questions all of the time but, again, she failed to give the witness any tools to deal with such questions. Finally, by instructing the witness not to volunteer information, and failing to provide any rationale, the attorney suggested to the witness hidden rules with hidden purposes. Again, none of this put the witness at ease.

13.2 BURDEN-REDUCING PREPARATION

Let's start the preparation session all over again; this time, the focus will be on taking burdens away from the witness and allowing him to focus only on the testimony.

Q. Good morning, John. Thanks for coming in for a final session about this deposition. I imagine that you are feeling a bit nervous?

A. Yes, I guess I am.

Q. Well, that's natural. It's just a little bit of extra adrenaline pumping getting you ready to do your best. I feel the same thing every time I go into a deposition or a courtroom. Let's talk about the setup for the deposition, so that you know just what to expect.

A. Okay.

Q. The deposition will be in the offices of plaintiff's attorney, but I want you to come here one hour before the deposition, so that we can go over there together. We'll take a cab from here so that we don't have to worry about parking. Is that all right with you?

A. Yes, that's fine.

Q. They have a comfortable conference room, and there will be water and coffee throughout the deposition. Do you know what a court reporter does?

A. Yes.

Q. Well, a court reporter will be there to swear you in and to record the questions and the answers. Later on, the reporter will type up those questions and answers and send them to us, so that we can read them and correct anything that we don't think is accurate. Any questions so far?

A. No.

Q. I will be sitting right alongside you at the deposition, and anytime you think that you need to talk to me, you just tell me. We can talk right there, or we can leave the room. You just tell me you want to talk with me, and I'll take care of it. Is that all right?

A. Yes.[1]

---

1. Of course, when a question is pending the witness normally should answer before he talks with counsel. On the other hand, because the witness must be given the opportunity to discuss questions of privilege with counsel before being compelled to answer, this rule must have some flexibility. In general, as long as you do not abuse this procedure, it should be permissible for the witness to check with you if a particular question raises a problem. Where appropriate, you can prevent that interruption from becoming an issue by explaining, on the record, why the witness had a problem with the question: "Ms. Jones asked me whether we were still talking about the first transaction or had jumped ahead to the second transaction. I told her that I would ask you." Or, "Ms. Jones asked whether this last question got into a privileged area, and I told her that she could answer."

The above instruction allows you to start off the preparation session by immediately putting the witness at ease about several of his concerns. First, you explain that his anxiety is natural. Next, you address logistics—where the deposition is and how he will get there. You then talk about what a deposition is—explain the procedure to the witness. Finally, you assure the witness about what you will do for him in the deposition.

How long this part of witness preparation lasts and what is said depends on the witness. Some witnesses have had their depositions taken before or are quite experienced with the way litigation works. Others are just not the nervous or worried type. But many witnesses are entirely ignorant of the whole process and are scared to death. Tailor your witness preparation to suit the witness.

A caveat: False or insincere reassurances do not work. Comments like "Don't worry, everything will be fine," do nothing to comfort the witness when the witness knows the wrong answer may cause him to lose his job, his house, and everything else he holds dear. Far better to be honest, but upbeat and confident. Avoid false promises.

13.3 MAKING WITNESS PREPARATION STICK

Before we get into other specifics about witness preparation, a word about style is appropriate. Too often witness preparation consists of the lawyer giving the witness a long, uninterrupted lecture which may go on for up to an hour. At the end of the lecture, the attorney asks the witness if he has any questions and then sends him on his way. The attorney is then surprised to see the witness quickly forget everything discussed during the witness preparation session and start violating all of the rules the attorney thought she had so carefully impressed on the witness.

The question is how to make all of the suggestions made during the witness preparation session stick with the witness during the deposition. The answer is to follow the five important rules of witness preparation:

1. Interact

2. Confirm

3. Repeat

4. Illustrate

5. Reinforce

INTERACT

Think back to your law school days and recall how interested you were in listening to the professors' lectures. For most of us they were boring. Think how your mind wandered during the lectures and how much you retained without going back and studying your notes. The same is true of witnesses. Straight lecturing is boring and not much of what you say will be remembered. But if you make the witness preparation session a discussion with give-and-take between you and the witness, then it is more likely the witness will internalize and remember what was said.

CONFIRM

Confirming means that you constantly check with the witness to make sure that what is being said is understood, and that the witness does not have any questions.

REPEAT

Repeating information several times makes it more likely to be remembered than if you mention it only once. Therefore, give key instructions more than once. But repetition does not mean you merely say the same thing twice. Instead, phrase the information differently but make the same point each time.

ILLUSTRATE

Illustrate means exactly what it says. Every time you give an important instruction to the witness, illustrate it by an example. This will make the instruction much more understandable to the witness.

REINFORCE

Finally, reinforcing means actually having the witness practice following the instructions given. This helps impress the instructions upon the witness and makes it much easier for the witness to recall and apply the instruction during the deposition. Usually reinforcing means just reminding the witness when she violates an instruction, but it can also mean actually having the witness practice answering questions in the correct way. Constantly reminding the witness of your instructions will make it easier for them to remember the instructions during the deposition.

13.4 ADDRESSING QUESTIONS ABOUT THE PREPARATION SESSION

Whether a lawyer's conversation with a particular witness is covered by the attorney-client privilege is beyond the scope of this book, but well before the witness preparation session you should know whether the other side will be able to discover what you and the witness say to each other. You should then explain to the witness how to deal with these questions, so that he is not surprised by them at the deposition.

If the witness is covered by the attorney-client privilege, the witness should be told this:

> "Let me tell you right now that whatever we say to each other in getting you ready for your deposition is confidential. The other side is not entitled to learn about what we say here, so I want you to feel comfortable in saying whatever you wish. Do you have any questions about that?"

If the witness is not covered, you should also explain this:

> "I want you to understand that whatever we say here can be asked about during the deposition and you will have to tell them what you remember about our conversation. What this means is that we should not talk about anything or say anything to each other we would not want the other side to hear."

More important than the explanation is that you not say anything to the witness that would be better kept confidential.

13.5 ANSWERING QUESTIONS

Now let's address answering questions. This part of your preparation session is very important. The following is an example of a recommended instruction:

> At the beginning of the deposition, you will be asked to swear to tell the truth, and then the plaintiff's attorney will start his questioning. The only thing that you have to remember during this whole time is to give the shortest, correct answer to each question. Let's just take a minute here for me to explain what I mean by the shortest, correct answer. There are seven answers that are the best response to 90 percent of the questions asked at deposition. Those seven are:
>
> > (1) "Green." "Two o'clock." "In the basement."
> > (2) "Yes."
> > (3) "No.
> > (4) "I don't understand the question."
> > (5) "I don't know."
> > (6) "I don't remember."
> > (7) "I'd like to take a break."
>
> We can go through them one by one.

(1) "Green." "Two o'clock." "In the basement." If you are asked what color your car is, or when you came home in the afternoon, or where you keep your canceled checks, these short answers are best, and you don't have to worry about what the questioner really wants to know, or where he is going. If he wants more information he will ask for it. The main reason that short answers are best is that attorneys are trained to chase down any paths that appear, just in case there is something relevant at the end. We don't have any desire to prolong this deposition unnecessarily, so it helps everybody if we keep the answers short and to the point.

(2) and (3) "Yes" or "No." You will find that most of the time the attorney will ask questions that let you answer "yes" or "no." When he asks those questions, go ahead and answer that way. If he wants more information, it's his job to ask for it. If I want you to explain some answer more fully, I will talk to you at breaks, and we can ask some questions of our own at the end of his questioning. Let me worry about that.

(4) "I don't understand the question." You do not have to try to answer any question that you don't understand. It's the other attorney's job to ask understandable questions, and we don't want to waste time guessing as to what he might mean. If he uses words you don't understand, tell him, "I don't understand the question." If he uses words that you do understand, but he uses them in a way you do not understand, tell him, "I don't understand the question." If the question just gets too long, or has too many different phrases in it, tell him, "I don't understand the question." Then, if he asks what you don't understand about the question, tell him that. You don't have to try to fix his question by saying, "Well, if what you mean by 'no profit' is that we had no net profit for that period, then my answer is such and so." Just tell him that you don't understand the question and wait to see how he wants to clarify it.

(5) "I don't know." This is often the hardest answer for witnesses to give, because they feel somehow as if they should know all the answers. You just don't have to feel that way. We haven't told the other side in this lawsuit that you have all the answers, and our case does not depend at all upon you having all the answers. What you do know, tell them; what you don't know, don't worry about. Just say, "I don't know." There is no need for you to try to guess what the answer is, or to try to figure out what it probably is, unless they ask you to do that.[2] If you don't have the answer in your mind, say, "I don't know."

(6) "I don't remember." Witnesses also find it hard to use this answer, perhaps because no one wants to admit that his memory is not perfect. You are not expected to have every answer or to remember every fact that the other attorney wants to ask about. If you don't remember at the deposition, and then later something reminds you of the answer, we can correct the transcript of the deposition or we can explain at trial that you remembered, if the question even comes up at trial. But, if you are asked for information that you can't remember at the deposition just say, "I don't remember." Then, if the attorney wants to try to help you remember by showing you documents or suggesting answers, he can do that. If those things help you remember, that's fine; if they don't, you just say, "I still don't remember."

(7) "I'd like to take a break." Sometimes in the deposition you may be asked a question and you just are not sure what you are supposed to do. Maybe you think the answer should be private; maybe you think the answer is likely to be long and you need a chance to stretch and collect your thoughts; maybe you think the question is unfair in some way and you want to talk to me. If, for any reason, you want to take a break just tell me, or tell the other attorney, and we will take a break. I'll worry about whether it's a good idea or not. It is much better to take a break and talk together, to figure out how to make you comfortable with giving an answer, or to decide whether the question is objectionable, than it is to go forward and perhaps give the other side some information that really is your private business or that they are not entitled to. So, if you have any doubt as to whether you should answer, talk to me right then or say, "I'd like to take a break."

These "shortest, correct answers" are intended to simplify the witness's job—to reduce his burden at the deposition. When you give these instructions, continually reassure the witness: "Don't worry

---

2. Some attorneys in preparing witnesses for deposition tell the witness, "Don't speculate." There is only one problem with this advice: it's wrong. There is no rule against seeking the witness's speculation in a deposition, so long as that speculation is reasonably calculated to lead to the production of relevant information. For example, suppose the question is, "Who was the last person to adjust the temperature settings on the boiler?" The witness answers, "Well, I'd really have to guess, based on who was there." The next question could quite properly be, "Okay, what's your guess?" There is no basis here for directing the witness not to answer, since there is no question of privilege or harassment and the question is not patently beyond the scope of proper discovery. Yet, if the witness is told that he should not speculate, he may be confused when speculation is properly called for.

about the procedure or what the other attorney might say or do; that is why I'm there; I'll take care of all those matters, so you don't have to worry about them. All you have to worry about is giving the shortest, correct answer."

13.6   EXPLAINING THE ISSUES

Witnesses who have an interest in the outcome of the case will naturally try to give answers helpful to their chosen side. This does not mean they will be dishonest or less than fully truthful. But they will try to phrase their answers in the most helpful way possible and to emphasize those facts they believe contribute to a winning outcome.

The danger is witnesses may misunderstand or not fully grasp the position of the side they wish to help. As a result, they end up emphasizing facts which actually help the other side and do harm to their own side's position.

To avoid such problems, you should spend some time explaining the issues in the case and each side's position regarding each issue. This does not mean giving a long legal explanation to the witness or attempting to have the witness achieve your level of understanding. Instead, your goal is to help the witness develop a basic grasp of what the case is about.

If the witness is also the client, you undoubtedly will have educated them early in the case and updated them many times since. But lower-level employees and others not directly interested in the outcome may have only vague ideas of what the lawsuit is about.

You should present this sort of explanation issue by issue. Don't give a long summary, but break the discussion down into manageable bites by focusing on one issue at a time. Then for each issue, give each side's position or what it is trying to prove. If the witness's role in the facts giving rise to the litigation is limited, limit the discussion just to those issues in which the witness was involved. Like every other aspect of witness preparation, tailor your explanation to fit the witness's intellectual abilities. Do not make the explanation more complex than the witness can understand and remember.

Lawyer:

> Let's now talk about what this case concerns and how you fit into it. As you know this is an antitrust action. Dr. Rimard is claiming Hospital Pathology, Inc. has unfairly taken all of the pathology business for itself and has prevented Dr. Rimard from getting any of the business. Have you heard about that?

Witness:

> Yes, there has been a lot of talk in the doctors' lounge about the case.

Lawyer:

> The reason your deposition is being taken today is to find out whether Hospital Pathology uses general practitioners such as yourself to steer pathology patients to themselves and away from Dr. Rimard. Dr. Rimard is claiming that when a patient requires pathology work, the hospital automatically refers the patient to Hospital Pathology without letting the patient or the patient's primary care physician know about alternative sources of pathology services. Hospital Pathology, on the other hand, is claiming it and the hospital always give a patient and the primary care physician a choice about what pathology services to use.

Witness:

> Okay.

Lawyer:

> Your deposition is being taken today because you are a primary care doctor, and Hospital Pathology wants to find out what your experience has been with the referral of patients for pathology services. Does this all make sense?

Witness:

> Yes.

13.7 WHAT TO DO WHEN OBJECTIONS ARE MADE

In a preparation session, witnesses often ask what to do if a particular topic comes up, or if the opposing counsel asks irrelevant questions, or if she asks the same question over again. The attorney's typical response is, "Well, if she does that, I'll object." Unfortunately, the attorney usually does not tell the witness that he will have to answer the question anyhow.

You should tell the witness that usually he must answer the question, even if it is objectionable, and that you will specifically direct or advise him not to answer when appropriate. Discuss privileged areas with the witness and describe the ways in which such issues could come up. Tell the witness that if he has any question about whether an answer will involve privileged matters, he should tell you that he needs to talk to you before he answers, so that you do not inadvertently lose the privilege.[3] If you recognize the privilege problem without the witness's consultation you can object ("Mr. Smith, objection; there may be a matter of privilege involved here; give me a moment with the witness, please.") and then consult with the witness.

During the preparation, you should tell the witness that if privileged matters come up, you will object and also direct or advise him not to answer the question. Tell the witness that you will object to questions that are designed to harass, annoy, and embarrass the witness and may also advise or direct him not to answer. Finally, if a question calls for information covered by a protective order, it may again be necessary to instruct him not to answer.

At that same point in the preparation session, instruct the witness that opposing counsel will frequently follow up on a direction not to answer by asking the witness directly whether he will answer the question. The witness should be prepared to state, "On the advice of my counsel, I decline to answer the question."

Beyond these three situations, however—privilege, harassment/annoyance/embarrassment and protective orders—you should advise the witness that he is expected to answer all questions truthfully, and preferably in accordance with the approach outlined above, even when you have made an objection, using the short answers where possible and appropriate. Other objections that you make in defending the deposition—form, foundation, beyond the appropriate scope of the deposition, misstatement of testimony, mischaracterization of testimony—do not justify a refusal to answer, and the witness should listen to those objections only to inform himself of problems with the questions which may affect his answers. Otherwise, you should tell the witness to ignore the colloquy or argument between counsel; not to become irritated by objectionable questions; and at all times to remain as calm and aloof from such discussions as possible.

13.8   HOW TO HANDLE DOCUMENTS IN PREPARATION

In the reasonably small case where there are twenty or thirty crucial documents, you should review those documents carefully with the witness before her deposition. Witnesses are sometimes unnerved

---

3. Of course, as mentioned earlier, the questioning attorney may object strenuously if you consult with the deponent while a question is pending. Because there is no better way to protect legitimate privileges, however, this consultation before the answer is given is appropriate. If the deposing attorney raises such a fuss that you cannot consult with the witness effectively, you can take a break and take the witness out in the hallway, to discuss the possible privilege. Sometimes we call this "elbow rule," since you take the witness by the elbow and lead him out of the room; normally, this effectively prevents answers from being given without adequate counsel.

by facing documents relating to their testimony which they have not seen in months or years. The pre-deposition review serves to assure her that her testimony is consistent with the important documents and that letters written long ago will not trap her out on a limb.

Larger cases pose a different problem, however. Faced with hundreds or thousands of "crucial" documents, the witness will not be able to use them in any effective way to prepare for the deposition. In a complex case, therefore, you should provide the witness with any documents or other materials with which you wish them to be familiar before the deposition is taken. This means giving the witness only the key documents relating to her expected testimony and not overwhelming her with boxes of material of varying importance. Some lawyers also provide witnesses with summaries of what other witnesses have said in their depositions. Remember that simply giving documents to a witness for review does not ensure she will actually look at them. Therefore, you must still go through the documents with the witness at the preparation session. Here, the task falls to you to organize and review those documents and to prepare the witness by leading her through the events, using the documents to assist where necessary.

Assuming that there are several issues on which the witness is likely to be questioned at her deposition, you should arrange the documents chronologically within each issue. Then thoroughly familiarize yourself with the documents, outlining the issues and noting in the outline where the documents are relevant. (This same outline, obviously, can become the primary basis for arranging the witness's direct examination at trial.) In preparation, you should then ask the witness to describe the events pertinent to each issue and ask for clarification where the witness's description seems at variance with the documents. After this exercise, the witness should have some confidence that she has not forgotten something important shown in the documents, but she has not had time to try to review and incorporate all of the documents at one time. Preparation in this fashion is a time-consuming task for you, but it greatly eases the load on the witness.

As has been discussed elsewhere[4] a standard question at depositions is, "Have you reviewed any documents in preparation for this deposition?" The logic behind this question is that, by analogy to the procedure at trial, under the Federal Rules of Evidence, the questioner is entitled to know whether the witness has used documents "at or before trial" to refresh her recollection. Especially at a deposition, this logic fails because "reviewing a document" and "refreshing recollection" are different activities. If a witness reviews a document

---

4. See § 9.5.

under the direction or in consultation with her attorney and the witness finds the document to be consistent with her recollection, or finds that she still has no recollection, then the document has not been used to "refresh her recollection," and no basis exists, at deposition or trial, to reveal that those documents were reviewed with the attorney's assistance. That review remains privileged work product. Therefore, in preparation, you should tell the witness that in response to this question she should answer, "Yes, I have reviewed documents with my attorney in preparation for this deposition," but that you will probably direct her not to identify particular documents reviewed unless the questioning attorney can establish that some document did in fact refresh her memory on some relevant point.

13.9   PRACTICING ANSWERING QUESTIONS

The heart of witness preparation is having the witness actually practice answering questions. Only through practice will the witness fully understand how to phrase the answers to questions, how to respond to an aggressive cross-examination style, how to behave during the deposition, and how to apply the instructions given about keeping answers short, and the many other instructions given during the witness preparation session.

You cannot, however, rehearse every question you expect to be asked during the deposition nor is it necessary to do so. You need only identify the key areas on which you expect the witness to be examined and have the witness practice answering questions about these. But remember this is not just a time for practicing answering, but also to refine and improve the answers given. Listen to the witness's answers and give suggestions about how they can be phrased to better state the witness's knowledge. Then have the witness practice answering again until you are satisfied the response accurately and clearly states what the witness intends. Here is an example of what should occur.

Lawyer:

Okay, let's imagine again I am the lawyer for Hospital Pathology and let me ask you some questions about your efforts to generate pathology patients. Ready?

Witness:

Yes.

Lawyer:

Dr. Unitas, please tell me all of the things you did to get pathology patients of your own.

Witness:

Well, I contacted all of the hospitals and told them I had left Hospital Pathology and was now accepting patients of my own. And I also sent a letter to all of the primary care physicians telling them about the availability of my services.

Lawyer:

Is that all?

Witness:

That's about it.

Lawyer:

Okay, let me become your lawyer again. Those were good answers, but I think we can phrase your answer better. Didn't you tell me that when you went out on your own, you sat down and tried to figure out the best way of generating patients?

Witness:

That's true.

Lawyer:

And as I recall, you also did some research on how to start your own practice and made some phone calls to doctors to let them know you were now taking patients?

Witness:

That's true.

Lawyer:

Did you ever tell other doctors at parties and Medical Association meetings that you were now out on your own and accepting patients?

Witness:

Sure, it would come up and I would let them know.

Lawyer:

Let's see if you can incorporate this information into your answers. Here is an example of what I mean. If you were asked the question of what did you do to generate patients, based on what you've told me, a more complete and accurate answer would be this: "When I started my own practice I thought about the best way of getting patients, so I did a lot of reading on the subject such as books and articles in medical economics journals. I also talked with other doctors who were practicing on their own and received a number of suggestions about how they were able to generate patients. Another thing I did is to carefully study how Hospital Pathology went about getting patients. When I went into practice, I systematically visited all of the hospitals in the area where I met with the surgeons and other hospital staff to let them know of my availability. I explained my background and experience to them even though I had worked with many of them through the years and they were well familiar with my skills. I also sent a personally signed letter to all of the primary care physicians in the area again explaining I was available to take patients and about my experience. Finally, when I determined that a personal contact would be helpful, I followed the letter up with a phone call to the physician in which I emphasized the same things.

I think you have told me in previous interviews everything I just included in that answer, but you can add other things you did that I left out or subtract anything I got wrong. Okay?

Witness:

Yes. That's a better answer. That's what I really meant.

Lawyer:

Let's try it again. Imagine again I am the lawyer for Hospital Pathology. Tell me everything you did to generate patients when you went out on your own.

Note what is going on here. The lawyer is actively suggesting how the answer should be phrased and is not relying on the witness to think of what should be said. *The lawyer is being very careful to suggest only those facts the witness has previously related or has confirmed as true.* The information must come from the witness or documents, otherwise the danger of improper "coaching" arises. Most importantly, the lawyer does not just suggest a better way to answer, but has the witness actually practice until the lawyer is satisfied.

The witness's answers during the deposition will never be as perfect as they were during the preparation session, but they will be better for having been practiced. Even if not phrased exactly the same way as in the witness preparation session, the witness is now better aware of what facts should be included in the answer and is more likely to give the information in a persuasive manner when asked the question.

13.10 GETTING USED TO AGGRESSIVE CROSS-EXAMINATION

You do not want the witness to suffer the shock of an aggressive cross-examination for the first time during the deposition. Instead, let the witness get comfortable with this type of questioning during the witness preparation session so the witness will be more comfortable when it actually occurs during the deposition. If the witness knows what to expect, the witness is less likely to become angry or intimidated when the opposing counsel tries this tactic.

Lawyer 1:

> Sometimes aggressive questions may make you upset. The important thing for you is not to get angry or intimidated by what is happening. Just remain cool and answer the questions as best you can. Let me show you what I mean by this. Pretend we are at the deposition and Mary, my partner here, is opposing counsel. Go ahead, Mary.

Lawyer 2:

> Now Doctor, you never ran any advertisements in the Nita Medical Association Journal saying you were available to accept patients?

Witness:

> No.

Lawyer 2:

> You know every doctor in the area receives a copy of the Journal?

Witness:

> Yes.

Lawyer 2:

> A three-by-five-inch ad would only cost $250?

Witness:

> I don't know what the advertising rates are.

Lawyer 2:

> You never checked?

Witness:

> That's right.

Lawyer 2:

> You would agree this is an inexpensive way of making sure all of the physicians in the area would know about your services?

Witness:

> Well, quite frankly, I don't think many doctors read those ads nor take them seriously. I have talked with lots of doctors through the years and I have never heard of any of them bothering to read those ads. And when I talked with other doctors who had started their own practices, none of them thought it was a good idea to run an ad like that.

Lawyer 1:

> Let me become your lawyer again. You are doing the right thing. Just remain calm and answer the questions. But with the last question Mary asked whether you would agree that the ads are an inexpensive way of making sure all of the doctors know about your services. If you don't agree, just say "I don't agree." What you did was natural. You wanted to explain why you didn't think so. Don't give the explanation unless it is asked for. Okay?

Witness:

> Yes. I am afraid I was starting to get angry.

Lawyer 1:

> That won't help you focus. You may say more than you should. Keep calm and listen to the question.

Keep the examples of aggressive cross-examination short. Even though the witness understands intellectually that you or your colleague is merely playing the role of opposing counsel, being treated in such a hostile fashion is still irritating. You do not want the witness to become angry with you, but only to be prepared to deal with this type of questioning. Using one of your colleagues to conduct the cross if possible will reduce the possibility of any damage to your relationship with the witness.

13.11 USING VIDEOTAPE TO PREPARE

Some witnesses require intensive work to prevent speech habits or mannerisms from distracting from their testimony first at deposition, then at trial. While they might not always believe an attorney's comments about their demeanor or speech habits, they will find it difficult to argue with videotape showing those problems. Stuffy corporate executives, pompous experts, and mumbling fact witnesses can all have their performances improved markedly if they are shown videotape of the problems.

Lengthy taping sessions are not necessary; the witness will more likely improve in his delivery if you tape a fifteen-minute segment, then review and discuss it, and then tape another segment with your suggestions for improvement in mind. For key witnesses, communications consultants can assist in identifying and curing problems that interfere with the witness effectively presenting his evidence.

The question arises, of course, whether such videotape rehearsals are discoverable: they are, after all, verbatim statements by the witness. Nevertheless, the better rule is that these videotapes, just like an attorney's notes on preparation sessions, constitute attorney work product and are protected from discovery. The order of questioning, the subjects prepared, the suggestions from the attorney or consultant— all reflect the attorney's approach to and preparation of the case. The fact that videotape technology provides an especially effective way of accomplishing preparation does not reduce the protection courts should accord such effort by the attorney. While courts should uphold a claim of privilege, counsel and the client should be prepared to discuss such preparation if the privilege is denied.

A more subtle question is whether using videotape to prepare a witness for deposition or trial makes that witness more vulnerable to effective cross-examination at trial on the use, if not the content of video preparation. Assume that your opponent has discovered your use of videotape in a witness's preparation session; consider the following approach to cross-examination on such "rehearsals."

Q. Mr. Shadis, you spent quite a good deal of time reviewing and preparing your testimony with your lawyer before you came to court, didn't you?

A. Yes, I did, I suppose.

Q. And you went over and over that testimony, your story, because you wanted to get it just right, isn't that true?

A. Well, we did go over it several times, yes.

Q. Several times, until your attorney thought it was just right?

A. Well, until she was satisfied that it was clear.

Q. In fact, you gave these answers again and again in your attorney's office, so you could get them just the way she wanted them?

A. Well, as I've said, we went over my testimony.

Q. And then she actually videotaped you, giving your answers, didn't she?

A. Yes, we used videotape to prepare.

Q. And then you reviewed the videotape, and looked at what you said, and how you said it, and what words you used, and how you looked while you were answering, right?

A. We did review the videotapes, yes, but I don't see anything wrong with that.

Q. Then your testimony here this morning is actually the result of very careful rehearsal, isn't it?

A. I don't think I would use the word rehearsal.

Q. You prepared as though you were playacting, and delivering lines that had been written for you, isn't that right?

A. No, no, I think that presents the wrong picture entirely.

No matter how the witness protests, the impression that the jury receives to this point is that they have somehow been "conned" by having a set piece of theater presented when they thought that they were hearing the spontaneous testimony of the witness in his own words.

The witness can dispel this impression, however, if he makes it clear to the jury why this videotape preparation was necessary:

A. No, no, I think that presents the wrong picture entirely. I am nervous about testifying here; I've never done it before, and I don't speak in public often. I don't think that it would be fair if that nervousness made me mix up my testimony and kept me from telling the jury what really happened. So my attorney and I decided that we would try to do everything that we could, including going over my testimony several times on videotape, to get the truth of what happened across to the jury.

The simple fact is that if a witness needs the assistance that videotaped practice can provide so effectively and efficiently, the concern about disclosure at trial should not by itself be a sufficient argument against that assistance.

13.12 FINAL INSTRUCTIONS

Never conclude the witness preparation session without taking care of all of the necessary housekeeping details. Let's look at a few of those details.

WHAT TO WEAR

As was discussed in § 2.3.1, depositions influence the settlement value of a case by giving opposing counsel a chance to assess the impression a witness will make upon a judge or jury. A strong witness on your side—a witness whose testimony is believable and who can withstand the rigors of cross-examination—will cause the opposing party to demand less or pay more in settlement than a witness who vacillates, is tentative, has memory problems, or otherwise makes a poor impression.

The witness's appearance is one of the factors affecting the impression a witness makes. If the witness is attractive (we are not talking about being handsome or beautiful, but about the impression made) and is dressed appropriately, this will enhance the witness's credibility. What dress is appropriate for a particular witness depends on the image to be projected and deserves careful thought on your part. Whatever the image you seek, instruct the witness on how to dress for the deposition, perhaps after consultation with a professional communications consultant.

WHAT TO BRING

When defending a deposition, one of the less pleasant experiences you can have occurs when a witness suddenly reaches into his pocket and pulls out a set of notes you have never seen. Not only are these notes a surprise, but when you take a look at them, you find the witness has scribbled on them all sorts of damaging comments about the strength of your case. If the witness used the notes to refresh his memory, you can do little to keep them away from opposing counsel.[5]

The scene just described happens more times than you would wish. Often, after the witness preparation session, a witness will go home and start worrying about what questions will be asked the next day. The witness logically thinks that a few notes will help him keep events straight. Then, if he forgets, he can also refer to the notes during the deposition. The witness may also figure it would not hurt to write down your comments about some of the problems in the case.

The easiest way to prevent this scenario from occurring is to instruct witnesses to bring nothing to the deposition—no notes, documents, or anything else. Don't, however, rely only on your instructions. On the day of the deposition, be sure to ask whether the witness has any notes or other papers and, if so, take them away before the deposition begins.

WHAT TO LOOK AT AND WHO TO TALK TO

Your witness can surprise you in many ways during the deposition. After carefully preparing him until you are satisfied with his answers, he may start coming out with new and unexpected information during the deposition. During a break you may ask where he got this new

---

5. See § 9.5.

information and why he never mentioned it before. You then find that after the witness preparation session, he decided to do some last minute investigation on his own. Instead of going home and having a quiet evening and a good night's sleep, he telephoned other witnesses or went to the office to track down new documents.

Sometimes the investigative efforts are for the good—new, helpful evidence turns up or the witness is better able to answer the hard questions during the deposition. But the danger is that you, as the lawyer, have never had the opportunity to discuss the new information with him.

You can help to avoid these nasty surprises by instructing the witness at the witness preparation session about who he should talk with and what he should look at between the end of the session and the time of the deposition. Again, on the day of the deposition you should check to see whether he has followed your instructions.

WHERE AND WHEN TO MEET

It hardly needs saying that the witness should not leave the witness preparation session without knowing where and when to meet you for the deposition. You may wish to meet at your office to do some last minute preparation and then drive over together. Or, meeting at the location of the deposition may be more convenient. Work out these matters with the witness in advance. But if you are meeting where the deposition is to be taken, be sure to give instructions about not talking with opposing counsel if the witness should arrive before you do. And do show up early so this will not be a problem.

13.13 CONCLUSION

The basic rules for preparing a witness to be deposed are simple:
- Try to reduce the witness's anxieties.
- Try to lift burdens from the witness, rather than to put burdens on the witness.
- Try to assure the witness that you are there to handle any problems that might come up.
- Try to persuade the witness that any procedural problems will be minor and will not interfere with effective testimony.

Chapter Fourteen

DEFENDING THE DEPOSITION

"They have no lawyers among them,
for they consider them as a sort of people
whose profession it is to disguise matters."
— *Sir Thomas More*

The attorney defending the deposition must preserve certain objections in the record for the court's later ruling, and protect the client from the disclosure of privileged information. Your first step in fulfilling these responsibilities is to determine whether the deponent is, indeed, a client.

Determining whether a witness is a client is usually quite simple: Has that person retained you to represent them? More difficult problems arise, however, when the party who has retained you is, for instance, a corporation and the witness is an officer of the corporation or, at the opposite extreme, is a low-level employee at the bottom of the organizational chart. Even though these individuals may not be clients, they may nevertheless be covered by the attorney-client and work-product privilege that extends to you and the corporate client. To further complicate matters, the witness's legal interests may be different than, and possibly inconsistent with, those of the party you are representing. For instance, the defendant bank and its president may both be accused of wrongdoing and each may have an interest in showing that the other committed malfeasance.

Determining whether a witness is a client and is covered by the attorney-client privilege is difficult, complex, and beyond the scope of this book. The answer may depend on the rules of professional responsibility as well as on state and federal law.[1] The important thing is, when in doubt, research the applicable law to determine whether the witness is considered protected by the attorney-client privilege accorded to the party who is clearly your client and whether you may properly represent the witness at the deposition.

---

1. See Fed.R.Evid. 501 which states that matters of privilege, when jurisdiction is based on a federal question, is determined by the common law as "interpreted by the courts of the United States in light of reason and experience." In diversity actions and actions where state law supplies the rule of decision, matters of privilege are determined by reference to state law.

When the deponent is a client or someone who can properly be represented by you at the deposition, the witness retains the protection of all of the benefits of the attorney-client relationship. For example, the preparation sessions are privileged, and the deponent can consult privately with counsel during the deposition (although normally not when there is a question pending). As counsel for the deponent, you are responsible at the deposition for:

1. supporting and protecting the witness;

2. entering into any necessary stipulations;

3. preserving the record;

4. conferring with the witness;

5. stating objections;

6. instructing the witness not to answer when appropriate;

7. adjourning the deposition to seek a protective order; and,

8. questioning the witness and clarifying and correcting answers.

Even when the witness is neither a client nor covered by any attorney-client privilege, you may still be performing many of the same roles in the deposition room that you would with a client. With friendly witnesses, you may be providing emotional support and protection. Even with witnesses who are hostile, you have the responsibility of making necessary objections and clarifying the record. The important difference between witnesses covered by the attorney-client privilege and those who are not is that any conversations between you and the uncovered witness may have to be disclosed upon questioning by opposing counsel.

14.1 SUPPORTING AND PROTECTING THE WITNESS

Anyone who has ever been deposed can attest that it is almost always an anxiety provoking, unpleasant experience. Most witnesses are nervous about the prospect of being deposed. If witnesses are parties, they are worried about whether they are answering correctly or in a way that might cause them to lose the case. Even when not a party, they may be concerned that their answers might cause them to lose their jobs or that people whose opinion they value may think they did something wrong. The interrogating attorney often challenges and argues with the witness, asks personally embarrassing questions, and even suggests, directly or indirectly, that the witness is a scoundrel and a liar. In short, being a witness at a deposition is a horrible experience.

One of the most important tasks of defending counsel is to provide emotional comfort and support to the witness. Your job is to make an unpleasant situation as bearable as possible. In large part, you can accomplish this merely by insuring that the witness perceives you as being there to take care of him and to look after his interests. Witnesses rely upon you to make sure that nothing bad happens.

This is not just a matter of handholding and client service. A witness who feels secure and protected will feel more comfortable in defending his or her actions, in fending off the questioning attorney's efforts to shake his story, or to lull him into making unfortunate admissions. Not only is this good client service, but also good deposition strategy to have the witness see you as his guardian during the deposition.

At the deposition, you and the client-deponent will be seated next to each other, normally across from the questioner. In order to participate effectively in the deposition, you should locate yourself slightly forward of the deponent, that is, closer to the table, so that you are always in the deponent's view. By taking that position, you can halt the witness's answer merely by raising your hand slightly, and you can thereby preserve your opportunity to make objections before answers are given. Sometimes you may want the witness to wait before answering so you can have a moment to think about the question, its propriety, and its ramifications. By holding up your hand between the witness and the reporter, and saying, "Give me a moment, please," you obtain some reasonable time to consider whether an objection or direction not to answer is appropriate. No rule says that you must, without thought, immediately object upon a question being asked; just as the questioner is entitled to pause and consider between an answer and his next question, so should a defender be allowed to think about possible objections to questions.

By staying up at the table at the witness's elbow, you will also find that you stay much more involved in the deposition, and that the witness is less likely to fall into a "conversation" with deposing counsel which can lead to ill-considered volunteering. When you make objections, the witness will be able both to see *and* hear you, and more readily perceive the significance of the objection.[2] In that position, at the witness's elbow, you are also positioned to exercise two of your most important—albeit, limited—rights at the deposition: consultation with the client-witness at the table and recessing the deposition briefly for a conference in the hallway.[3] Protecting the client is not confined to the deposition room.

Be cautious about allowing the witness to converse with opposing counsel before the deposition begins, while everyone is filling up their coffee cups and getting comfortable. Even if substance is not disclosed, these casual moments with opposing counsel tend to lower the witness's guard. As a corollary to this, never leave the witness alone in the deposition room. Follow the rule that the witness is never left without counsel: If you must leave the room for a telephone call or a restroom break, take the witness out of the room with you. During restroom breaks, if you are female and the witness male, or vice versa, ask the witness to wait in a vacant office and strictly instruct him not to speak with anyone—opposing counsel, paralegals, strangers, or secretaries. Even though it is clearly inappropriate, deposing counsel frequently try to engage the witness in conversation when defending counsel is absent or occupied. Although deposing counsel always try to defend those conversations as "merely trying to make the witness comfortable," they are improper when the witness is represented.

14.2 ENTERING INTO STIPULATIONS

The wisdom of various stipulations has been discussed in § 6.1.

---

2. In the authors' opinion, attorneys in trial or deposition may not object for the primary purpose of coaching a witness or otherwise affecting the witness's testimony; but a good-faith objection—that is, one which has an arguably valid basis in evidentiary considerations—does not become improper merely because the witness, on hearing it, may adjust his answer.

For example, consider a good-faith objection that a question is ambiguous:

Q. Tell us about the regular procedure.

OBJECTION: At what time, counsel? The question is ambiguous. I object. The witness will certainly review the "regular procedures" in his mind, to determine whether there have been changes since the relevant time. That review by the witness does not render the objection improper or unethical. On the other hand, an objection clearly raised to cue the witness, and for no valid evidentiary purpose, is improper:

Q. Did your company earn any profit the first year of operation?

OBJECTION: I object. I don't understand the question. I don't see how anyone could understand the question. It's completely ambiguous as to what you mean by "profit" and "operation." Can you understand the question, Mrs. Banis?

THE WITNESS: No, I don't understand the question. See Rule 30(d)(1).

3. See § 14.4.

14.3 PRESERVING THE RECORD

Depositions usually result in a transcript of the testimony that you can use for various purposes including at trial.[4] Like an appellate record, the deposition transcript may be clear and understandable or a muddled jumble of words incomprehensible to both judge and jury. The question you must answer is which is better—clear or muddled. Is the client's best interest served by a clear record, or is the client better off if the transcript is a mass of confusion? The answer to this question may change with the topics under examination and also with whether the deponent's answers are favorable or unfavorable to your client's position. Helpful answers should be clear and understandable; harmful answers are better left obtuse and incomprehensible. Making this decision—clear or muddled—requires you to be alert during the deposition and to listen carefully to the answers being given.

Such answers as "It was from here to there" or "It was right here at this point on the map that I first saw the other car," are useless if the deposition is later used at trial. Even though everyone in the deposition room could see exactly where the witness was pointing when these answers were given, the judge or jury will be left without a clue as to where "here" and "there" are or to which point on the map the witness was referring.

If that is the way you prefer it—the judge and jury in the dark—because the answer is harmful to your claim or defense, sit quietly. However, if the answer is helpful, then you should state for the record what is occurring. "Let the record reflect that the witness is indicating from his chair to counsel's chair, a distance of approximately five feet" or "Counsel, let's have the witness mark with the letter A where he is pointing on the map which has been marked as Deposition Exhibit 12."

14.4 CONFERRING WITH THE WITNESS

One reason you should sit next to the witness is to enable you and the witness to confer quickly and easily about a question or answer when necessary. Assuming you do not abuse this "right" to obstruct discovery, there is no limit on the number of times or frequency with which it can be used.[5]

---

4. See chapter 16, "Using Depositions."

5. Several courts have held that, except about matters of privilege, conferring with the witness off the record, even during breaks and recesses, is prohibited. *See, e.g., Hall v. Clifton Precision,* 150 F.R.D. 525 (E.D. Pa. 1993); *Chapsky v. Baxter V. Mueller Division, Baxter Healthcare Corp.,* 1994 WL 327348 (N.D. Ill. 1994).

For example, after the witness has answered a question, you can lean over and remind the witness she should not volunteer information beyond that called for by the question, or that she should not attempt to argue the case, but should merely state facts. This conference is off the record because it is whispered and inaudible to the reporter and opposing counsel. Obviously, if this type of conference follows every important question and answer, deposing counsel will begin to "make a record" by commenting on each conference, with the result that the witness will grow uncomfortable and the judge, if asked to rule on this behavior, may grow skeptical. So long as you use this right to confer judiciously, it can be an effective and proper means of controlling the witness so that her answers are responsive without being overly generous.

Where some topics are off-limits in a deposition because they are privileged or because the court has previously issued a protective order, you can use these "mini-conferences" to remind the witness that the questions are getting close to those topics, so that the witness does not inadvertently provide protected or privileged information in an answer to an upcoming question.

Occasionally at a deposition, a witness will need some lengthier counseling—she has forgotten the basic rules of listening to the question and answering accurately and briefly, she has adopted the role of advocate rather than witness, or she is allowing the deposing attorney to goad her into intemperate remarks. In such situations, after an answer is completed you should use the "elbow rule": take the client-witness by the elbow and state, "We're taking a break here," and guide her from the room into the hallway or a vacant office to straighten her out.

Deposing counsel will probably try to prevent this interruption by saying something like, "You can't do that," or "You can take a break after I finish this line," or "Let's break after this next question," but you need not even respond to those suggestions. The questioner cannot prevent you and the deponent from leaving. You should also not wait if you believe the witness is starting to get out of control. You at least know this: deposing counsel will get no information from the witness while the witness is out of the room, so you should march him out and re-instruct him in the proper behavior of a deponent.

As stated, you can hold these conferences *sotto voce* at the table or out in the hallway without much concern that they will lead to a ruling by a judge that discovery has been illegitimately frustrated. Sometimes, however, you and the client-deponent must confer before an answer is given—when you think privileged information might be disclosed in an answer or when the witness is unsure about how he may answer without divulging confidential or personal information. In such a case, you have little choice but to confer with the witness while the question is pending in order to determine whether you should object on the grounds of privilege.

In fact, you cause no added interruption by this conference since the alternative is for you to lodge an objection and direct the witness not to answer, in order to protect her opportunity to find out if a privilege objection must be raised. After that objection and direction, you and the witness would have exactly the same conference as just discussed.

14.5 STATING OBJECTIONS

The process of making and responding to objections at depositions probably consumes more energy, causes more frustration, and wastes more time than any other aspect of discovery. Perhaps because of their lack of confidence in their own knowledge of the rules of evidence, or because they are unsure about what objections are waived and what objections are preserved, attorneys at depositions object and battle over objections, by actual count, 517 percent more than is necessary to represent their clients properly.

Consider a typical exchange in the deposition of an opposing party:

Q. Now, Ms. Vardas, you've told us that you ran this company for the last seven years. During that time, how profitable was your company?

DEFENDING ATTORNEY:

I object. You are misstating her prior testimony. Also, we don't know what you mean when you say, "how profitable." You know that's a term that hasn't been defined, so your question is ambiguous. Nobody can understand it. Besides that, none of this is relevant to this case. I mean, what does this have to do with your claim that the company somehow mislabeled? Besides that, you haven't shown any personal knowledge.

DEPOSING ATTORNEY:

The question is not ambiguous; it is perfectly clear. Anybody could understand it, and you know that. Besides that, we've been over this before and I'm not misstating anything. The witness can tell me if she understands the question or not. And you know perfectly well that this has a lot to do with this case. Those profits properly belong to us, or at least a share of them do. So, why don't you let her answer?

DEFENDING ATTORNEY:

> Well, I have a right to understand the question so that I can protect my client's interests. You're trying to trap her with these trick questions, and that's not fair. Why don't you just ask a reasonable question without trying to force your views on her? Besides that, your question assumes facts not in evidence. It sounds like you are referring to some document. If you have a document, you should show it to her.

DEPOSING ATTORNEY:

> I'll ask whatever questions I want, and not what you want me to ask. I'm not trying to trap anybody, and I resent your suggesting that. Why don't you just state your objection for the record, and let's get on with the deposition. Ms. Vardas, would you please look at what I am having marked as Vardas Deposition Exhibit 73? Would you please read the first paragraph into the record?

DEFENDING COUNSEL:

> Objection. Come on, counsel. You know that the document speaks for itself.

Of course, we all know that this is not the end of it. This time, or the next, this discussion may go on for pages, without resolution, without purpose, and without profit to the clients. In such discussions, there is no light, only heat, and there is therefore no possibility that one or the other of the attorneys will suddenly throw up his hands and say:

> You're right. I've been a fool. I do hate myself when I get like this. How pigheaded of me not to see that your question [or your objection] was perfectly proper and clear! I'll pay for the extra pages of transcript that all took.

In fact, if an attorney ever said such a thing at a deposition, not only would her reputation around town suffer badly, but the opposing attorney would immediately suspect some sort of clever ruse, and probably become even more argumentative.

To cure this problem and to put objections in their proper role at a deposition, we must first look at the purpose of discovery in our system. Rule 26(b)(1) explicitly states about discovery:

> Parties may obtain discovery regarding any matter, not privileged, that is relevant to the to the claim or defense of any party, including the existence, description, nature, custody, condition, and location of any books, documents, or other tangible things and the identity and location of persons having knowledge of any discoverable matter.

> For good cause, the court may order discovery of any matter relevant to the subject matter involved in the action. Relevant information need not be admissible at the trial if the discovery appears reasonably calculated to lead to the discovery of admissible evidence. All discovery is subject to the limitations imposed by Rule 26(b)(2)(i), (ii), and (iii).

The rules are consistent to the effect that absent a protective order, "a party may obtain discovery."[6] The history of the rules and their amendments makes it clear that *discovery*, not *suppression*, was being promoted. The "sporting theory of justice" and "trial by ambush" were intended to fall under the onslaught of the discovery rules.[7] Yet we continue to raise generations of young lawyers to believe that a deposition is successfully defended only if substantial and important information is hidden from the opponent.

The results are discouraging. Defending attorneys, if unsure of the rules of evidence and procedure, raise and argue objections which would be preserved even if they were not raised and which will merely have to be raised again in the designation process or at trial. Deposing attorneys, if motivated by a misplaced pride of authorship of their questions, respond vociferously to sound and unsound objections alike, even though the witness has not been instructed not to answer and no judge is present there to rule on their responses. No profit can be gained from this arguing: No ruling will be obtained and there has been no real obstruction, to this point, of discovery. Furthermore, these counsel are not serving their clients well as the clients pay the attorney's fees and the transcript costs for all of this time and useless verbiage. All in all, in the objection and response pattern at depositions we probably see the trial attorney at his worst.

The rules clearly state what objections you must make at the deposition and how to make them. Following those rules will help you avoid many of the problems just described.

14.5.1 What objections must be made at or before the deposition?

Objections as to Notice

Rule 32(d)(1) states that you waive all errors and irregularities in the notice of deposition unless you promptly serve written objections on

---

6. The matter of discovery against experts is the single exception and is dealt with separately in chapter 19, "Overview of the Expert Deposition."

7. "The pretrial deposition-discovery mechanism established by Rules 26 to 37 is one of the most significant innovations of the Federal Rules of Civil Procedure." *Hickman v. Taylor*, 329 U.S. 495, 500 (1947).

the party giving notice. The purpose of this provision is to prevent technical irregularities from destroying the utility of depositions at trial. If the irregularities are not corrected and present some substantial question of the deponent's rights, the objecting party should seek a protective order; otherwise, if he merely fails to attend, he may have to justify his noncompliance with the notice at a hearing on a motion to compel discovery.[8]

Counsel will usually have agreed upon a time and place for the deposition, and the fact that the witness showed up is usually a demonstration that the notice has been adequate. Sometimes, however, the notice should contain some additional information—the subject of a 30(b)(6) deposition, or the specifications for the subpoena *duces tecum* accompanying the subpoena to a non-party witness—on which counsel may not agree. Because these are matters of notice which can be corrected—cured or obviated—during the deposition, you must raise them or any objections are waived.

Objections as to Qualifications of the Officer

Rule 32(d)(2) states that unless you object before the deposition begins, or as soon thereafter as the disqualification becomes known or could be discovered with reasonable diligence, you waive any objection to the qualifications of the officer before whom the deposition is being taken. Occasionally, the reporter provided by the reporting service is not a notary in the jurisdiction in which the deposition is being taken. Sometimes this occurs because the notarial powers are granted for limited geographical areas, like counties, and the reporting service was not aware that the deposition was across a county line. Nevertheless, you can easily cure this by having a notary come in to swear the witness. As a technical matter, the "officer" notary would then have to remain in the room, because the deposition is to be recorded "in the officer's presence."[9] By stipulation, of course, the parties could waive this requirement so the officer could leave.

Objections to Cure Problems

Rule 32(d)(3)(B) requires that failure to object at the deposition waives errors of any kind occurring at the deposition which might be obviated, removed, or cured if promptly presented at the deposition. This includes, but is not limited to, errors in the taking of the deposition, in the form of the questions or answers, in the oath or affirmation, or in the conduct of the parties. The vast majority of deposition objections are made under this provision.

---

8. See 7 James W. Moore, et al., *Moore's Federal Practice* ¶32.43[1] (3d ed. 2000).
9. Fed.R.Civ.P. 30(c).

While not intended to be a definitive list, the most common types of problems that can be cured at the deposition are:

- **Vague question.** A vague question is one where it is not clear what is being asked. "How large is XYZ Corporation?" is a vague question because it is not clear whether the question is asking for the number of employees, the gross sales, net profits, or what. Because the questioner could rephrase the question to be specific about what is being asked, it is a curable problem.

- **Ambiguous question.** Ambiguous questions are similar to vague questions; exactly what is being asked is unclear. Because the questioner can rephrase ambiguous questions to be clear, they are, therefore, curable.[10]

- **Unintelligible question.** As the objection suggests, the question does not make sense.

- **Complex or confusing question.** Closely related to the unintelligible question, complex or confusing questions are difficult to understand because of their phrasing or length.

- **Compound question.** Compound questions are actually two questions combined into one making it impossible to tell to which question the witness is responding. Q. "You were driving at thirty-five miles per hour and on the left side of the road?" A. "Yes." Whether the witness was driving on the left side of the road or going thirty-five miles per hour or both is unclear. Compound questions can be rephrased into two or more separate questions and are, therefore, are curable.

- **Misleading question.** You will encounter two primary forms of misleading questions. One is the question which, when answered, provides erroneous information to the trier of fact. The classical example of the misleading question is, "Have you stopped beating your wife?" If the witness answers yes, the implication is that he at one time did beat his wife; if he answers "no," it sounds as though he continues to beat her. By seeking a yes or no answer to such a misleading question, the questioner does not allow the witness to explain that he has never beaten his wife.[11] The other form of a misleading question is one which asks the witness to accept certain facts as true when they are not. For example, "Mr. Kaunas, we have already talked to many witnesses who believe that your

---

10. Often, such questions suffer from what grammarians call "ambiguous antecedents." For example: "When Jones met with Smith, did he give him the contract?" We cannot know from a yes answer to this question, whether Jones gave it to Smith or Smith gave it to Jones. Therein lies the ambiguity.

11. In formal logic, this is sometimes referred to as the "principle of the excluded middle," because the question by its terms excludes the third, or middle, possibility.

car was over the center line. Now, don't you agree that you weren't in your lane?" If the deposing attorney has not, in fact, talked to many witnesses and obtained this information, he is misleading the witness and committing a breach of ethics to boot.

- **Question calls for speculation.** Asking the witness to speculate is not objectionable;[12] it is objectionable, however, not to make clear that you are asking the witness to speculate. "What was Mr. Jones thinking when he told you to leave the premises?" is objectionable as calling for speculation. "Tell me what you think Mr. Jones was thinking when he told you to leave the premises?" is not.

- **Lack of foundation or no showing of authenticity.** Foundation and authenticity are discussed in § 9.4. Since the questioner can always ask the necessary foundation questions, the problem is curable.

- **Best evidence rule.** Fed.R.Evid. 1001 *et seq.* requires the use of the original or a copy of the original when proving the contents of a writing, recording or photograph. The objection can be cured by using the original or a copy.

- **No showing of personal knowledge.** Fed.R.Evid. 602 requires that a witness, other than an expert witness, has personal knowledge of the matters about which he testified. Since the witness can be asked if and how he has personal knowledge, this is a curable problem.

- **Unfair characterization.** An unfair characterization occurs when the questioner characterizes a previous answer as part of asking a question. "Q: How fast were you going? A: Fifty miles per hour. Q: When you were speeding at fifty miles per hour, were you looking ahead of you?" The objection is curable.

- **Misstating prior testimony.** The objection is made when the question misstates a witness's prior answer. "Q: How far away from the intersection did you start braking? A: About 500 feet away. Q: When you started braking 300 feet away from the intersection, how hard did you apply the brakes?"

- **Question assumes facts not in evidence.** This objection is used when the question assumes a fact to which the witness has never testified.

- **Argumentative question.** An argumentative question is one that does exactly that—argues or comments on the evidence rather than asking a true question. In other words, the question is a conclusion by the interrogator. "That was very reckless driving

---

12. See § 6.3.

on your part. Weren't you worried you might have an accident?" The question can be cured by deleting the argumentative portion.

- **Question calls for an improper lay opinion.** Fed.R.Evid. 701 permits certain types of lay opinions, but when the question asks the witness for an opinion which cannot be given or given only by an expert, it is objectionable. "Do you have an opinion about whether the failure to administer blood thinners contributed to your stroke?" Depending on the type of opinion being elicited, the problem may or may not be curable.

- **Question calls for a legal conclusion.** "Was the defendant, by driving fifty miles per hour in a thirty-five mile per hour zone, negligent?" You cannot ask a witness to testify about the legal significance of actions or documents nor can he be asked about what the law states. You can ask a witness, however, about what he believes to be the law or the legal significance of some act or document if evidence about the witness's belief would be admissible at trial or is reasonably calculated to lead to the discovery of admissible evidence.

- **Asked and answered.** The objection is directed to a question that has been previously asked and answered. While a proper objection at trial, it is unlikely that a judge will ever sustain such an objection made during a deposition. If the witness's answer is the same, no harm is done. If different, then asking the question the second time proved useful.

- **Question calls for an opinion beyond an expert's qualifications.** A physician qualified as an expert in the field of hematology should not be permitted to express an opinion about the prognosis for the plaintiff's carcinoma unless also qualified to give that opinion as well. If the expert can be so qualified, the objection is curable.

- **Leading (if not an adverse or hostile witness).** Fed.R.Evid. 611(c) states that leading questions should only be used on direct examination when the witness is hostile, an adverse party, or identified with an adverse party. No one usually has difficulty identifying when a witness is an adverse party or identified with an adverse party.[13] But for other witnesses, the examining party must first establish through the witness's answers or attitude that hostility exists. Until this is done, you can make the leading objection.

---

13. Although there may be an issue about when a party is adverse.

- **Hearsay (if answer can be put within a hearsay exception).** A hearsay objection usually cannot be cured, but if the hearsay statement can be placed within the exceptions of Fed.R.Evid. 803 or 804, then the objection is conceivably curable.

- **Non-responsive answer or volunteering.** Many courts permit only the attorney asking the question to make this objection while some courts will permit either party to object. The objection is made when the witness's answer exceeds or is outside of the scope of the question being asked. Since an unresponsive answer can be cured by either counsel asking a question to which the answer is responsive, this is an objection that is waived by not being made at the deposition.[14] Some courts also expect the objection to be accompanied by a motion to strike (even though there is no one at the deposition to rule on the motion).

14.5.2   The rule for making objections.

The rule for making objections at a deposition is basically the same as for trial: Only object if you will gain by the objection; that is, when unfavorable evidence to your position may be made inadmissible. For example, if the witness is asked about what occurred at a meeting with your client without first being asked whether he was present at the meeting, you could properly object that there has been no showing of personal knowledge. But should you make such an objection? Certainly you should if you know that the witness was not at the meeting or even if you are unsure *and* you expect the answer to be unfavorable ("They discussed how to breach the contract."). If the questioning attorney then cures the objection by asking if the witness was present and the answer is no, any statement about what occurred at the meeting will be inadmissible at trial. On the other hand, if you expect the answer to be favorable ("There was a discussion of how to avoid breaching the contract.") *or* you know the witness was present at the meeting, you gain little from the objection. Worse, you can harm your client's interests by making what would be an admissible, helpful answer inadmissible if the witness should become unavailable and you wish to introduce the answer at trial. The questioning attorney may also in the face of a curable objection end up making the witness's answers more persuasive and harmful. Assume that the witness is now unavailable for trial, but at the deposition the following occurred:

Q. Mr. Vilas, what was said at the meeting that occurred in the corporate offices on May 5, 1994?

---

14. See *Kirschner v. Broadhead*, 671 F.2d 1034 (7th Cir. 1982).

OBJECTION:

>   Objection. No showing of personal knowledge and lack of foundation.

Q. All right, were you present at the meeting?

A. Yes.

Q. Who else was present at the meeting?

A. Johnson from corporate and Ted Smith from purchasing.

Q. When did this meeting take place?

A. Ten o'clock in the morning on May 5, 1994.

Q. Where exactly did it take place?

A. In the boardroom on the second floor of the corporate building.

Q. Were you able to hear everything that was said during the meeting?

A. Yes.

Q. Did you leave at any time during the meeting?

A. No.

Q. Do you remember clearly what was said at that meeting?

A. Yes.

Q. What was said at that meeting?

If defending counsel had not objected, it is possible that the questioning attorney would have learned what was said at the meeting and moved on to a new topic. By objecting, however, the questioning attorney clearly established the witness's accuracy of recall about what happened. In the event this portion of the transcript is read to the jury, the testimony is now likely to be much more persuasive than if the objection had never been made.

Having given the general rule—do not object unless you will gain by the objection by keeping unfavorable evidence from being admitted at trial—there is one difference between objections made at deposition and those made at trial. Objections made at trial will be ruled on by the judge before the questioning proceeds further. In contrast, no judge is present at the deposition to rule on objections and the questioning will proceed subject to the objections. Therefore, if in doubt, make the objection. If you later decide that the objection was not valid, nothing requires you to assert it at the time the judge rules on objections (and there will be no opportunity to assert it later unless one of the parties attempts to introduce the deposition testimony). But if the problem with the question is curable and you fail to make an objection, the objection is waived forever.

14.5.3   Objections that do not have to be made at the deposition.

Rule 32(d)(3)(A) states that objections to the competency, relevancy, or materiality of deposition testimony are not waived by failing to make them at the deposition unless the objection could have been cured. Similarly, Rule 32(d)(3)(B) only states that curable objections are waived by failing to make them at the deposition. In short, you need not assert any objection that cannot be cured at the deposition; you can assert them for the first time when one of the parties attempts to introduce the deposition at trial or in support of or in opposition to a motion.[15] What kinds of objections cannot be cured? Again without attempting to be definitive, the usual non-curable objections are:

- **Relevancy (including materiality).** Obviously, relevance is a matter which cannot be cured by further questioning or by re-phrasing the question; it may be disclosed, but it is not cured. It depends solely upon the relationship between the facts sought and the issues in the case.[16] Furthermore, Rule 26(b)(1) allows discovery of relevant information and defines it to include information which may not itself be admissible but which is reasonably calculated to lead to the discovery of admissible evidence.

- **Prejudicial.** Whether, under Fed.R.Evid. 403, the probative value of the evidence is outweighed by the danger of unfair prejudicial effect cannot be determined until trial when the evidence is weighed in relationship to all of the evidence in the case.

- **Hearsay (unless the testimony can be placed within a hearsay exception).** Hearsay is not a curable objection and therefore you do not waive it if not made at the deposition. If a statement is hearsay under Fed.R.Evid. 801, no amount of further questioning will convert the statement into non-hearsay. If, however, the hearsay statement can be placed into one of the hearsay exceptions of Fed.R.Evid. 803 or 804, then arguably the objection is curable. Whether the statement is admissible under a hearsay exception depends, of course, on the statement.

- **Confusion of the issues, misleading to the jury, undue delay, waste of time, or needless presentation of cumulative evidence.** As with unfairly prejudicial evidence, these objections under Fed.R.Evid. 403 can only be evaluated in the context of trial or

---

15. At least one court has said that it is improper to make objections at the deposition to competency, relevancy and materiality. *Hall v. Clifton Precision*, 150 F.R.D. 525, 528 n.3 (E.D. Pa. 1993).

16. See Fed.R.Evid. 401: "Relevant evidence means any evidence having any tendency to make the existence of any fact that is of consequence to the determination of the action more probable or less probable than it would be without the evidence."

a motion *in limine* and not at the discovery stage. Therefore, you do not waive these objections by failing to make them at the deposition.

- **Competency.** Fed.R.Evid. 601 provides that every person is competent to be a witness unless otherwise provided in the rules. However, when state law supplies the rule of decision for an element of the claim or defense, then the competency of a witness will be determined in accordance with state law. Rule 32(d)(3)(A) expressly states that you do not waive objections to competency if you do not make them at the deposition.

14.5.4 How to make objections.

There is not much of a trick to making objections. Wait until the question or answer is completed and then state the objection: "Objection, vague." "Objection, ambiguous." "Objection, compound question." But while there are few tricks, there is much potential for abuse. As a result, Rule 30(d)(1) requires that "[a]ny objection during a deposition must be stated concisely and in a non-argumentative and non-suggestive manner." Thus, the coaching objection, long the favorite of the unethical lawyer, as well as the time consuming speaking objection, are now prohibited.

14.6 INSTRUCTIONS NOT TO ANSWER

When defending a deposition one of the most difficult decisions to make is whether to instruct or direct a witness not to answer a question. Rule 30(d)(1) sharply curtails the situations in which such an instruction is proper: "A person may instruct a deponent not to answer only when necessary to preserve a privilege, to enforce a limitation directed by the court, or to present a motion under Rule 30(d)(4)." Paragraph 3 refers to adjourning the deposition to seek an order terminating or limiting the deposition because it is being conducted in bad faith or in such a manner as unreasonably to annoy, embarrass, or oppress the deponent. The decision is difficult because if you make the wrong choice, the penalties can be great. If you instruct the witness not to answer a question which the court later determines is proper, the attorney or her client can be required to pay the reasonable expenses, including attorney's fees, of the questioning attorney in obtaining the order compelling an answer.[17] On the other hand, if you allow the witness to answer the question, you risk losing both the protections of the privilege or court order, at least for that question, and may waive them for the future as well.

---

17. See § 12.2.1 and § 12.2.5.

The calculus of deciding whether to instruct the witness not to answer runs as follows: (1) If I instruct the witness not to answer, how likely is it that opposing counsel will bring a motion to compel? (2) If opposing counsel brings a motion to compel, how likely is it that the court will sustain the motion and compel an answer? (3) If the court sustains the motion, how likely is it that I or my client will be required to pay the reasonable expenses of opposing counsel bringing the motion and resuming the deposition? and (4) How important is it to prevent discovery of the information to which the question is directed compared to the amount and probability of having to pay the opposing side's expenses? If you are giving the instruction not to answer so as to adjourn the deposition to seek a protective order, then your calculation must focus on how badly the protective order is needed and the prospects for the court granting it.

Having decided to instruct the witness not to answer, the actual instruction should sound like this:

> Now, Mr. Vasys, did you ever receive any advice from your attorney concerning whether it was proper to terminate the contract?

OBJECTION:

> I object to the question on the grounds that it asks for information covered by the attorney-client privilege, and I instruct the witness not to answer.

Q. Mr. Vasys, will you answer the question, please?

A. No, I'll follow my counsel's advice.

Several additional comments. First, one of the matters that must be covered in preparing a witness to be deposed is what to do when an instruction not to answer is given. You must instruct the witness that the question is not to be answered and if asked whether he will answer, the response is "No." Second, you should place a hand on the witness's arm and speak directly to the witness when giving the instruction. If the witness then starts to answer, you can start squeezing the witness's arm, which is usually an effective way to get the witness to stop talking, and quickly interrupt by cutting the witness off with a stern "Don't answer that question." Third, Rule 26(b)(5) requires that when instructing a witness not to answer based on a claim of privilege or work product, you must do so expressly and "shall describe the nature of the documents, communications, or things not disclosed in a manner that, without revealing information itself privileged or protected, will enable other parties to assess the applicability of the privilege or protection." In the example given, the question itself makes evident the nature of the communication. Finally, be alert to questioning counsel's tactic of coming back later in the deposition, often toward the end when everyone is tired, to an area about which you have instructed the witness not to answer. Unless you have decided that the previous instruction not to answer was a mistake, you should persist in closing off the inquiry.

Instructions not to answer for purposes of adjourning the deposition to seek a protective order occur for many different reasons. The questioning attorney may be abusing the witness by yelling at her, the questions may be asking for trade secrets, the questioning attorney may be asking questions about matters that have absolutely nothing to do with the issues in the case, a 30(b)(6) deposition witness is being asked questions about subjects not listed in the notice of deposition or subpoena, etc. While Rule 30(d)(1) suggests that you should immediately adjourn the deposition to seek a protective order, the lawyers often agree to complete the deposition before moving the court. An exception occurs when the questioning lawyer engages in abusive tactics; then you should adjourn the deposition immediately.

A problem that often occurs is when, at least in the eyes of the defender, the questioning attorney has gone so far beyond the scope of the complaint and answer that the information sought no longer "appears reasonably calculated to lead to the discovery of admissible evidence," which is the outer bound for discovery defined in Rule 26(b)(1). Problems arise, however, because what the questioner believes is "reasonably calculated" will almost surely be seen by the defender as unreasonable and intrusive. The result is an argument between counsel that probably accounts for most of the heat and none of the light at discovery depositions.

The practical solution is this: Defending counsel should recognize her own bias in favor of a narrow interpretation here, and therefore should give the questioner a bit of latitude; the questioning attorney should recognize he need not turn over every rock in the field in order to find enough worms to go fishing.[18] If the questioner still wants what the defender will not give, the areas should be postponed until the defender can bring the matter to the court in a motion for a protective order.

---

18. Controversies on scope can be better understood if we recognize that attorneys at a deposition take such positions in large part because they believe their clients expect them to, and not because they believe in the need for the discovery or the protection. Thus, the deposing attorney is intent upon pressing her inquiries to the limits of reasonableness because she does not want her client (or senior partner, or government supervisor) to think she gave away the store; the defending attorney has the same concerns about allowing too much latitude. In fact, these are exactly the kinds of judgments trial attorneys get paid to make, and if their focus was on the genuine needs of the litigation, rather than on how their actions will be second-guessed later on, the purposes of discovery would be better served.

14.7 QUESTIONING AND CLARIFYING AND CORRECTING ANSWERS

Defending counsel usually does not ask any questions at the deposition of the witness. The reason is simple. If the witness is friendly or a client, the best place to ask questions is in the privacy of the lawyer's office where opposing counsel cannot overhear what is being said. There is no sense sharing information with the other side when there is no requirement of doing so. But exceptions to this rule do arise.

When a witness refuses to cooperate or to be interviewed informally, you should ask questions at the deposition for the same reason that the other side is asking questions: to find out what the witness knows. When the witness is uncooperative with both sides, both have an incentive to ask questions. Even though the other side has noticed the deposition, the "defending" counsel may also question the witness. Defending counsel will also want to question a deposition witness, even though friendly, if she expects the witness to be unavailable for trial and that she will use the deposition instead.

Sometimes the opposing party will notice the deposition of its own party or of a witness friendly to that side. This usually indicates that the witness will be unavailable for trial and the deposition is being taken to preserve their testimony. Prudent counsel will prepare to cross-examine the witness in the same way they would if they were noticing the deposition.[19]

Finally, if you are defending counsel you may want to question the witness using an off-the-record conference if he has misstated an answer or has given a confusing or incomplete answer which might later cause trouble. An example of how you might do this follows:

Q. Mrs. Matulis, what marketing plans did you have for the Green Boy lawn sprinkler for its second year on the market?

A. For the second year? There, we intended to consolidate our first year market penetration by using point-of-purchase manufacturer's rebate coupons, and, I think, that was when we were going to heavy-up our spot TV advertising, probably doubling our television budget.

DEFENDING COUNSEL:

Mrs. Matulis, have you finished your answer?

Q. Yes, I have.

---

19. See § 17.3.

DEFENDING COUNSEL:

Let me talk to you a moment, then. [Aside and off the record, whispered.] I thought that you told me last night that the increased TV advertising was intended to begin in the first quarter of the third year of sales? You've just said it was going to start in the second year.

WITNESS:

[Still off the record.] Oh, oh. No, I didn't mean to say that. I meant that we were planning in the second year. Can I correct that?

DEFENDING COUNSEL:

Of course. Just say that you want to correct your answer.

THE WITNESS:

[Aloud.] Let me correct something I just said. I was a bit confused. During the second year, we were making plans for that heavy-up in television advertising, but the heavy-up itself did not begin until the third year of sales.

Q. Is there anything else about your answer you would like to correct or change?

A. No, I think that is accurate now.

Alternatively, defending counsel could wait until the attorney taking the deposition had finished questioning. The defending attorney could then ask:

Q. Do you recall earlier answering to a question by counsel that you began marketing the heavy-up in the second year?

A. Yes.

Q. Was that a correct answer?

A. No.

Q. What was incorrect about your answer?

If deposing counsel asks the witness about the content of the conversation with counsel, the attorney-client privilege protects that information from disclosure and you should object and instruct the witness not to answer. Of course, the deposing attorney could ask whether the change was made as a result of the conference, a slightly different and probably legitimate question.

In the last example given, the correction occurred after examining counsel had completed her questioning. Nevertheless, if the witness has misstated an answer you can most efficiently clear it up at the same point in the transcript, rather than pages or days later.

The examining counsel may follow up any questions by defending counsel or by other parties with "redirect" examination to be followed by recross and re-redirects and re-recrosses until everyone reaches the point of exhaustion.[20]

14.8 CONCLUDING THE DEPOSITION

Under Rule 30(e), the deponent or a party must demand before the conclusion of the deposition the right to review the deposition transcript or recording and to make corrections. As discussed elsewhere,[21] it makes little sense to give up the right to correct mistakes the witness has made in answering or the court reporter in transcribing. Therefore, you should always demand the right to make corrections before ending the deposition.

---

20. Fed.R.Civ.P. Rule 30(c) provides that "Examination and cross-examination of witnesses may proceed as permitted at trial under the provisions of the Federal Rules of Evidence...."
21. See chapter 15 and § 6.1.

Chapter Fifteen

REVIEWING, CORRECTING, EDITING, AND SUPPLEMENTING THE TRANSCRIPT

"You can't always get what you want,
But if you try sometimes,
You just might find
You get what you need."
— The Rolling Stones

15.1 REVIEWING, CORRECTING, AND EDITING

Under Rule 30(e), a party or the witness must request before the completion of the deposition the right to review and change the deposition. The witness then has thirty days, once the deposition officer has given notice that the deposition is available for review, to carry out the review, and to make and sign any changes. In those jurisdictions following the pre-1993 version of the Federal Rules of Civil Procedure, the parties and the witness must *waive* the right to review and make corrections to the deposition, and the parties must waive the right to sign the deposition. In those jurisdictions, the witness must join in any waiving of the right to read the deposition if the parties wish to do so; a failure to have the witness join in the waiver may make the deposition unusable at trial even though the witness is now unavailable. Obviously, if the deposition is of a party then only the parties need waive the reading. No penalty attaches under either the current rules or pre-1993 version of the rules if the witness fails, under the thirty-day period for doing so, to review the deposition or, under the pre-1993 rules, to sign the deposition; the court will treat it as admissible to the same extent as if the witness had reviewed it and, when necessary, signed it.

Normally both sides have an incentive for the witness to review the deposition, a matter more fully discussed in § 6.1. Under Rule 30(e) you must request this right. Under the pre-1993 version of the rules you simply must not waive it by agreeing to do so, or by failing to have the witness read and sign the deposition afterwards.

In practice, the correcting and editing process usually begins when the reporter creates the transcript and sends it to the attorney who defended the witness at the deposition. That attorney then arranges for the witness to read the transcript, either at the attorney's office or at a convenient location for the witness. If the witness reviews the transcript on her own, she should note changes and then review the changes with her attorney.

Many attorneys have the misconception that the witness may only "correct" mistakes made by the reporter or transcriber, but may not make substantive changes. In fact, under both the current version of Rule 30(e) and the pre-1993 version, the witness may make changes to both "form and substance," but shall give the reasons for doing so. The witness, however, may be subject to further examination, especially if the changes are so extensive or so substantive that they destroy the utility of the deposition.[1] You should exercise caution before allowing the witness to make changes in deposition answers and should avoid making wholesale changes in the deposition transcript. Changes in the original transcript are treated as though they resulted from examination by counsel for the witness at the deposition. Thus, the deposing attorney can obtain an order permitting further examination of the witness.[2] Moreover, the additional examination may inquire into the reasons for the changes.[3] The deponent may also bear the costs and attorney fees associated with re-examination.[4]

Indeed, in the extreme case where a witness makes extensive changes to the transcript which render the deposition virtually useless, the court may, on application of the deposing attorney, order that the original transcript be deemed an accurate record of the deposition testimony, as though the witness had waived reading and signature.[5] For example, a *pro se* Title VII civil rights plaintiff crossed out the answer to almost every deposition question. The plaintiff noted in the margin, "This question was never asked," or "Plaintiff never gave this answer." After an evidentiary hearing at which the court reporter confirmed the accuracy of the transcript, the court imposed sanctions under Rule 37(b)(2), and ruled that the original transcript would be considered an accurate representation of the plaintiff's testimony, as though the plaintiff had waived reading and signing.[6]

---

1. See *Colin v. Thompson*, 16 F.R.D. 194 (D.C. Mo. 1954).
2. See, e.g., *DeSeversky v. Republic Aviation Corp.*, 2 F.R.D. 113 (D.C.N.Y. 1941); *Colin v. Thompson*, 16 F.R.D. 194 (D.C. Mo. 1954).
3. *Sanford v. CBS, Inc.*, 594 F.Supp. 713, 715 (N.D. Ill. 1984).
4. See, e.g., *Lugtig v. Thomas*, 89 F.R.D. 639 (N.D. Ill. 1981).
5. See *Barlow v. Esselte Pendaflex Corp.*, 111 F.R.D. 404 (M.D.N.C. 1986).
6. *Baker v. Ace Advertisers' Service, Inc.*, 134 F.R.D. 65, 73 (S.D.N.Y. 1991).

In practice, the standard procedure for correcting the deposition transcript is for the witness and defending counsel to review the transcript and create a sheet which notes the page and line numbers of the deposition testimony and the corrected testimony (errata sheet). The witness then signs the errata sheet and also may have the signature notarized. The errata or corrections sheet is then returned to the officer/reporter who, under Rule 30(e), will attach the sheet to his certification under Rule 30(f)(1). The certificate will also indicate within it whether any changes were made. Under the pre-1993 version of the Federal Rules of Civil Procedure the corrections are included in the final bound transcript of the deposition. A typical errata sheet under either version of the Rules looks like the following:

Corrections to Vardas Deposition of May 17

Page 17, ll. 2–5:

"should have been considered a possible sort of supplier, but never really came to a close on supplying," should read, "should have been considered a possible source of supply, but never really came close to supplying."

Page 43, l. 13:

"now that I see a difference" should read, "not that I see a difference"

Page 51, l. 20:

"Harry Schmidt and Russell Trover" should read, "Harry Schmidt, Russell Trover, and Jane Vilnius."

Page 73, ll. 15–18:

"and lumber. I cannot remember the other person at the meeting. It may have been George Estus, but I am not certain" should read, "and lumber. The other person at the meeting was George Estus."

Page 114, l. 10:

"No" should read "Yes."

Page 165, ll. 7–10:

"if you understand the document, and I can read it to you and we'll discuss" should read, "if you understand the document, and I cannot, read it to me and we'll discuss."

The best practice always is to satisfy Rule 30(e) by including the witness's reason for the change after the new answer even though the reason for the change is readily apparent from the context and the change itself. This prevents opposing counsel from moving to strike the correction because of a failure to give the reasons for the change. For example, the page 114 change above might read:

Page 114, l. 10:

"No" should read "Yes." Reason: The deponent did not understand that the question had been phrased in the negative.

Some attorneys prefer to provide the changes in a brief form which requires the reader examining the changes to refer back to the original transcript more often in order to understand the context. For example, two of the above changes in this case would instead be:

Page 43, l. 13:

"now" should be "not"

Page 165, ll. 7–10:

"I can read it to you" should be "I cannot, read it to me"

A better practice, however, is to include enough of the unchanged material that the readers can understand the significance of the change without referring back.

An important point that some attorneys do not appreciate is how corrected answers are used at trial. If the deposition is used to impeach the witness or to present a party admission, the deposing attorney is entitled to read the original, uncorrected transcript. The defending attorney can then request, under Rule 32(a)(4), that the corrected response be read immediately thereafter. In this situation, the corrections are simply additional statements by the witness and the original testimony does not lose its testimonial value, but remains the prior statements of the witness. While the corrections and the trial testimony may be inconsistent with the original deposition statement, this merely means that both of the later statements can be impeached by the original deposition statement.

15.2 SUPPLEMENTING THE DEPOSITION

The Advisory Committee Notes to Rule 26(e) clearly state that, with two exceptions, a witness has no duty to supplement deposition testimony by correcting or adding to the answers given. The first exception is depositions of expert witnesses, if the expert is of the type required to file a report under Rule 26(a)(2)(B). The depositions of such experts must be supplemented if the answers are in any way incomplete or incorrect, provided that the new information has not previously been made known to the other parties during the discovery process or in writing. Second, the court may order any witness to supplement his deposition if it deems appropriate.

The duty to supplement under the pre-1993 version of Rule 26(e) extended to:

1. the identity and location of persons having knowledge of discoverable matters;

2. the identity of expert witnesses who will testify at trial, as well as the subject matter and substance of their testimony; and

3. the party acquires new information such that the party knows an answer in the deposition was incorrect or, even though correct when given, is no longer true and a failure to amend the answer would be in substance a knowing concealment.

Under the current Rule 26(e)(1), a party must supplement the information provided under the mandatory disclosures of Rule 26(a) "if the party learns that in some material respect the information disclosed is incomplete or incorrect" and the new information has not been given to the other parties through the discovery process or in writing.

Of course, as with almost all discovery rules, the parties can stipulate to different obligations for supplementation.[7] Therefore, when defending a deposition you should recognize that your casual agreement—to provide further information, additional documents, or to check on the accuracy of an answer—does in fact impose an enforceable obligation.

---

7. Fed.R.Civ.P. 29 and 26(e)(3) (pre-1993 version).

PART FOUR:

USING DEPOSITIONS

Chapter Sixteen

USING DEPOSITIONS

"How use doth breed a habit in a man!"
— William Shakespeare

Testimony from depositions, especially that of parties to the lawsuit, can be used in many ways in pretrial and trial. You can use such testimony to support or to oppose motions (such as summary judgment and other motions) as a source of admissions, as a substitute for the testimony of absent witnesses, to control witnesses at trial, and to prepare for trial. Therefore, if you view depositions solely as a source of impeachment material you are not getting your client's money's worth from the deposition process.

16.1 MOTIONS FOR SUMMARY JUDGMENT

A common use of witness statements from depositions is, just like affidavits, to support or oppose motions for summary judgment.[1] Deposition testimony are statements made under oath, so they have all the trappings which give weight to an affidavit, and logically, you should treat them in the same way.

Some attorneys are concerned about asking open questions at depositions of the opposing party's witnesses because they feel this gives opposing counsel the opportunity to create a record to use for summary judgment purposes, and perhaps in some small part because they believe that if they do not discover unfavorable information, the other side will not discover it either.

In simple fact, opposing counsel has the opportunity to create a favorable record in any event, either through her own questioning at depositions or through affidavits from the party or friendly witnesses if the subject is avoided at the deposition. Therefore, you should proceed

---

1. Fed.R.Civ.P. 56(c) says that the court will consider depositions along with the affidavits, pleadings, admissions, and responses to interrogatories in determining whether a genuine issue of material fact exists. Rule 56(e) says "the court may permit affidavits to be supplemented or opposed by depositions, answers to interrogatories, or further affidavits," and the response shall be "by affidavits or as otherwise provided in this rule. . . ." See *Weldon v. Kraft, Inc.*, 896 F.2d 793 (3d Cir. 1990); C. Wright & A. Miller, *Civil Procedure* § 2142 (West 1994).

with the normal "funnel" approach at the discovery deposition, using open questions to try to uncover all the relevant information the witness has. You should discard the idea that unfavorable information can be left undiscovered. The safest assumption, especially when dealing with witnesses who are parties or closely identified with parties, is that the opposing attorney already knows all of the information that hurts you, and you might as well find it out as well, along with any additional information which may lessen its impact.

Occasionally when one side has to defend a motion for summary judgment early in the pretrial schedule, depositions are scheduled explicitly to permit response to the motion.[2] At such a deposition the deposing attorney's focus is clearly on discovering "genuine issues of material fact." The emphasis, however, remains on "discovering," since relying solely on a cross-examination style with narrow, leading questions may leave entire areas of dispute unrevealed. Just as for a normal discovery deposition, the last portion of the deposition may be used to sharpen positions and issues so that the court may see the "genuine issues" and the "materiality of the facts" more clearly. The approach for summary judgment or simple discovery is the same.

You can also use deposition testimony to support or oppose any motion where the court would consider affidavit evidence. As previously noted, a deposition, being under oath, resembles an affidavit and courts will generally give the same weight to the two.

16.2 PREPARING FOR TRIAL

Perhaps the most important use of depositions is in preparing to cross-examine witnesses at trial. The late Irving Younger in his famous lecture, *The Ten Commandments of Cross-Examination*, gave as his fifth commandment, "Never ask a question to which you do not already know the answer." One of the ways to know the answer is through the witness's deposition.

Many trial lawyers construct their cross-examinations based on the answers given in the witness's deposition. The difference, however, between the deposition answers and trial is that the questions asked at trial can be reorganized to make the intended points in the most effective way possible. For example, you may not have covered an important point until toward the end of a deposition, but nothing prevents you from leading off the cross-examination with this point. Not only can you change the order of points and questions, you can also

---

2. Rule 56(f) specifically provides, among other things, that where it appears that a party opposing a motion needs discovery beyond affidavits to support its opposition, time for depositions may be allowed.

delete unimportant or harmful information in the deposition and reword unartfully phrased questions.

When dealing with important admissions by a witness, the cross-examination questions should mirror the deposition questions as closely as possible in meaning, if not actual wording, so that you can use the deposition to impeach the witness if the answer changes. A minor change in wording between the deposition and trial may permit an intelligent witness to avoid the sting of impeachment and may make you look foolish in the process. Consider the following example:

Q. Isn't it true, sir, that you never even bothered to read the contract?

A. No, that's not true.

Q. Are you telling this jury that you did read the contract?

A. Yes.

Q. Well sir, do you remember having your deposition taken?

A. Yes.

Q. Showing you that deposition, do you see on Page 14, Line 6 that you were asked, "Did you read the contract before you signed it?" and your answer was "No"?

A. Yes, but that is different than what you just asked me. You asked whether I had ever read the contract and I did read it about two weeks after the signing.

Q. Oh, let's move on.

Many trial lawyers, when preparing both their direct and cross-examination outlines for witnesses, will annotate the outline with the line and page of the deposition confirming the expected answer. Such an outline, this one for cross-examination, might look like this:

Was going approximately 50 mph as approached the intersection. (28:32)

Started braking about 200 feet away. (30:14)

Baby was crying in the back seat. (12:4)

Was expected to be at work at 8:00 A.M. (72:12)

Was running late that morning. (73:30)

Thus, if impeachment is necessary on cross-examination or a witness's memory needs to be refreshed on direct examination, the exact page and line of the deposition can be quickly located.

You should usually have depositions abstracted or summarized shortly after they are taken to facilitate preparing for motions and trial, as well as for locating impeaching answers in the heat of trial. Paralegals or new associates usually do the abstracting, but experienced attorneys also do it as a way of becoming more familiar with what was said during the deposition.

There are a number of methods of abstracting depositions such as page/line and subject methods. The first is a straight summary of the deposition; the second organizes the summary by topics. Some attorneys, instead of abstracting, now rely on computer searches for key words and phrases, having used a reporting service that provides a computer disc of the deposition. This method is more expensive and requires bringing a computer to trial, but can sometimes be quicker and more efficient than reviewing a lengthy abstract. A typical abstract might look like the following:

14:6   Formed own construction co. after graduation from college.

14:12   Had only 5 to 10 employees for 1st 10 years.

14:16   Now has 50 employees.

14:20   Does all engineering work and bidding on contracts.

Many times witnesses will be testifying at trial months and even years after they gave their deposition testimony. It is not uncommon for their trial testimony to change in minor ways from what they said at the deposition, not because of any intent to lie or deceive, but because memories fade. Nonetheless, these deviations in the hands of a skillful attorney can be used in a way to discredit a witness's integrity and honesty.

You can avoid many of these problems if you ask every witness you expect to call during a trial to review their deposition carefully before they take the stand. You should emphasize the dangers of changing their testimony from what they said in the deposition.

16.3 SEVEN WAYS TO USE A DEPOSITION AT TRIAL

Whether you have originally taken a deposition for discovery or trial purposes, you can use it at trial in many ways. Among the most common uses are: (1) as the testimony of an absent witness; (2) as a source of admissions; (3) as a basis for a proffer; (4) as a means of refreshing recollection; (5) as the testimony of a witness who is unable to testify because of lapse of memory; (6) as a means of impeaching a witness; and (7) as a means of accomplishing a "phantom" impeachment. Each use of a deposition has a different foundation, deriving from the evidentiary rules which control that use. Since depositions are out-of-court statements which the attorney may be offering for their truth, the rules restricting the use of hearsay are often involved in determining the proper foundation. Here are examples of each use of a deposition at trial.

16.3.1 The testimony of an absent witness.

In many cases by the time of trial some witnesses will have become unavailable, even though you may not have anticipated this when the absent witnesses' depositions were taken. In that event, the depositions may be used to replace the live testimony of the missing witness under Rule 32(a)(3) and Fed.R.Evid. 804(b)(1). Here is what that process would sound like in court:

PLAINTIFF'S COUNSEL:

> Your Honor, Mr. Theodore Barker was scheduled to be our next witness, but he has been called out of the state due to an illness in his family. Counsel for the defendant has been kind enough to stipulate to Mr. Barker's unavailability, and to the fact that this is his deposition testimony.[3] In place of Mr. Barker's live testimony, we would like to read certain limited portions of his deposition testimony for the jury. In total, there are about fifteen pages, Your Honor.

THE COURT:

> That's fine, Mr. Moreland. I presume that these portions have been redacted pursuant to the pretrial rulings?[4]

PLAINTIFF'S COUNSEL:

> Yes, Your Honor, and defendant's counsel also has had an opportunity to review the portions we intend to read. And with the court's permission, we would like to have Mr. Richkus, a paralegal who works with us, read Mr. Barker's answers from the witness stand, as I read the questions.

THE COURT:

> All right. There being no objection, you may proceed.

---

3. By this statement reciting the stipulation, counsel has laid the foundation for use of the deposition under Fed.R.Evid. 804: The witness is unavailable, not through the fault of the proponent of the evidence, and this is in fact his deposition. If opposing counsel refuses to stipulate, it may be necessary to offer evidence establishing the witness's unavailability.

4. Normally during the pretrial proceedings parties will have designated the deposition portions which they intend to use and presented objections for ruling by the court. In addition, any objection to the witness's unavailability would have been raised as part of the mandatory pretrial disclosure scheme. See § 16.6, The Designation Process and Obtaining Rulings on Objections. The portions that the court rules are not admissible are "redacted," or deleted.

PLAINTIFF'S COUNSEL:

Mr. Richkus, if you will go up to the witness stand, we can start with page 27, at line 17.

Q. (By defendant's counsel:) Mr. Barker, what was your position with Vitas Industries in 1987 and 1988?

A. I was the vice-president for purchasing for the company.

Q. What were your responsibilities in that position?

A. I oversaw the purchasing of all materials that we required to manufacture all of our products. That included everything from the copper wire that we wound around the cores to make the armatures for the generators to the decals that we put on the transformer boxes telling about the high voltage.

Q. During that time, from whom did Vitas Industries purchase refined copper?

A. We had several suppliers, but the main ones for those two years were Chilean Copper Conglomerate, Incorporated and Python Industrial Metals.

PLAINTIFF'S COUNSEL:

Now, Mr. Richkus, will you please turn to page 43 in the deposition of Mr. Barker? We'll begin with line 4.

Q. Mr. Barker, why do you think that Chilean Copper and Python Industries were engaged in some kind of agreement to fix copper prices to your company, as is alleged in the complaint in this case?

A. Well, during that time, I often tried to get one or the other of them to give me a better price, you know, to bid against a price I had from the other. But they'd never break the line. Right in lockstep, all the time. On my other metal purchases, I could make deals by going from one supplier to the next, but on copper, those two never gave even a penny off.

DEFENDANT'S COUNSEL:

Your Honor, at this point, we ask that the next two questions and answers be read, pursuant to Rule 32(a)(4), because they contain material which, in fairness, the jury ought to be allowed to consider along with this last answer.

THE COURT:

Well, let me just look at that material for a moment. Yes, I agree, we'll have that read at this point, please, Mr. Moreland.

PLAINTIFF'S COUNSEL:

Yes, Your Honor.

Q. Mr. Barker, isn't it true that there was a terrific demand for copper during that period, and a shortage of supply due to unrest in the government of Chile?

A. Well, there were some political problems down there that made the supply of copper a little less predictable. But we were getting all that we needed.

Q. And isn't it also true, Mr. Barker, based on your experience in the purchase of metals, that no one discounts their prices on metals during periods of shortage, because they can clear their inventories without price reductions?

A. Yes, I suppose that is true in general, but I still think that Chilean Copper and Python were fixing prices.

The process continues until all selected portions of the deposition have been read. At that point, opposing counsel may read in as her cross-examination additional portions of the deposition, either with another "witness" on the stand, or perhaps with this same one, to lessen the likelihood of jury confusion.[5]

Some courts rule, erroneously, that 32(a)(4) material can just as well be presented during cross-examination. If the conditions of these rules have been met, that is, that the proffered material is so closely related to what has already been read, the jury "ought in fairness" to consider the two selections together, then they should be presented together, and not separated by the remainder of the main examination. These rules promote the jury's understanding of the evidence; the fact that the additional material *could* be presented on cross-examination does not mean that is the *best* way for the jury to understand it.

16.3.2 As a basis for a proffer.

Often you must persuade the court that certain evidence is relevant or certain lines of questioning have a good-faith basis. Sometimes you can use depositions to provide this foundation for going forward. Consider the following example from a cross-examination:

Q. Mr. Taras, isn't it true that you never saw the plaintiff before he went into the hospital?

A. No, that's not true at all. I saw him several times. We were good friends, and visited a lot.

---

5. The use of Fed.R.Civ.P. 32(a)(4) deserves comment. This rule allows additional portions of depositions to be read into the record which ought "in fairness to be considered with" portions which have been read by the other side.

Q. Mr. Taras, you were good friends a year before the plaintiff's car accident, weren't you?

A. Yes, yes, of course.

Q. And you are good friends now, aren't you?

A. Yes, that's true, of course.

Q. But at the time of the accident, you and the plaintiff were not even on speaking terms, were you?

A. I don't understand what you're saying. He's my friend and I see him all the time.

Q. Mr. Taras, you used to play poker with the plaintiff once a week, didn't you?

PLAINTIFF'S COUNSEL:

I object, Your Honor. This is irrelevant and prejudicial, and I request that counsel be directed to move on to another area.

DEFENSE COUNSEL:

Your Honor, may we approach the bench?

THE COURT:

Yes, step up, counsel. Now, where are you going with this, Mr. Kaunas?

DEFENSE COUNSEL:

Your Honor, based on this witness's deposition testimony, which I can show you here at 34 and 35 of the deposition transcript, I believe that he will testify that he and the plaintiff used to play poker once a week, but that two weeks before the accident, they had an argument over a poker hand, and that they didn't speak to one another for several months. That testimony impeaches his testimony on direct that he visited with the plaintiff in the weeks after the accident and could see the pain and limited movement that the plaintiff now claims he had.

THE COURT:

Let me see the deposition. All right. Based on this deposition testimony, I am going to overrule the objections and permit the questioning. You may proceed, Mr. Kaunas.

DEFENSE COUNSEL:

Mr. Taras, the question is, didn't you and the plaintiff play poker once a week before the accident?

A. Yes, but he was never very good.

Q. But just a week or so before the accident, you stopped playing poker, right?

A. Yes, that's true.

Q. You had an argument about a poker hand, didn't you?

A. Yes. He never had a pair of aces. He had one ace, and he took the other from his pocket.

Q. And because of that argument, you and the plaintiff didn't talk to each other for almost a year?

A. Yes, that's the truth. It was silly. I've had aces in my pocket, too.

Q. And you didn't spend time with him and visit with him right after the accident, did you?

A. No, I didn't. But he has told me that he was really in a lot of pain then.

16.3.3 As a source of admission.

You can introduce admissions of a party opponent in their deposition under Rule 32(a)(1) and (2) as though the statements were given as live testimony from the stand. Rule 32(a)(2) specifically authorizes using the deposition of a party, depositions of an officer, director or managing agent of a party, or the deposition of a person designated to testify under Rule 30(b)(6). Further, Fed.R.Evid. 801(d)(2) defines admissions by a party opponent to include not only the party's own statements, but also statements made by the party's agents, employees, and persons authorized to speak on behalf of the party. All of these statements are classified by the Federal Rules of Evidence as non-hearsay and are admissible as substantive evidence.[6]

Thus, a plaintiff may use portions of the defendant's deposition to establish the plaintiff's *prima facie* case, without calling the defendant as an adverse witness. Assume in the following assault and battery case, that an element of plaintiff's case is the fact that the guard was an agent of the company at the time of the assault.

(QUESTIONING BY PLAINTIFF'S COUNSEL:)

Q. And what was the defendant Sugis wearing when he came out of the building and struck you with the nightstick?

---

6. Fed.R.Civ.P. 32(a)(1) states that depositions can be used for any purpose permitted by the Federal Rules of Evidence. Party admissions, direct or vicarious, should not be confused with "statements against interest," which are defined by Fed.R.Evid. 804 as exceptions to the rule excluding hearsay if the declarant is unavailable. This confusion has probably persisted much longer than it otherwise would have because of the unfortunate habit of some courts of using the hybrid phrase, "admission against interest."

A. He had on a guard's uniform, you know, like a rent-a-cop kind of outfit, that said, "Ace Security" on a patch on his shoulder.

BY COUNSEL:

Your Honor, at this time we would like to read a section of one page of the defendant Sugis's deposition, which is a party admission under Federal Rule of Evidence 801(d)(1). The depositions have been stipulated as authentic.

THE COURT:

With that stipulation, you may proceed, but let's keep it short, since you have this witness on the stand.

COUNSEL:

Yes, Your Honor. The portion appears on page 17 of the deposition. Quote:

Q. Mr. Sugis, when you saw the plaintiff marching down the street with the group carrying the antiwar signs, what were you doing?

A. I was at my desk in the lobby of the Metropolitan Building.

Q. Why were you there?

A. I was on the job; that's my responsibility, to provide security for the clients of the company.

Q. You say, "the company." Is that the Ace Security Company?

A. Yes. That's who I work for, Ace Security.

Of course, use of a deposition as an admission is not limited to matters that are elements of the *prima facie* case. You can use selections for any purpose, as long as they are relevant and otherwise unobjectionable.

Rule 32(a)(4) applies to this use of depositions also. Thus, in the above situation involving Ace Security, counsel for the company might say:

ACE DEFENSE COUNSEL:

Your Honor, may we read the next two questions and answers, under Rule 32(a)(4)? Let me give you a copy.

THE COURT:

Well, let's see. Yes, I see what you're saying. Yes, you may read the next two questions and answers.

ACE DEFENSE COUNSEL:

Thank you, Your Honor. Let me quote:

Q. Mr. Sugis, what time was it when you went out onto the street and had this confrontation with the plaintiff?

A. Well, it was about 9:30 in the morning.

Q. And what shift were you working for Ace Security at the Metropolitan Building?

A. I was on the midnight to 8 shift, but, you know, I heard there was going to be this demonstration, so I kind of stayed around so that I could see these people with their signs and things.

16.3.4 As a means of refreshing recollection.

You may refresh a witness's recollection with anything from a simple leading question to a photograph, a snatch of song, or a letter from Mom. The question which the court must decide is not, "What was used to refresh recollection?" but rather, "Is the witness actually testifying from refreshed recollection?" Depositions are useful tools to refresh recollection, since they have often been taken months or years closer to the relevant events. The foundation at trial for using depositions in this way is essentially the same as that for any attempt to refresh present recollection:

Q. Now, Ms. Vardas, what was the next step in trying to persuade United Lumber and Hardware to finance the expansion of your business?

A. Well, I think that I met with Mr. Shadis at the bank. No, that wasn't it. Maybe . . . I'm sorry, I'm just not sure what was next. There were a number of meetings.

Q. Is there anything that might help you remember?

A. I think that we discussed this, you know, at my deposition. It seems to me that we went over this in the deposition.

Q. Okay, let me hand you your deposition, and ask if you would turn there to page 73. Read that to yourself, please, and tell me when you've finished.

A. All right . . . yes, I've read it.

Q. Now, just let me have the transcript back, please. Having read that portion of your deposition, do you now recall what the next step was in trying to negotiate financing through United Lumber and Hardware?

A. Yes, I do. I met with their accountant, and brought my accountant and architect with me. It was at that meeting that United told me, "Go ahead with obtaining the permits and negotiating with your general contractor. We'll work something out."

Notice Rule 32(a)(4) does not apply here, since no deposition, writing, or other recorded statement is being *offered*; only the refreshed memory of the witness provides the evidence.

16.3.5 As the testimony of a witness whose memory cannot be refreshed.

When a non-party witness[7] or your own client testifies at trial and cannot remember what color the traffic light was even though the witness testified in her deposition that the light was red, another method of introducing the statement, other than impeaching the witness with the deposition testimony, is available. Fed.R.Evid. 804(a)(3) defines a failure of memory as unavailability for purposes of admitting statements that would otherwise be hearsay.[8] The witness's deposition testimony then becomes admissible as substantive evidence under Fed.R.Evid. 804(b)(1), the provision allowing the use of "former testimony."

The foundation under Fed.R.Evid. 804(a)(3) and 804(b)(1) is quite simple. You need merely show the witness's memory is currently inadequate for the matters on which the deposition is being offered and the deposition was in fact given. An example of cross-examination (but the same thing could also occur on direct examination using non-leading questions) using the deposition testimony in this way follows:

Q. Now, isn't it true that, as his friend, you were advising the defendant not to break this contract with the plaintiff?

A. Well, I don't remember doing that.

Q. You don't remember having a conversation where you told Mr. Shadis that you thought it was a fair contract and that he shouldn't breach it?

A. No, I don't remember that.

Q. Mr. Barker, in that same deposition we discussed earlier this morning, you were asked this question and you gave this answer—page 46, counsel: "Question: What did you discuss about the McLean contract? Answer: Well, I told Shadis that he seemed to be getting his money's worth, and that it looked to me like Vardas was doing a good job. I mean, he asked if I thought it

---

7. We focus here on non-party depositions because the deposition of an adverse party can be used as an admission, regardless of his present recollection or his availability, as we have discussed above.

8. Fed.R.Civ.P. 32(a)(1) states that a deposition may be used by any party for any purpose permitted by the Federal Rules of Evidence.

was a fair deal, and I said, 'Yeah, it looks fair to me'." That was your answer, wasn't it, Mr. Barker?

A. Yes, that's what I said.

16.3.6 As a means of impeachment.

Under Rule 32(a)(1) you can also use depositions as prior inconsistent statements to impeach a witness at trial. In fact, under Fed.R.Evid. 801(d)(1)(A), deposition testimony used to impeach a witness with a prior inconsistent statement is classified as non-hearsay and may be considered by the judge or jury as substantive evidence as well as reflecting on the witness's credibility.[9] Such testimony may also qualify under 801(d)(2)(A) as an admission of a party opponent.

Early on, we discussed the commitments extracted at the outset of the deposition in some detail and made the point that those commitments were made to aid in control and impeachment at trial. Now, presented with the opportunity to impeach at trial, that groundwork comes into play. A full-blown impeachment of a non-party witness at trial follows, at the first time an impeachment of the witness has been necessary:

Q. Mr. Lapitis, on your direct examination you said that you saw the traffic signal when the defendant's Cadillac started into the intersection, is that right?

A. Yes, sir, I said it and it's true. I saw that light.

Q. Isn't it true that the light was red for the defendant?

A. No, like I said, it was green for him. No question about it.

Q. No question about it?

A. No question about it.

Q. Mr. Lapitis, you remember coming to my office a few months ago?

A. Yes, I remember that.

Q. You came there to have your deposition taken, right?

A. Yes. Well, I got a subpoena, so I showed up like I was supposed to.

---

9. In contrast, prior inconsistent statements not under oath can be used only for impeachment, i.e., reflecting on the witness's credibility, and cannot be considered as substantive evidence. Thus, if the defendant's running of a red light is an element of the plaintiff's *prima facie* case, a letter in which the witness wrote, "the light was red" can impeach his testimony that the light was green, but it cannot prove the light was red to satisfy the plaintiff's burden on that point. A deposition from the same witness in which he previously testified the light was red, can impeach his trial testimony that the light was green and can also provide the necessary substantive element that the light was red.

Q. And the defendant's attorney was there, wasn't she?

A. Yes.

Q. In fact, you met with her before the deposition, didn't you?

A. Well, yes, she asked me to come to her office the day before, so I went in and talked with her.

Q. When you came to my office for your deposition, we met in a conference room; do you remember that?

A. Yes.

Q. And the defendant's lawyer sat right next to you during the deposition, didn't she, and talked with you?

A. Yes, she was very nice.

Q. I told you that you could have breaks when you wanted them, and we had coffee and water there for you, isn't that right?

A. Yes, it was very pleasant.

Q. There was a court reporter there who gave you the same oath that you took here in court today?

A. Yes, that's right.

Q. And you promised then to tell the truth?

A. Yes, I swore to tell the truth as best I could.

Q. And you did tell the truth in your answers, didn't you?

A. Yes, I did.

Q. And after the deposition was over, the court reporter typed up my questions and your answers into a booklet, and he sent you that booklet, didn't he?

A. Yes, I went over it with the defendant's lawyer.

Q. And after you made corrections of some errors, you signed the corrections and sent the booklet back to the court reporter, right?

A. Yes.

Q. Let me show you that deposition, Mr. Lapitis, and I'd like you to look at page 76, the correction page. That's your signature right there at the bottom?"

A. Yes.

Q. Mr. Lapitis, at that deposition, page 16, line 32, I asked you this question and you gave this answer: "Question: Sir, what color was the traffic light for the westbound car, the defendant's

Cadillac? Answer: For the Caddy, let me see, for the Caddy it was red." I have read your answer correctly, haven't I, sir?

A. Well, yes, that's what I said then.

Q. And you did not change that page of the deposition when you read it later with the lawyers, did you, Mr. Lapitis? Take a look at the page of corrections here.

A. No, we didn't change it.

That completes the impeachment, and under Fed.R.Evid. 801(d)(1)(A) that puts in front of the jury the substantive evidence the light was red for the Cadillac, as well as the evidence that this witness has told two different stories under oath.

Sometimes, especially when there is nothing about the stories to distinguish them—that is, to make the favorable deposition statement apparently more truthful than the later, trial testimony—impeaching counsel might want to provide the motive:

Q. Mr. Lapitis, since the deposition, you have met with the defendant's counsel a couple times, haven't you?

A. Yes.

Q. You met with her to review the deposition and you met with her to prepare for your testimony today in court, isn't that right?

A. Yes.

Q. And both those times, you discussed what you were going to say here today, didn't you?

DEFENDANT'S COUNSEL:

Objection, Your Honor. This calls for hearsay and attorney work product.

PLAINTIFF'S COUNSEL:

Your Honor, these are conversations with a non-party witness. There's no privilege here. And these conversations are relevant and admissible for impeachment, Your Honor, and therefore do not constitute hearsay.

THE COURT:

Objections overruled. Please answer the question, Mr. Lapitis.

A. Well, yes, we discussed what was going to happen at trial, and what questions I'd be asked.

Q. And you practiced your answers to those questions, didn't you?

A. Well, yes.[10]

16.3.7 As a means of accomplishing a "phantom" impeachment.

The "phantom" or "ghost" impeachment is so-called because no impeachment actually occurs but the witness answers truthfully because he thinks impeachment is possible. This tactic's success depends upon convincing the witness at trial that the cross-examiner has absolute mastery of the facts in the deposition, coupled with ability to call them up virtually instantaneously.[11]

Some attorneys put the witness's deposition in bright covers with the witness's name two inches high across the front so that, perhaps, during the direct examination, but certainly during the cross, the witness comes to recognize the cross-examiner has that deposition readily available. Then, when impeaching during the cross-examination you would make conspicuous use of the brightly bound volume using notes in your examination notebook to go directly to the right page and line without fumbling.

After a number of such impeachments, the witness will become "disciplined," that is, will be much less willing to fight over testimony. At that point, you may be able to force the witness to tell the truth by making apparent use of the deposition, even though the deposition does not contain testimony on the point in question. If you have a good faith basis for believing a particular fact is true—for example, that the witness's car is green—but that fact is not in the deposition, you might conspicuously leaf through the deposition, settle on one page, appear to read it for a moment, and then say to the witness who has been watching:

Q. And, sir, your car is green, isn't it?

The witness, now believing that the color of his car is mentioned in the deposition because the attorney has not been wrong yet, would rather admit the truth the car is green than lie and be impeached again.

---

10. One caveat is appropriate here, however. This impeachment for bias depends for its success upon the latent (or patent?) mistrust which lay jurors have for attorneys—their belief that an attorney can make a witness say that red is green. If the cross-examiner establishes this as a premise, he indeed weakens that particular witness's testimony, but he also weakens the testimony of all of his own witnesses. And, since he is an attorney, he risks weakening his own credibility as well if the jury analyzes this form of impeachment logically.

11. In *The Art of Cross-Examination*, Francis Wellman writes, "A witness, in anger, often forgets himself and speaks the truth." Francis Wellman, *The Art of Cross-Examination*, 4th ed. at 135 (Macmillan Publishing Co.). A similar phenomenon occurs with the phantom impeachment.

16.4 THE DESIGNATION PROCESS AND OBTAINING RULINGS ON OBJECTIONS

Discovery depositions, unlike examination at trial, contain many misstatements, false starts, irrelevancies, and arguments between counsel. The procedures for cleansing the transcript of such problems have arisen not so much from the rules of procedure as from common practice and common sense. The designation and counter-designation conventions are intended to avoid arguments at trial about objections and to provide all parties with the opportunity to respond to deposition testimony which has been selected for use at trial.

If the case is sufficiently complex, at some point before trial most courts will normally order the parties to designate those depositions or portions of depositions each intends to offer at trial. In U.S. District Courts, Rule 26(a)(3)(B) requires as part of the mandatory pretrial disclosures that each party designate those witnesses whose testimony is expected to be presented by means of a deposition, except for impeachment testimony, and, if the deposition was not recorded stenographically, also to provide a transcript of the deposition portions to be used. Each party must make these disclosures at least thirty days before trial unless the court orders otherwise. Each party then has fourteen days, unless the court sets a different time, in which to file a list with any objections to the use under Rule 32(a) of the deposition testimony designated by any other party. You must be careful to include all objections you intend to urge since any not listed are waived. The only exceptions are for objections made under Fed.R.Evid. 402 (relevancy) and 403 (prejudice, cumulative, etc.) or if the court permits the objection to be added later for good cause shown.

In those jurisdictions following the pre-1993 version of the Federal Rules of Civil Procedure as well as those under the current rules, no required procedure for the actual designation and ruling on objections exists. Some general observations apply, however. Simultaneous designations are common: first, each side identifies the portions of depositions it intends to offer, either by making a list of witnesses, pages, and lines (the procedure under the current Federal Rules) or by marking on a copy of the transcripts with a particular color; red for plaintiff's designations and green for defendant's designations, for example. The parties then exchange the lists or transcript volumes and make counter-designations, either with additional lists, or by marking with additional colors; blue for plaintiff's counter-designations, yellow for defendant's. (Of course, the parties keep duplicate color-coded copies, so that each can know what it designated and counter-designated and what the other side designated and counter-designated.) That normally is the end of it—counter-counter-designations normally do not occur.

Once the designation and counter-designation process has occurred, the court will usually order a submission on objections to any designated portions and then may hold a hearing to resolve them. Some judges prefer to postpone a ruling on these objections until trial, but that does not provide the attorneys with any certainty as to what portions will be admitted. On the other hand, ruling pretrial on all objections to the designated portions can be very time consuming and will result in the court spending time on objections to portions which may never be used at trial.

The best procedure may be to ask the court to review designations a few days before their intended use at trial, after the jury has left for the day. That will be close enough to the presentation so that the attorneys will have a relatively firm idea of what they actually want to use at trial, and yet far enough in advance so that they can plan based on the judge's rulings.

As a practical matter, however, courts are very unwilling to set aside time for ruling on these objections to designated portions, and seem to hope that if they postpone looking at the designations long enough those designations may never surface at all. To a great extent this is true, because, far in advance of trial, attorneys tend to designate more than they will ever need. By refusing to turn to rulings on designations until near trial, or during trial, the courts may be dealing with the attorneys when they are able to evaluate their needs more realistically.

After the parties have made their designations and registered their objections, no other designations or objections should be considered by the court for admissions or testimony of an absent witness. (Uses for impeachment, proffers, and refreshing recollection of course remain unaffected.) Even for use of the depositions under Rule 32(a)(4), those materials ought to have been counter-designated, since those rules deal with use in response to an opponent's original use. The court should allow additional deposition material to be used only on a showing by the proponent that the need to use that portion of the deposition could not reasonably have been anticipated.

16.5 PRESENTATION OF DEPOSITION TESTIMONY AT TRIAL

We have already discussed one method of presenting written deposition transcript in court by having an associate or paralegal read the answers from the witness stand.[12] Although suitable for lengthier

---

12. Supra, § 16.3.1.

portions of the written deposition, this method is much too cumbersome for short excerpts and, of course, is inapplicable to videotaped depositions.

Using an associate to read answers from the stand, however, is clearly preferable to the attorney standing and reading pages to the jury; even though it is a "re-enactment," the give-and-take of questioning of a live witness has a dramatic content that is not present in a straight reading. You should consider, however, some subtle problems.

The court will expect the deposition readers, attorney, and employee to avoid inserting emotional content into the deposition through exaggerated intonation or pauses. Nevertheless, the jury itself will "add" content to the deposition reading by reacting to the appearance and personality of the witness-reader. In the instance where a friendly witness is unavailable and you are reading his deposition, you will want to select a witness-reader who presents an appropriate and attractive demeanor in terms of age, appearance, and bearing. Thus, if your absent witness is a middle-aged executive, select a middle-aged reader dressed in a suit and tie; if the witness is an assembly line worker, select a reader who looks as though he could make a living with his hands, and perhaps should wear a sports coat and open shirt; if the witness is a woman who owns a small business, select a reader who presents the appropriate appearance of experience, competence, and success.

Obviously, the opponent must guard against abuse by the attorney presenting the reader. If the actual deponent is a twenty-five-year-old high school dropout who happened to be present when his boss discussed contract terms, it is misleading to present to the jury a reader of his deposition who looks and speaks as though he has a graduate degree in business administration. The opponent should object, under Fed.R.Evid. 403, that use of that particular reader will mislead and confuse the jury by inviting it to associate greater credibility with the testimony than would have occurred had the actual witness been available. The court may have a hard time appreciating this objection because it will not have seen the actual deponent, but the attorney could present the educational background of the witness from the deposition, so that the court has some understanding of her concern.[13] Sometimes you suspect your opponent is taking the deposition because the witness will be unavailable for trial and is deliberately choosing to stenographically

---

13. As mentioned, courts already understand that the weight given the testimony can be affected by the manner in which it is read, and they will instruct readers to avoid adding any emphasis or drama. The same concern logically applies to adding substance or weight by selecting readers from "Central Casting."

record the deposition because the witness will be less persuasive on videotape. While expensive to do so, Rule 30(b)(3) allows you to defeat your opponent's strategy by arranging for the deposition also to be recorded by videotape. At trial when your opponent presents the deposition to a jury, you have a right under Rule 32(c) to insist on showing the videotape recording instead of your opponent using associates or actors to read the stenographic version.

The opponent of the deposition testimony may have no advance notice of the identity of the reader selected by the other side, so it would be wise for you to keep a "generic" bench brief in your trial notebook. This brief would remind the court of its power to control the mode of presentation of this deposition testimony and of the need to prevent confusing and misleading the jury.

PART FIVE:

SPECIAL TYPES OF DEPOSITIONS

Chapter Seventeen

DEPOSITIONS FOR USE AT TRIAL

"It took me forty years on earth
To reach this sure conclusion:
There is no Heaven but clarity,
No Hell except confusion."
— Jan Struther

One talent of attorneys who are "good deposition takers" is that they are able to hear, as the deposition record is created, how the deposition testimony will sound months later when portions are read at trial. Testimony read from a transcript is not as interesting to a jury as testimony presented by live witnesses; therefore you must take care to make the deposition testimony as clear and interesting as possible in its later use.

Any deposition can be used as a substitute for the live testimony of a witness if for some reason the witness becomes unavailable to testify at trial.[1] One inherent risk of taking a deposition of a potentially adverse witness is that, if the witness later becomes unavailable to testify at trial, the deposition that you take for discovery purposes may end up being read into evidence by your opponent. Thus, questions that you ask to gather as much information as possible later come back to haunt you when the other side uses the answers. This becomes an even greater problem when you have refrained from aggressively cross-examining the witness during the deposition, planning to reserve such attacks until trial to avoid giving the witness experience on how to respond. If the witness has become unavailable, then the other side can present the deposition testimony to the jury mostly unchallenged.

But depositions sometimes are taken specifically because you anticipate that a witness will not be available at the time of trial. These are called "preservation depositions" or "depositions *de bene esse*." The plan is to present the witness's testimony through deposition. For instance, if a witness is moving to another state or is expected to die before the trial, the deposition is not being taken for discovery purposes, but to perpetuate the witness's testimony for use at a later time.

---

1. Fed.R.Civ.P. 32(a)(3); Fed.R.Evid. 804.

Usually you will want to take such a deposition of friendly witnesses; that is, witnesses who you expect to testify favorably for your side. Because the witness is friendly, you can often prepare the witness for his or her deposition in the same way you would prepare the witness to testify at trial. Occasionally, however, a witness is known to have important information that may be favorable, but neither side is quite sure and the witness refuses to be interviewed. When you expect the witness to be unavailable for trial, you must make the hard decision of whether to take the witness's deposition and thereby preserve potentially favorable testimony, or forgo taking it because of the risk that the testimony will turn out to be unfavorable and the deposition will ultimately be used against you.[2] Of course, the other side can short circuit all of these plans by noticing the witness's deposition.

When a witness refuses to be interviewed or when it is otherwise impossible to pin down a witness's story in advance, the deposition must, by necessity, be a combination of discovery (finding out what the witness has to say) and perpetuation (putting the testimony in a form that can be used for trial). The risk, of course, is that all of the information will be harmful and there is nothing to put into shape for trial. However, your opponent, who has now had the benefit of your discovery efforts, will no doubt be pleased to arrange the testimony in a way most favorable for presentation at trial.

Despite the risks of preserving unfavorable testimony, you will often find it necessary to take a witness's deposition in anticipation of that witness being unavailable for trial. Preparing for and taking these depositions is at least as important, and sometimes more so, as taking a discovery deposition.

17.1 PREPARING TO TAKE THE TRIAL DEPOSITION

In preparing to take a deposition for purposes of perpetuating the witness's testimony for later use at trial, remember that reading the deposition testimony almost always renders juries slightly comatose. Even placing an associate in the witness box to play the role of the witness only minimally increases the interest level of the jurors. Thus, if finances and logistics permit, consider recording the testimony on videotape.[3] The jury's attention span and retention are likely to be much greater than with the use of a stenographic deposition.

---

2. In some states, attorneys control this risk by conducting a discovery deposition first, then proceeding with a "trial" or *de benne esse* deposition if the evidence is favorable and should be preserved.

3. See chapter 18, "Videotape Depositions."

You should schedule the deposition of the potentially unavailable witness as early in the litigation as possible. If you have not had adequate time to prepare for taking the deposition, schedule it for a later date. If the witness is seriously ill or is transient, however, be cautious and schedule the deposition as soon as possible.

If the witness is friendly and cooperative, preparing him or her for the *de bene esse* deposition is the same process as preparing a witness to testify at trial. You should carefully explore the witness's story and attempt to resolve any internal discrepancies or weaknesses. More importantly, you should review the expected questions and the witness's answers and make suggestions for improving the presentation through better word choice, order, or emphasis. Finally, you should discuss potential cross-examination and give the witness a flavor of what it is like. Remember, however, that your preparation conference with the witness will not likely be privileged unless the witness is a client or an agent of a client.

One difference between preparing a witness for a trial deposition and preparing that witness to testify at trial is that there will be no jury or judge at the deposition to evaluate the witness's demeanor (unless, of course, you are taking a videotape deposition). Thus, the witness's dress is not particularly important. Nor is whether the answers sound memorized, and so on, except to the extent that you might cause opposing counsel to find out what you said to the witness in advance. But the transcript gives no indication of demeanor or tone and therefore preparing on these matters is unimportant (Obviously, this is not true for a videotape deposition where preparation on dress and demeanor is very important).

For the same reason, it does little harm to write out your questions in advance. The transcript will not show whether you are reading your questions or composing them on the spot. Nor does it much matter with most friendly witnesses whether you are making eye contact with them while asking the questions or looking down at your script. Writing the questions gives you the opportunity to make sure they are correctly worded and that you cover all of the topics. The negative aspect of writing out the questions is that if the witness deviates from the prepared answers, the questions may prove useless. Also, written questions may sound prepared rather than the sort of thing that you would ask in a natural oral exchange. However, reviewing the questions with another person, such as a secretary, can usually protect against the use of stilted lawyers' language.

17.2 TAKING THE TRIAL DEPOSITION

The examination of a witness whose deposition is being taken to perpetuate the testimony is conducted as if the witness were testifying at trial, with several important differences. First, because the jury or judge will not have an opportunity to observe the witness's demeanor and to make judgments about credibility on that basis, you should provide other indices of veracity. The most important is a longer and more complete accreditation of the witness. Providing details about the witness's personal background is helpful, such as whether the witness is married, has children, and has lived in this community for a number of years. Similar information about the witness's education and employment history will also aid the jury. If the witness's testimony relates to his or her job, add some detail about the job and the witness's experience. Finally, if the witness is neutral and has no ties to either side of the dispute, you should bring this out.

Because there is no opportunity to ask the questions again at trial, it is important that your questions and the answers be clear and understandable. Carefully thinking through the best method of explaining complex matters and even writing out the questions help ensure that the jury or judge will comprehend the witness's testimony when it is read at trial. An effective trial lawyer learns how to "self-monitor." In other words, learn to listen to your own questions and the witness's answers and judge whether they are clear, understandable, and successful in bringing out all you were hoping to extract from the witness.

Techniques such as using tone of voice and facial expressions to convey meaning do not work for stenographic depositions. Make sure that all questions and answers are understandable without reference to these factors. Similarly, hand gestures and other body language do not come across in a transcript.

If it will be necessary for the witness to give distances or illustrate movements, plan in advance how to do this in such a way that the jury listening to the testimony later will understand what is going on. Thus, you should clarify all hand gestures and descriptions such as "from here to there."

When opposing counsel makes an objection at a deposition being taken for discovery purposes, you may choose not to respond in any way to the objection except to direct the witness to answer the question. Since you have no intention ever to introduce the testimony at trial or use it for a summary judgment motion, it does not really matter that the question was objectionable; your only interest is the answer. However, this is not the case with a deposition being taken for use at trial.

You should avoid objectionable questions by carefully reviewing the testimony in advance. If objections are then made at the deposition, the advance review will put you in a better position to decide whether you should rephrase the question. If the objection is valid, or if you think it may be sustained, rephrase the question. If in doubt as to the basis of the objection, do not hesitate to ask opposing counsel to state the grounds. You will not have the opportunity to ask the question again at trial if the objection is sustained and the witness is unavailable. Even if you doubt the validity of the objection, rephrase the question once it is answered the first time. Then, if the objection ultimately turns out to be unfounded, you can choose which of the two phrasings to read to the jury. If the objection is sustained, you will still have a good question and answer remaining.

Sometimes it is necessary to take a deposition for use at trial when you have had no opportunity to interview the witness in advance. In those situations, it may be necessary to first ask discovery-type questions to find out what the witness knows. Once you have explored the witness's knowledge, you may then want to go back over some of the prior answers to place the information in a more useable form for presentation at trial. For instance, if the witness, in answering a question about what happened, provides a long answer with neutral information and a few items of importance, you should probably ask several additional questions to highlight the favorable information. That the useful questions are separated by several questions and answers with unhelpful information does not matter. When you read the deposition at trial, you can omit the irrelevant questions and answers and present only the useful ones.

Remember also that you can use leading questions only with an adverse party—a witness identified with an adverse party, or a witness who has demonstrated hostility. There should be no question about who is an adverse party, but you should establish through your questions that a witness is hostile or identified with an adverse party. The foundation for asking leading questions is usually laid at the beginning of the deposition.

17.3 DEFENDING THE TRIAL DEPOSITION

Nothing in a notice of deposition indicates whether the deposition is being taken for use at trial, for discovery, or for both. But any time you receive a notice of deposition from the other side for a witness who you know to be friendly to that side, it is probably being taken to preserve testimony. It generally makes no sense to take the deposition of a witness who can be interviewed out of the presence of opposing counsel unless that witness is likely to be unavailable for trial. If this occurs, be prepared to cross-examine the witness in the same way as you would at trial.

If the witness is friendly to the other side, you probably have not had an opportunity to interview them and to determine what the witness has to say. Thus, while your opponent is conducting the deposition to preserve testimony for use at trial, you will be taking the deposition for discovery purposes *and* to preserve testimony. Unless you are able to determine from other sources what the witness will be saying, it will be difficult to prepare cross-examination unless you have first done some discovery questioning.

The usual procedure in preparing to cross-examine is to conduct information-gathering questioning to determine what the witness knows and to develop possible areas for cross-examination. While normally you would worry about preserving unfavorable testimony, such information is likely to be brought out on direct examination unless opposing counsel is equally ignorant of what the witness will say. Your task is to discover the testimony favorable to your side that your opponent has failed to bring out.

Besides cross-examining, you must also object when appropriate. Since any objection to a problem which can be cured is waived if not made, you must be alert in your role as opposing counsel. The transcript will be read at trial and this is the only opportunity to make curable objections.[4]

Naturally, the same strategic considerations that govern objections at trial also govern in defending the trial deposition; therefore, you may choose to forgo some objections. For instance, objecting to a lack of foundation is rarely helpful unless the questioner cannot establish the necessary foundation.[5] Otherwise, the opposing lawyer is likely to ask the necessary questions resulting in the evidence being more persuasive than it would otherwise be.

17.4 USING THE DEPOSITION AT TRIAL

How you present deposition testimony to the trier of fact is very much a matter of local custom and procedure. In a bench trial, the offering party usually will merely designate the pages and lines that the court is to consider, and the judge will actually read the testimony at some later time. In a jury trial, however, the testimony is almost always read to the jury and the actual deposition transcript is never given to the jury to consider during its deliberations.

---

4. See § 14.5.1.
5. See § 14.5.2.

The procedure for reading the deposition to the jury also varies from jurisdiction to jurisdiction. Some courts have the bailiff read the designated portions to the jury while in others one of the attorneys for the offering side reads it. The preferred method with many attorneys, however, is to have a person sit in the witness box—usually an attorney—who reads the deposition answers while another attorney reads the questions. This makes the deposition reading resemble actual trial testimony as much as possible. As discussed before, some attorneys attempt to select an associate or other person to play the role of the witness who presents the desired image to the jury.[6]

If lawyers will be reading the testimony, they should animate their voices and, within reason, accent those questions and answers they particularly wish the jury to focus upon. While the reading of depositions is boring, reading in a monotone turns an experience that is otherwise unpleasant for the jury into torture.

Before you can present the deposition at trial, two steps are necessary: first, editing; and second, ruling on objections.[7]

The judge must rule on objections only if objections are made. Usually the judge's ruling is done as part of the pretrial conference or during the trial.[8]

Deposition readings are invariably a tedious experience for the jury. One study of jury comprehension noted that "[t]he jurors' response to reading of depositions into evidence was uniformly negative. They found it boring, difficult to follow, and uninformative."[9] The more mercifully brief the experience, the more likely the jury will understand, remember, and be persuaded by what they hear.

A mistake many lawyers make is reading the entire deposition to the jury, not because all of it contributes to their cause, but because of desire for context or completeness. Don't. You should carefully edit depositions for reading so that you present only those questions and answers that contribute to the jury's understanding and persuasion. The other side can request that additional portions be read, but whether this occurs as part of your reading or during the opponent's case is discretionary with the judge.[10] Use brevity as your guiding principle.

---

6. See § 16.5.

7. See § 16.4.

8. *Id.*

9. Special Committee of the ABA Section of Litigation, Jury Comprehension in Complex Cases, 37 (1990).

10. Fed.R.Civ.P. 32(a)(4).

Chapter Eighteen

VIDEOTAPE DEPOSITIONS

"A picture may instantly present what a book could set forth only in a hundred pages."
— *Ivan Sergeyevich Turgenev*

Presenting a witness on videotape, for impeachment or in place of live testimony, has much greater impact than testimony read from a transcript. Because of that greater impact, you must take special care to create the visual record that conveys the desired message. As a corollary, if defending the videotaped deposition, you must protect your client from sometimes subtle techniques which can unfairly diminish his performance and credibility.

18.1 WHEN TO TAKE A VIDEOTAPE DEPOSITION

You should almost always prefer testimony from a live witness in the witness box to presenting evidence through depositions. An actual person on the stand answering questions holds the jury's interest better and is more understandable and persuasive than listening to the reading of a deposition. Juries also expect that the testimony of key witnesses, particularly that of a party, will be presented live. The assumption is that a party or witness must not think the case important if they are not willing to testify at the trial. This preference for live testimony is reflected in the requirement in most jurisdictions that deposition testimony may only be used if the witness is unavailable.[1]

Sometimes, however, a witness cannot be available for trial or strategic considerations dictate using deposition testimony rather than a live witness; some examples include when a witness is seriously ill or elderly, a company executive is required to be out of the country at the time of trial, or a key witness is beyond the subpoena powers of the court and refuses to appear voluntarily. Expert witnesses present a particular problem. The best are usually busy, as well as expensive. The problem of coordinating the expert's schedule with the court's is

---

1. Fed.R.Civ.P. 32(a)(3); Fed.R.Evid. 804(b)(1).

oftentimes insurmountable, and the expense of having an expert witness waiting to testify is more than many clients can bear.

Even though a witness's testimony must be presented by deposition, you can capture many of the advantages of live testimony by using a videotape deposition. The jury can see the witness testifying as well as hear what the witness is saying. The jury can evaluate the witness's demeanor and credibility almost in the same way they could if the witness were in the courtroom sitting in the witness box. In short, videotape technology now provides the ability to bring distant witnesses into the courtroom and have the jury hear their testimony as if the witness were testifying live.

18.2 ADVANTAGES OF VIDEOTAPE DEPOSITIONS

Just as live witnesses are more interesting and persuasive than deposition testimony, so too are videotape depositions in comparison with stenographically recorded ones. Consider the following advantages of videotape depositions:

–Videotape depositions permit the jury to see the witness's demeanor. Videotape allows the jury to judge a witness's sincerity and trustworthiness almost in the same way it can with live testimony at trial. Reading a stenographic deposition deprives the jury of this opportunity.

–Videotape depositions allow the jury to see the witness's physical condition. A videotape deposition can capture the physical condition of a witness who is terminally ill and who you expect to be dead by the time of trial. For example, a videotape deposition of a plaintiff with asbestosis allows the jury to see the effects of the disease on his health in a way the bare transcript of a stenographic deposition cannot.

–Videotape deposition testimony is more entertaining and easier to follow; reading stenographic depositions is often the most boring part of the trial. Stenographic deposition testimony is usually presented by one or two lawyers reading the questions and answers to the jury. No matter how well you present it, juries repeatedly confirm that it leaves them confused and bored. While not as easy to follow as live testimony, videotape depositions are an improvement over the reading of depositions. The jury gets to watch as well as listen, and is more likely to follow the testimony and remain interested in what is occurring.

–Videotape depositions allow for the better presentation of exhibits. Consider what happens in a stenographic deposition when a witness refers to an exhibit, for example an anatomical diagram about which a doctor is testifying. The witness might say, "The fracture occurred here," and the lawyer will then attempt to make the record clear by saying, "You are pointing to the upper portion of the ulna?" and so on. If the deposition is read at trial, a copy of the exhibit must be shown to the jury with the hope the jury can understand from the deposition testimony at what part of the exhibit they should be looking. The procedure is cumbersome and there is always a risk that the jury will not understand to what part of the exhibit the witness is referring.

A videotape deposition solves most of these problems because the camera can take a close-up of the exhibit and show the viewer exactly where the witness is pointing when she testifies, "The fracture occurred here."

–Videotape depositions permit the witness to demonstrate large pieces of equipment, work with materials, and show a scene when these cannot be brought into the courtroom. Sometimes you may want the jury to see how the plaintiff in a products liability case was operating the machine when the injury occurred or how, for instance, a piece of scaffolding was assembled. When the exhibit is too large or inconvenient to bring into the courtroom, the best way of having the jury understand the witness's testimony is through a videotape deposition taken where the witness can demonstrate exactly what happened. Similarly, a videotape deposition permits the witness to visit the scene of an accident or a construction site to point out where events occurred. Of course videotapes can also be used as an exhibit during the testimony of a witness appearing at trial.

–Videotape depositions can show tests and experiments being conducted while in the laboratory when they cannot be shown in court. Where an expert witness has conducted a series of experiments but will be unavailable to testify at trial, a videotape deposition permits the jury to see exactly what the expert did and what results were reached.

–Videotape depositions can be more effective for impeachment; the jury can see as well as hear the prior inconsistent statement. The dramatic impact of impeachment is heightened when the jury can not only hear, but also see the witness actually speaking the words of the prior inconsistent statement. While it is cumbersome to set up and use the videotape deposition, under the Federal Rules of Evidence you need not do this while the witness is on the stand so long as the witness is given the opportunity at some time to explain or deny the statement and the opposing party is afforded a chance to interrogate the witness about it.[2]

---

2. Fed.R.Evid. 613(b). This requirement does not apply to admissions of a party opponent.

–Videotape depositions highlight an opposition witness's evasiveness, fumbling, or pauses before answering. Some witnesses do not perform well in the courtroom. They come across as evasive or disingenuous, and the jury will not likely believe their testimony. This is wonderful if they are an important witness for your opponent. Presumably opposing counsel in such a situation will make the same evaluation of the witness as you and, if the witness is beyond the subpoena power of the court, prefer to present the testimony by stenographic deposition rather than live testimony. But if you choose to use a videotape deposition, the jury will be able to see the witness and make the same judgment about the witness's credibility as if it were live testimony.

–Videotape depositions can be edited for use during the closing argument and, with the court's permission, during the opening statement. Courts increasingly permit the use during closing argument of selected portions of videotape depositions that were shown to the jury during the course of the trial. Some courts also permit segments of videotape depositions to be shown during the opening statements in the case. Consider the effect on the jury of actually showing them a key question and answer in the deposition during the closing rather than asking them to recall what was said at some earlier point in the trial.

–Videotape depositions are more likely to control the behavior of disruptive opposing counsel. Lawyers who are willing, in front of a court reporter, to disrupt the deposition and act completely inappropriately are often much more reluctant to do so when you capture their actions on videotape. Even for those lawyers who are not deterred by the presence of the camera, the existence of the tape will make it much easier when you request sanctions to convey to a judge how counsel has interfered with taking a deposition.

18.3 DISADVANTAGES OF VIDEOTAPE DEPOSITIONS

While videotape depositions have many important advantages over stenographic depositions, they do have drawbacks. When considering whether a deposition should be taken stenographically or by videotape you must carefully consider the advantages and disadvantages of each and decide which method provides the greater benefits in light of your objectives. The drawbacks of videotape depositions are:

–Videotape depositions are usually more expensive than stenographic depositions, require more effort to arrange, and may involve editing costs as well. As a general rule, videotape depositions are more expensive than stenographic records. In addition to the cost or rental of the equipment, an operator must be paid, a special room may be required, and the tape may require editing before it can be presented at trial. Rules 26(a)(3)(B) and 32(c) as well as the deposition rules of many states also require that a stenographic transcription be prepared of the portions of the deposition to be offered at trial in order to facilitate making rulings on objections and to ensure accuracy.

Videotape depositions can be comparable in cost to stenographic depositions if the deposing lawyer already owns the necessary equipment, the deposition can be taken without arranging additional space, and the lawyer acts as the operator. Even where an accompanying stenographic transcription is required, the parties often agree the deposing lawyer's secretarial staff may do the typing.

–Videotape depositions are more likely than stenographic depositions to have technical or mechanical problems. Videotape equipment occasionally breaks down or malfunctions, the operator forgets to turn on the tape at the proper time, or no one notices the tape has run out. When this happens in the middle of a deposition, the results can be disastrous, particularly if the malfunction or error is not discovered until the deposition is completed and the witness has departed. Careful checking of equipment before the deposition begins and using a monitor while the deposition is occurring help minimize the problem, but the risk is always present.

–Videotape depositions are more difficult to use for trial preparation. One of the more important uses of depositions is to help you prepare for trial. You can use them to review what evidence is available for and against your position, to plan the deponent's cross-examination, or to sketch out the closing argument. Using a stenographic deposition is far more convenient than reviewing a videotape when preparing for trial. Not only does it take more time to review the tape, but you must arrange for the necessary equipment, it is difficult to go back to an earlier question and answer, and it is harder to keep track of what has been said. You can always have an accompanying stenographic transcription, but its preparation will add to the deposition's expense.

–Videotape depositions are a waste of money if the deposition is being taken for discovery purposes only. You need not incur the expense of a videotape deposition if you are taking it for discovery purposes only. The strength of videotape is in presenting evidence at trial. If you do not intend to show the tape at trial, then a stenographic deposition is easier to take and even easier to use for trial preparation. The one exception to this rule is where you are taking the videotape deposition to record or control the behavior of an obstreperous opposing counsel.[3]

–Videotape depositions require special equipment and extra arrangements for use in court. Reading a stenographic deposition in court does not require any special preparation or equipment, but the same is not true for videotape depositions. You must arrange for a monitor and deck (although many jurisdictions now have them as part of the courtroom equipment), check lighting and viewing conditions, line up extension cords, allow for equipment malfunction, and set up everything before the tape can be shown.

–Videotape deposition witnesses may be more attractive or unattractive than the person used to read to the jury the answer portions of a stenographic deposition. Where the deposition is of a witness aligned with the other side but who you expect to give favorable testimony for your position, the pleasant manner of the witness may dilute the impact of that favorable testimony. In such a situation, the persuasive impact of the deposition may be higher if you have it read to the jury by someone who is less appealing than the actual witness who would appear on the videotape.

–Videotape depositions are more difficult and cumbersome to use for impeachment purposes than stenographic depositions. Videotape depositions are not usually taken for discovery purposes, but to perpetuate testimony because a witness is expected to be unavailable to testify at trial. When, however, the witness does end up testifying and testifies differently than at the deposition, using the videotape deposition to impeach is difficult. You must have the equipment setup, locate the proper portion of the tape, and the jury has to watch the tape being played. You can avoid these problems by either using a stenographic transcription of the videotape, in other words converting the videotape deposition to a stenographic form, or by presenting the impeaching portion of the case at a later time in the case, such as during rebuttal. An option that allows much greater flexibility is presenting the video deposition on laser disk. This allows you instant access to any portion and great control of the displayed material. The cost of such storage and retrieval is declining rapidly.

–Videotape depositions may preserve evidence harmful to your side more effectively than stenographic depositions. All depositions have the potential of preserving evidence that is helpful to your position, but also potentially harmful evidence. When you preserve the harmful evidence on videotape, the impact of showing the

3. Many lawyers who are willing to act in an outrageous manner during a stenographic deposition, feel constrained to behave reasonably when their actions are being recorded on videotape.

tape to the jury will be higher than if the questions and answers are read from a transcript.

–Videotape depositions allow an opponent's witnesses to hone their performances if they later testify at trial. Sometimes you take a videotape deposition of an opposing party's witness because you expect the witness has helpful information but will not be testifying at trial. Remember, however, the witness can always decide later to testify and use the videotape as a guide on how to improve. If the witness came across badly on videotape, for instance, because of poor eye contact or appearing to be evasive when answering questions, the videotape will help him to correct these problems.

–Videotape deposition witnesses may not talk or film well. Remember Richard Nixon in the 1960 Presidential Debates. Poor preparation and hot lights made him look like a gangster and may have lost him the election as well. When a witness cannot testify at trial, consider how they will appear and sound on the tape. Some witnesses are more persuasive and credible if the jury cannot see and hear them. Reading a stenographic deposition will not give any hint of a witness's halting answers, furtive looks, and nervous manner, but a videotape deposition will.

18.4 THE LAW

The Federal Rules of Civil Procedure favor the use in jury trials of videotape depositions over stenographic depositions. Under Rule 32(c), on the request of any party, deposition testimony offered other than for impeachment purposes must be presented in non-stenographic form, e.g., videotape, if available, unless the court for good cause orders otherwise. In bench trials, deposition testimony may be offered in stenographic or nonstenographic form. Whenever a videotape deposition is used at trial or, for instance, in support of a motion for summary judgment, the offering party must provide the court with a transcript of the portions being offered.

Rule 30(b)(2) states that videotape depositions may be taken as a matter of right unless the court orders otherwise. The only requirement is that the notice of deposition shall state that videotape will be used to record the testimony. The cost of the videotaping is borne by the taking party, but any party may arrange for a transcription to be made from the videotape.[4] Any party may also, after giving notice to the witness and other parties, designate another method, in addition to the noticed method, for recording the testimony. In short, even if the taking party

---

4. Fed.R.Civ.P. 30(b)(2).

notices the deposition to be taken by stenographic means, any other party may, as of right, require that the deposition also be videotaped. The cost of videotaping shall be at the requesting party's expense and is also arranged by that party.[5]

Rule 30(b)(4) specifically instructs that the appearance or demeanor of the deposition witness shall not be distorted through camera or sound-recording techniques. In other words, the videotaping must be done through fair and accurate means.

Rule 26(a)(3)(B) states that if a party is intending to use videotape deposition testimony at trial, this fact must be disclosed to opposing counsel, as part of the required pretrial disclosures, at least thirty days prior to trial or by a date set by the court. In addition, a transcript of the pertinent portions of the deposition testimony must be provided to the other parties.

Many states have adopted specific rules or legislation concerning videotape depositions, but in those jurisdictions following the pre-amendment version of the Federal Rules the parties may stipulate in writing, or the court may upon motion, order a deposition be taken by videotape.[6] The stipulation or order shall also designate: before whom the deposition is to be taken; the manner of recording, preserving, and filing the deposition; and other provisions necessary to assure that the recorded testimony will be accurate and trustworthy.

18.5 SCHEDULING THE VIDEOTAPE DEPOSITION

You schedule videotape depositions in the same manner as other depositions, but be aware that editing may be necessary before you can use the final tapes at trial. Also, the potential for mechanical or technical problems is always present. Therefore, take the deposition sufficiently in advance of trial to leave adequate time for any necessary editing or to retake the deposition if technical difficulties do occur.

As previously discussed, most videotape depositions are taken of a party's own witness who expects to be unavailable for trial. Since the deposition will be the only opportunity for opposing counsel to cross-examine the witness, it makes sense to schedule the deposition on as short notice as possible and as early in the litigation as feasible. Short notice and early scheduling may reduce the opposing counsel's abilities to prepare effectively for any cross-examination.

The converse of this is that if you receive a notice of a videotape deposition you should anticipate the witness will be unavailable for

5. Fed.R.Civ.P. 30(b)(3).
6. Fed.R.Civ.P. 30(b)(4).

trial and you will need to be fully prepared to conduct any cross-examination of the witness at the deposition. To prepare adequately for cross-examination, you must consider all discovery that might provide you with potential sources of cross-examination before the deposition occurs. You may even want to postpone the videotape deposition either by agreement or by requesting a protective order from the court until preparation is complete.[7] While expensive, it may also be desirable, either by agreement or with the court's permission, to conduct a stenographic deposition before taking the videotape deposition. Since this would be the procedure if the witness were to be testifying at trial, a strong argument can be made that a similar procedure should be followed with a videotape deposition.

18.6 PREPARING TO TAKE THE VIDEOTAPE DEPOSITION

Videotape depositions being taken for use at trial more resemble a movie of a trial than they do a traditional deposition. Like a witness's trial testimony, the videotape deposition should be entertaining and persuasive, but to accomplish these objectives you must prepare as carefully as you do to examine a witness at trial.

Effective videotape depositions must be carefully planned productions. Keep in mind that when the tape is being shown, the jury is concentrating on every word and action occurring on the screen in a way that does not occur with live testimony. When you are examining a witness at trial and briefly stop to search for a document, the jury can look at the judge, opposing counsel, the witness, or entertain itself in other ways as long as the interruption is short. With a videotape deposition the television monitor becomes the center of attention and that same pause to find a document will now seem to last interminably.

18.6.1 Hire a capable operator to conduct the videotape deposition.

Using an experienced and capable operator to conduct the deposition avoids most of the difficulties that can occur with the use of videotape. An experienced operator can provide guidance in planning room setup, lighting, positioning the camera, editing, and the many other considerations that do not exist with a stenographic deposition, but which are crucial to taking an effective videotape deposition.

If you do not know the name of a good operator, ask around. Many court reporting firms now advertise themselves as having videotape

---

7. Fed.R.Civ.P. 26(c).

capability, but before making the decision to hire one be sure to check on what actual experience they have had. Get the names of several lawyers they have worked for in the past and check with these lawyers on the quality of the work.

18.6.2 Decide on taping options.

When you decide to take a videotape deposition, you become the director of a movie. Like any director, you must decide on how the movie will be shot. And like any director, you will also need to make compromises between keeping expenses reasonable and making the deposition entertaining and persuasive.

Type of camera and format: VHS is now the standard format and should be used for the videotape deposition unless a good reason exists for doing otherwise. A camera with a date/time generator, required by some courts, will provide increased security against tampering or unauthorized editing of the tape and can also be added to any accompanying stenographic transcription of the tape.

Single camera versus multiple cameras: In deciding on the taping, an important decision is whether to use a single camera or multiple cameras. Multiple cameras allow a variety of shots and angles that help to maintain the jury's interest. But multiple cameras are also more expensive and invite the other side to complain about unfair taping and distorting the evidence.

Distance: Most videotape cameras have zoom lenses which permit a range of shots from full to close-ups. Even without a zoom lens, the camera can be positioned to capture a range of shots from the entire room to a close-up of the witness's face. Before deciding on the taping distance, check whether local court rules or practice require a particular method. Depending on your opponent, you may also want to attempt to agree before the deposition on camera placement and the types of shots to be used. Finally, it is worth running some test shots to see which type of shot is most flattering to the witness.

Panning: Unless the preferred camera distance will take in both the examining attorney and the witness, you should decide whether the operator should pan back and forth between the lawyer as the question is asked and the witness for the answer or remain focused on the witness the entire time. Panning is more entertaining and is better able to hold the jury's interest. If, however, the deposition is of an opposing witness, remaining on the witness will show the witness's reaction to the question.

Camera angle: As with taping distance, you should select a camera angle that is most flattering to your witness. Usual choices are either straight-on or at a three-quarters angle. Usually an angle shot is best for your own witness while a straight-on shot is best for an opposing witness.

Zooming: Zooming can be used both to provide visual interest to the videotape and to show close-ups of exhibits, demonstrations, or the witness's features while a critical answer is being given. The danger of zoom shots is that unless agreed upon in advance, the court may consider them misleading to the jury and require you to delete portions of the tape. Close-ups of exhibits and demonstrations are normally permitted, but you should use other types of zoom shots with caution and attempt an advance agreement with opposing counsel.

Black and white or color: Juries are used to watching color television at home and they expect the same in the courtroom. Color also usually makes witnesses more attractive and better holds the jury's interest. On the other hand, black and white is better for showing detail in an exhibit and is often less flattering to a witness.

Arrangement of microphones: Think about the number and arrangement of microphones before the deposition. Normally you should have one microphone for each participant. If this is not possible, work out an agreement with opposing counsel in advance about sharing the available microphones.

Always check the microphones before the deposition to ensure they can adequately pick up the voices of all the participants. Directional microphones attached to the camera can be a particular problem. If the witness is some distance from the camera, or if someone off the camera is speaking, such as opposing counsel, the voices may not be picked up clearly and it may be difficult to identify who is speaking.

18.6.3 Selecting a suitable location for the deposition.

Unlike a stenographic deposition, the jury will see the location where a videotape deposition is conducted. As with everything else connected with the deposition, you will want to ensure that the surroundings present the witness in the best possible light. For instance, a cluttered or messy background with stacks of old files and paper coffee cups distract the jury and cause it to think less of the witness's testimony. Often the court reporting firm will have a room where the deposition can be conducted, but you should check this with the same thoroughness that you would give if you were selecting the room.

Size: The room should be large enough to permit all of the participants to be comfortably seated and to hold all of the necessary equipment. Allow adequate room to position the camera and for the operator to move about.

Lighting: Always check whether the lighting is adequate. Also check whether the lighting causes glare, whether curtains or shades should be open or closed, and whether additional lighting is necessary.

Temperature: If the deposition room is too hot, a witness's perspiring will show on the tape and may cause the jury to believe it is because of nervousness or lying. Make sure the room is cool enough, particularly if additional lights will need to be brought in.

18.6.4 Planning the questions.

Since the videotape deposition will be used in place of live testimony at trial, your deposition questioning should be as carefully organized as if it were occurring before a jury. A videotape deposition is not the place for stream-of-consciousness questioning or for asking questions on the fly. The goal is to present the fact finder with a clear, persuasive, and memorable story. To do so requires that you carefully plan the questions.

Organizing and drafting the questions: How to draft and organize trial testimony is beyond the scope of this chapter,[8] but you should present the witness's testimony in the same way as if the witness were in the witness box. The witness's background is usually brought out at the beginning of the testimony, questioning should move smoothly and logically from topic to topic, and the witness's story is normally presented in a chronological fashion.

Avoid interruptions: Long pauses and interruptions during a videotape deposition are far more noticeable than if the same thing occurred at trial. The jury focuses on the television screen and anything that occurs becomes the center of attention. Therefore, maintain a quick pace and avoid interruptions as much as possible.

One method of avoiding pauses and interruptions is by carefully outlining your questions. Using an outline will not be distracting to the jury if the camera is focused only on the witness, and will prevent you from having to grope for your next question.

Dynamic questions and visual aids: The usual videotape deposition shows what in the television industry are called "talking heads" and talking heads are boring. Make every attempt to enliven the testimony without sacrificing the witness's credibility. Putting more modulation in your voice and making the questions as dynamic as possible is one method of doing this. But do not stray far from your usual

---

8. See Steven Lubet, *Modern Trial Advocacy,* 2d ed., chapter 4 (NITA, 1997).

courtroom demeanor or it may appear false or contrived. Run a test tape of your questioning to make sure you are not overplaying your role.

Exhibits and visual aids help to make otherwise flat testimony more interesting. If possible, space exhibits throughout the testimony in order to maintain interest to the end. Concentrations of exhibits can be as boring as uninterrupted testimony.

You should arrange exhibits so they are quickly accessible during the deposition and are in the order in which they will be used. You can also avoid delays during the deposition by pre-marking exhibits and having extra copies for your opponent.

Minimize objections: Objections during the deposition can be edited out before the presentation of the videotape at trial, but such editing can be expensive and can make the testimony appear choppy. Therefore, carefully review your proposed questions and expected answers before the deposition to avoid objections. While an excessive number of objections may cause the judge to place the editing costs on the objecting party, the party offering the deposition most often will bear the cost, particularly if the objections are sustained.

18.6.5 Preparing the witness.

Factors that often are not important in a stenographic deposition become critical in a videotape deposition. For instance, a stenographic deposition does not show the witness's dress or demeanor, the tone with which questions are answered, or a witness's movements and nervous habits. However, you should carefully review all of these with the videotape deposition witness a day or more before the actual deposition to minimize the witness's anxiety.

Dress: Usually dark clothes and pastel shirts film best, but a test shot is advisable. Avoid checks and small prints that do not come across well on the camera. In general, the witness should dress as if for court.

Demeanor: The witness should be courteous and responsive to all questions. Evasiveness, particularly on cross-examination, will be readily apparent to the jury and should be avoided. Similarly, jousting with opposing counsel and displays of anger or irritation will come across poorly, and you should coach witnesses to avoid this type of conduct.

Movement: Natural movements in the courtroom may come across in a videotape deposition as jerky and distracting or as signs of nervousness. Advise witnesses to avoid unnecessary or distracting movements or gestures. One particular area to caution about is drumming on the table, particularly if table microphones are being used. On tape, the drumming sounds like a stampeding herd of elephants.

18.6.6 Preparing the operator.

Without close cooperation between the questioning attorney and the video operator, a videotape deposition can quickly turn into a disaster. Start working with the operator from the earliest possible moment to make sure that the operator fully understands your needs and what you want her to do during the deposition.

Check equipment in advance: Have the operator check thoroughly all of the equipment in advance to make sure it is in operating condition. Waiting until a few minutes before the deposition to discover that a key cord is missing is courting disaster.

Camera set-up and lighting: Discuss with the operator the lighting needs for the room and the camera angles and distances to be used during the deposition. Check these out in advance to make sure the image on the videotape is what you want and that the operator understands your instructions.

As part of the review, you should check that x-rays, photographs, and other exhibits will tape well. If they do not, you may need to arrange for enlargements, positive images of x-rays, or other steps to ensure exhibits come across on the videotape in a comprehensible way.

Arrange operator cues: The operator should know when you want to zoom in on an exhibit and when to shift angles or distances. Work out a series of cues which the viewer will not notice, but which the operator will clearly understand. Similarly, the operator may need to give cues to you. One such important cue to be arranged in advance is the signal by the operator that the tape is coming to an end. If the necessary cues are few and the viewer will easily understand them, it may be better to place them on the tape. For instance, when the witness points to an exhibit, it will appear quite natural for you to say, "Why don't we have the camera do a close-up of where you are pointing?"

Arrange for a deposition officer: As a matter of economy, the operator should also be a notary public able to serve as the deposition officer. But if one is not available, be sure to arrange for a notary to be present to swear the witness and preside over the deposition.[9]

18.6.7 Working out agreements.

Resolving with opposing counsel as many matters as possible before the deposition helps you avoid expense and disruption of the deposition and facilitates your future use of the deposition at trial. Agreeing on

---

9. See § 1.11.1.

such matters as the number of cameras, the angles and distances of shots, and whether to shoot in color or black and white are all matters that are best resolved by agreement beforehand.

One particular area that you should discuss in advance is the lawyers' conduct during the deposition. Deciding on the ground rules helps maintain the quality and usefulness of the deposition for both sides. Some topics that you should cover are:

- All the participants should avoid speaking while another participant is still speaking. The lawyers should avoid stepping on the witness's lines.

- Objections should be made only after the examining attorney has finished the question or the witness has finished the answer.

- Avoid finger drumming on the table, rustling papers, or otherwise causing distracting noise.

18.7 CONDUCTING THE VIDEOTAPE DEPOSITION

You can work out most details of conducting the deposition during the preparation stage, but thinking through how the deposition will actually progress is important to its success.

18.7.1 Beginning the deposition.

The taping of the deposition should follow a set sequence to anticipate the jury's curiosity about what is happening and to satisfy the requirements of Rule 30(b)(4):[10]

> A. Start out with a full shot of the room with the deposition officer giving his or her name and business address, and announcing that this is a videotape deposition and giving the name of the witness, and the date, the time, and the place of the deposition and the title of the case. This should be repeated at the beginning of each new videotape of the deposition.
>
> B. The deposition officer should identify every person present for the deposition while the camera focuses on that person using a full or medium shot.
>
> C. The officer should swear in the witness.
>
> D. If the camera will be panning between the examining lawyer and the witness, the camera should start with a full shot of the lawyer asking the first question and then go to a medium or close-up shot for the remainder of the question. All further

---

10. See § 1.11.3.

questions and answers should be medium shots unless it is necessary to do a close-up of an exhibit or demonstration.

18.7.2 Questioning.

Maintaining interest: Remember that long questions and answers are difficult for a jury to follow and understand. Therefore, keep your questions short and simple in the same manner as a stenographic deposition. Similarly, break up lengthy answers with questions calling for clarifications or additional information.

Information-gathering questions versus perpetuating questions: Sometimes a videotape deposition is taken for discovery purposes as well as for perpetuating testimony. For instance, you may believe that a particular witness who is beyond the subpoena powers of the court has valuable information helpful to your side, but has rebuffed your attempts to interview her. One response is to take a videotape deposition so that any useful information from the witness can be presented in the most persuasive manner at trial.

With such a witness, first ask information-gathering questions necessary to find out what the witness knows. Once familiar with the witness's story, go back to the beginning and ask only those questions you would ask at trial. Editing the tape for use at trial is easier, and the final tape will appear less choppy if the information-gathering questions are grouped at the beginning of the deposition rather than intermixing them with questions for perpetuating the testimony.

Demeanor and conduct: You should be careful to present a pleasant and authoritative image. Irritation or anger, whether with an opposing witness or your own, is rarely appropriate. The jury will appreciate a courteous approach even more if the witness is acting in an obnoxious manner.

The jury will also be favorably impressed if you ask appropriate and logical questions and maintain a suitable pace to the examination. Long pauses and a disorganized approach will present an image of incompetence and demonstrate a lack of preparation. Finally, both you and the witness should avoid distracting movements or sounds that will be magnified on the film.

Going off the record: One way of controlling interruptions and delays on the tape is to go off the record when it appears the witness will need to look for an exhibit, read a long document, or otherwise slow down the questioning process. When going off the record, it is appropriate to give a short explanation of why you are doing so and to repeat the explanation when going back on the record. "Doctor, while we were off the record you were looking for the plaintiff's x-rays. Have you found them now?"

18.7.3 Concluding the deposition.

Rule 30(b)(4) requires that at the end of the deposition, the officer shall state on the record that the deposition is complete and shall set forth any stipulations agreed to by the parties.

18.7.4 Post-deposition review.

Under Rule 30(e), if the witness or one of the parties makes a request before completion of the deposition, the witness shall have thirty days after having been notified by the deposition officer of its availability, to review the videotapes of the deposition and to make written changes.[11] Making corrections to a videotape deposition is more difficult than writing an errata sheet for written deposition testimony. First, the "incorrect" testimony will not be erased from the tape (just as the "corrected" testimony is not erased from the written copy). Thus, the jury will see the videotape of the testimony at the deposition, while the jury only hears the corrected version of a stenographic deposition as it is read in court. Visual testimony clearly has more impact.

If a stenographic record of the video deposition has been created,[12] that transcript can be corrected using the standard rules and procedures for a written deposition transcript. However, without a written transcript the attorney and the witness will have to review the deposition videotape and create a "corrected script," which indicates the time or footage of the material to be corrected, and states the correction and the reason for the changed testimony. As a general rule, counsel should have a transcript of the videotaped deposition made simultaneously. This will save money in the long run, because it obviates the need for repeated real-time viewings of the video.

18.8 PREPARING TO USE THE VIDEOTAPE DEPOSITION AT TRIAL

18.8.1 Transcribing.

In those jurisdictions that require a stenographic transcription to be prepared, it will be necessary to have the videotapes transcribed or arrange to have a court reporter attend the deposition (who can also serve as the deposition officer). It is usually cheaper to have the

---

11. See § 15.1.
12. Fed.R.Civ.P. 30(a)(4).

transcription made from the videotapes or from audiotapes made simultaneously with the videotapes.

A stenographic transcription is useful even when not required. Taking a simultaneous audiotape recording of the proceedings will permit your secretarial staff to prepare a transcription at a lower cost than having a court reporter prepare one.[13]

18.8.2 Editing.

While videotape depositions are more entertaining and will hold the jury's interest better than stenographic depositions, even the best videotape deposition can be terribly tedious. The jury's exposure to all depositions, both videotape and stenographic, should be kept as short as possible, consistent with the jury hearing the necessary testimony and being persuaded of its truthfulness. You can accomplish this with prudent editing.

As a practical matter, many more questions are asked at a deposition than are necessary for the effective presentation of that evidence at trial. In selecting the testimony to be presented at trial, you should critically examine each question and answer with an eye to deleting any that do not advance your theory of the case.

18.8.3 Ruling on objections.

The pretrial conference is the usual and best time for the court to rule on objections, but this is a matter of local practice and court rules. Whatever procedure you use, do it sufficiently in advance of trial so that you can edit out any portion of the videotape ruled inadmissible.

Having the judge watch the tape to rule on objections is a time consuming and wasteful procedure, and most judges will refuse to do so unless the objection is to the taping or the conduct of the deposition. But if the objection is to a question or answer, the court can much more conveniently make these rulings by examining a stenographic transcription of the tape. Once the excluded portions have been edited, you should always review the tape to ensure that the editing was done correctly.

18.9 USING THE VIDEOTAPE DEPOSITION AT TRIAL

The usual method of showing a videotape deposition to a jury is to position a monitor and tape deck in front of the jury box for viewing.

---

13. The Advisory Committee Notes to Rule 26(a)(3)(B) suggest that the transcription required by this rule and by Rule 30(b) can be prepared by a lawyer's own secretarial staff.

Like all other aspects of the trial, showing the tape should proceed as smoothly as possible. A few simple steps will make this possible:

- Check out the equipment in advance to make sure it is in proper working order.
- Know how to operate the equipment or have a competent operator present for showing the tape.
- Check out the courtroom in advance to determine how far away from the jury box the monitor should be positioned, where the electrical outlets are located, whether you will need extension cords, and whether glare on the monitor screen or other problems cause the jury difficulty in viewing the tape.
- Determine whether the judge will require a separate monitor.

Try to show the tape following a break so you have an opportunity to set up the necessary equipment without disrupting the trial. During the actual showing, either you or the judge should explain to the jury in the same way that you would explain a stenographic deposition what they are about to see and that the witness is unable to testify at the trial.

Leave the courtroom lights on during showing unless darkness is necessary to prevent glare on the television screen. A dark room and the hypnotic effects of television are too much of a temptation to sleep.

Often the lawyers, having already seen the tape, will leave the room or prepare for the next witness during the videotape showing. Do not do this. If you are asking the jury to pay attention to the tape, then you should demonstrate that the tape is worth watching by also paying attention.

Since appellate courts will rarely take the opportunity of reviewing the videotape testimony shown to the jury, it is wise to introduce into the record a stenographic transcript of the tape for purposes of appeal.

There is a temptation in presenting videotaped depositions to use the biggest television screen available in order to make an impression and to capture the jury's attention. Several negative aspects of this approach should be considered.

A large screen is where Americans, including jurors, watch movies; it is where *Star Wars* and *Indiana Jones* take us on fantastic flights from reality. The simple fact that the image is larger than life serves to remove it from reality and, since the jurors probably do not have such a giant screen television in their homes, its unfamiliarity also makes its images less real. Furthermore, the big screen tends to dominate the room, even the courtroom, so that the video portion of the trial might well be seen as completely separate from the rest of the trial. Additionally, the high-technology approach of the big screen television may distract the jurors from the content of the testimony. Finally, the time and effort needed to set up the large screen television is an intrusion which may be resented by the court and jury; it certainly raises greater expectations in the jury that the video will be entertaining and significant.

In comparison, the use of several small televisions avoids most of these problems. Average size televisions are where Americans, including jurors, get their news every evening. The technology is so commonplace that little attention is paid to the medium and it is so unobtrusive that it can be present in the courtroom throughout a trial without distracting the jurors' attention or diminishing the import of other portions of the trial presentation. Several small televisions give each juror a clear view, and additional sets can be provided to allow the judge and opponent to view at the same time without any awkwardness.

18.10 DEFENDING A VIDEOTAPE DEPOSITION

We have previously discussed some of the considerations concerning defending a videotape deposition. For instance, if your opponent schedules a videotape deposition of a witness before you have had adequate opportunity to prepare a cross-examination, you may wish to move for a continuance of the deposition date or to take a stenographic deposition.

Your major concern in defending a videotape deposition is to ensure the taping is fair and is not done in such a way as to make either the witness or you appear in an unflattering light. Be vigilant against distorting camera angles, close-ups of your witness that show the pores on their nose and every drop of perspiration, and other such tricks. If your opponent is less than fully trustworthy, you may also want to require continuous taping of the deposition with a time/date counter to avoid any later disputes about whether material has been inappropriately deleted.

Finally, while you should not hesitate to make any appropriate objections, courts have been known to saddle the defending attorney with the cost of editing out an excessive number of objections. Even more draconian is the practice of some courts of not permitting the tape to be edited, but allowing the jury to see the behavior of the defending attorney. Therefore, be particularly conscious of how your objections may appear to the judge or jury.

Chapter Nineteen

OVERVIEW OF THE EXPERT DEPOSITION[1]

*"An expert is someone from out of town
who carries a briefcase."*
— Anonymous

The liberal rules applied by most courts today allow expert witnesses great latitude in testifying to their opinions, bases, assumptions, and inferences. Their qualifications and the pomp with which they are presented and received in court combine to create an extraordinary, if not undue, emphasis to their testimony in front of the jury. The deposition of the expert therefore has become one of the most important events in the pretrial process.

The 1993 amendments to the Federal Rules of Civil Procedure have greatly simplified deposing expert witnesses. The first and most important change is that now Rule 26(a)(2) requires that not only must each party, without waiting for a discovery request, disclose the identity of any experts who will be testifying at trial, but the experts, with a few exceptions, must provide a report containing:

- A complete statement of all opinions to be given;
- The basis and reasons for the opinions;
- The data or other information considered by the expert in forming the opinions;
- Any exhibits to be used as a summary of or support for the opinions;
- The expert's qualifications, including a list of all publications within the last ten years;
- How much the expert is being compensated in this case; and
- The expert's experience testifying at trial or by deposition in the past four years.

The court will set the time for the experts' reports to be filed, usually in the scheduling order, but absent a stipulation or court order to the

---

1. Thorough treatment of the deposition of experts requires more space than is possible in this book; this chapter is intended to highlight some of the most important issues and approaches. The attorney who desires a more complete discussion of these and other expert deposition issues is referred to chapters 5–8 and 14–16 of *Effective Expert Testimony* by David M. Malone and Paul J. Zwier, NITA, 2000.

contrary, this must occur no later than ninety days before trial. If the expert is being offered solely to contradict or as rebuttal of an expert identified by another party, then the deadline is thirty days after the other side's disclosure of its experts. If the required information is not disclosed in the report and there is not a good excuse for failing to do so, Rule 37(c)(1) prohibits using the information as evidence as well as exposing the party to other sanctions.

The second change is that now under Rule 26(b)(4)(A) a party may depose as of right any person who has been identified as an expert whose opinions may be presented at trial. Before the 1993 amendments, an expert could only be deposed by stipulation or pursuant to a court order. In fact, this was rarely an obstacle to deposing experts because in any case where both sides were planning to present expert testimony, it was usually to everyone's advantage to stipulate to the taking of depositions; each side wanted to know what the other side's expert was going to say. Even when a stipulation was not forthcoming, most courts had permitted depositions upon a motion. The 1993 amendments do away with any doubt, however, and give an unqualified right to take an expert's deposition.

The third change is that Rule 26(b)(4)(A) now prohibits deposing any expert who will be filing a report until after the report is provided. This means that, unless the court sets an earlier date for providing reports, depositions of experts will not occur until within ninety days of trial.

The final change is that Rule 26(e)(1) now places a duty on the expert's party to supplement the Rule 26(a)(2)(B) report and any information provided through a deposition of the expert if the information disclosed is incomplete or incorrect and if the additional or corrective information has not otherwise been made known to the other parties during the discovery process or in writing. Unless otherwise directed by the court, supplementation must occur at least thirty days before trial.

Having the benefit of the expert's report greatly shortens the expert's deposition. Much of the information you would need to obtain during the deposition is now provided to you in written form. If, however, you are taking the deposition of an expert who has not provided a report or are practicing in a jurisdiction that is operating under a pre-1993 amendments version of the Federal Rules of Civil Procedure, the outline of what must be in the report is an excellent guide to the questions you need to be asking.

For ease of discussion, let's set out a recommended (albeit truncated) outline of an expert's deposition when you have the benefit of a report. Remember that if you do not have a report you will need to graft on to these categories the questions that are answered in the report.

OVERVIEW OF THE EXPERT DEPOSITION

1. Opinions: What other opinions, besides those given in your report, did you arrive at during the course of your work on this case? You have stated in your report, opinions X, Y, and Z. Are those all of the opinions you have developed regarding? . . .

2. Bases: Coming back now to the first opinion you told us about, that the chemical compound used in the laboratory was tainted with benzene, what did you do first in coming to that opinion? Why did you do that? How did you do that? What result did you get? What significance does that result have in coming to your conclusion that the compound was tainted? What other information did you look at? Why? What information was provided by your lawyers?

3. Assumptions: In coming to your opinion that the compound was tainted, was it necessary to make any assumptions? What were those assumptions? Why did you find it necessary to make those assumptions? Were there alternative assumptions that you decided not to make? On what grounds did you select the assumptions you made and reject the alternatives? Did you examine the impact those alternative assumptions would have made on your opinion that the compound was tainted?

4. Other experts: Are you familiar with other experts in this field who have analyzed this type of question? Have you looked at the approach that those experts used? Are there experts who make the same assumptions you did? Who are they? In what literature is their work reported? Are there experts who criticize the method of calculation that you used? Who are they? In what literature is their work reported? Why were they critical of that method?

5. Things left to be done: Have you completed your work on this project? What tasks are not complete? Are there any other tasks that are not complete? Do you intend to complete them? Why? When? Does your opinion depend upon those results? Is there literature which recommends that these tasks be completed before reaching an opinion on this question?

6. Things not done: In arriving at your opinion that the compound was tainted, did you visit the laboratory to observe the testing of the compound? Why not? In coming to that opinion, did you talk to all of the family members of the deceased lab workers? Why not? In conducting the work that led you to that opinion, did you review any of the medical records maintained by the veterinarians at the reptile house? Why not?

7. Evaluation of own expert's work: What is your opinion of the opposing expert's credentials? On what points do you disagree with what the opposing expert did? Are there errors in the opposing expert's methodology, results, conclusions, opinions? What are the reasons for your disagreements?

8. Qualifications: What work have you done; what articles or books or dissertations have you written more than ten years ago; what jobs have you held; what courses have you taken; what courses have you taught; what societies have you joined; what speeches have you given; what depositions or testimony have you given more than four years ago; what studies or consulting have you done; and, for all of these, how do they relate to the work you did for this case?

The above outline contains the essence of an expert deposition. We will now examine each of these areas in more detail.

Where the deposition is being taken without the benefit of first having a report, it will also be necessary to question about the information that would have been included in the report. Instead of merely asking about additional opinions, the expert will need to be asked about all the opinions arrived at, the bases and reasons for the opinions, the data or other information considered by the expert in forming the opinions, and what exhibits the expert may have prepared.

19.1   THE SUBSTANCE OF THE OPINIONS

The background questioning at the beginning of the typical lay-witness deposition is often counterproductive in an expert deposition. It allows the expert to warm-up to his topic, to take your measure, and to postpone answering the hard questions until he has become acclimated to the deposition process. The alternative is to get right into the substance of the deposition. Consider the following example from a construction delay case:

Q. (After the witness is sworn and the preliminary instructions about answering audibly and so forth are given:) Dr. Vilnius, you stated in your report that in your opinion one of the reasons why the warehouse construction project took longer to complete than had been originally estimated was because the contractor failed to allow for sufficient downtime due to bad weather?

A. That is correct.

Q. Isn't it true that 1993, the year of this project, was one of the wettest years on record?

A. It was a wet year.

Q. My question was whether it was one of the wettest years on record?

A. Yes, it was.

Q. Have you reviewed what figures other contractors were using for estimating downtime in their contracts in 1993?

A. I have looked at some of them.

Q. What figure were they using?

By going right to a substantive area of questioning, the expert has less time to guess at and adjust to your "game plan;" he has fewer opportunities to phrase his opinions to avoid certain theories or challenges; and he has had no opportunity to learn, from questions or objections, what words to use or to avoid.

As demonstrated in the above example, you must press the expert for *all* opinions. At this beginning point in the deposition, you want breadth, not depth. You want to be sure that you have left no area of opinion undiscovered because other areas consume all of the available time. Of course, the Rule 26(a)(2)(B) report will be used as the starting point in questioning the expert on her opinions and provides general notice of the areas of testimony, but those statements are most often written in general terms by the opposing attorney, in an attempt to preserve some flexibility for the attorney presenting the expert.

19.2 THE BASES

Once you are confident that you have obtained a broad statement from the expert of all of her significant opinions, you can then go back to the first opinion (or the most important opinion) to explore its basis. Your goal here is twofold: first, to discover whether the expert proceeded logically, on sound information, and applied her science, knowledge, or training to the facts at hand to reach a reasonable conclusion; and second, to allow your own expert to attempt to replicate the opposing expert's work, in order to check its accuracy.

The questions to ask are precisely those that you ask of your expert on direct examination because the goal of both efforts is the same: to provide an expert with an opportunity to explain her thought and work processes in a logical, step-by-step manner. Thus, you ask, "What did you do? Why did you do it? How did you do it? What result did you get? What significance does that result have in your conclusion that 'X'?" In context, these questions sound like this:

Q. Now, Dr. Vilnius, you have stated that, in your opinion, a proper critical-path methodology was not used by the general contractor. **What did you do** to come to that conclusion?

A. I examined all of the planning documents that the contractor prepared when he proposed to finish the work within the two-year contract period.

Q. **Why did you examine** those documents?

A. Those documents show the flow of the work over time; that is, the various activities that the contractor anticipated, and their relationship to one another in terms of when one starts, what is going on at the same time.

Q. **How did you examine** those documents?

A. I obtained the documents through the owner's attorneys, and then I studied them all with the help of my staff, which included two construction engineers and an accountant.

Q. Dr. Vilnius, let me show you what we will have marked as Vilnius Deposition Exhibits 17 through 34. Are these the documents that you studied relating to the use of the critical-path methodology?

A. Yes, that's them.

Q. Are there any other documents that you reviewed in coming to this conclusion on critical path methodology?

A. No, those are all of them.

Q. Let's look first at Vilnius Deposition Exhibit 17. How did you use that document in coming to your conclusion about the critical-path methodology?

A. That sheet is the first flow chart prepared by the contractor, on which he shows all of the job activities over time.

Q. **What was the result** of your examination of Vilnius Exhibit 17?

A. Well, I found one thing that is very important. You can see here that the structural work, primarily the steel girder installation, was planned to be completed by the end of the eighth week. You can also see that, before that eighth week, there were no plans to order the roofing members. In fact, those members were not ordered until the ninth week, and were not delivered until the fifteenth week, as you can see from my deposition Exhibit 20.

Q. **What significance does that information have** in your coming to the conclusion that a proper critical path methodology was not used by the contractor?

A. That seven-week delay could have been avoided by better planning, critical-path planning, which would have called for the ordering of the roofing members by no later than the second week, with delivery no later than the ninth week. Critical-path methodology requires the entire job to be scheduled out, so, for example, materials are delivered by the time they are needed.

The specific language of the questions here is not important; what is important is the structure of the inquiry which forces the expert to disclose in an organized, understandable way what she did, her reasons for doing it, and her results. Furthermore, by separating her work into these components, you can ask limiting or corralling questions (Are there other documents that you looked at? Are these all of the documents? Are these all of the results you obtained?) about each component. It is particularly important to ask about approaches considered, studies, investigations, tests or analyses that were undertaken by the expert but not used as the basis for her opinions.

19.3 ASSUMPTIONS THE EXPERT MADE

All experts make assumptions as they analyze data and come to conclusions. Some of the assumptions are logically beyond challenge: an accident reconstruction expert will assume that the normal laws of physics apply to the collision of a car and a tractor-trailer, so that the heavier vehicle will normally be deflected less from its course; an architect will assume that the laws of solid geometry apply, so that walls perpendicular to the same base wall will be parallel to one another. In more esoteric technical areas, where the logic of such proper assumptions is not quite so apparent, your own expert can identify such assumptions for you and keep you from wasting any time in trying to challenge them.

Another type of assumption, however, is not beyond challenge and arises where an expert must choose between two or more opposing possibilities without adequate empirical information to mandate the choice of one over another. In a case where the assumptions made by your expert produce significantly different results from those obtained using the opponent's assumptions, your goal in taking the deposition is to force the opposing expert to admit that other choices are reasonable (even if he does not prefer them), and to force him to acknowledge that, using those other possibilities, different results will follow.

An example that arises over and over in wrongful death cases involves what inflation rate and discount rate to apply to future earnings. The expert cannot "know" these numbers with any certainty;

she must make her best assumption and try to defend it. At deposition, the examination sounds like this:

Q. Doctor, how did you obtain this number labeled "discounted present value" in the third column of your Table 2?

A. After I calculated the income for each of those ten future years, in the manner that I have just described, I applied a discount rate to each of those amounts, to determine what amount of money one would need to invest at that rate today in order to generate those amounts in the future.

Q. Where did you get this discount rate?

A. From a review of financial information covering the past ten years.

Q. Dr. Vagris, what rate did you use for discounting this stream of income back to its present value?

A. I used 5 percent as the discount rate.

Q. Why did you use 5 percent?

A. I examined the past ten years of interest rate data and calculated some averages. From that information, 5 percent looked reasonable to me.

Q. What interest rate data did you examine?

A. I looked at ten-year Treasury Bills, thirty-year T-bills, and corporate bond rates.

Q. Why did you examine that data and not other data?

A. These are the type of data traditionally relied upon by economists for these purposes.

Q. What other data is available concerning historical interest rates?

A. I could have used a ten-year average to smooth out fluctuations, but most of the movement was recent, so I believed that created a distortion.

Q. Did you make any present value calculations using higher interest rates?[1]

A. Yes, I did. In fact, I bracketed my present value calculations.

Q. What do you mean, you "bracketed" your calculations?

---

1. The higher the assumed or applied interest rate, the lower the present value of the future income stream. For example, if you need to generate $100 ten years in the future, you will have to invest more now at a lower rate, or less at a higher rate. Therefore, plaintiff's experts try to justify a lower future interest rate, in order to increase the award now.

A. I made calculations where I used lower rates and higher rates, to determine the sensitivity of my results to the choice of a particular rate.

Q. What higher rates did you use?

A. I performed calculations using 5.5 percent, 6 percent, and 7 percent.

Q. At 5 percent, your final present value amount was $125,000, is that correct?

A. Yes, as shown on my worksheet that we've just looked at.

Q. What was your result at 6 percent?

A. $110,000.

Q. And what was your result at 7 percent?

A. $101,000.

Q. Before you picked 5 percent to use in your table, you looked at the results with higher discount rates?

A. Yes, that's what I've just said.

Q. Tell me all of the reasons you had for selecting 5 percent.

A. Well, if we look at the last ten years of data, we can see that for most of the period the interest rates were declining. If we project that decline into the future, we can see that we would have prevailing interest rates much lower than 5 percent. I took a much more conservative approach and leveled that decline off, so that the average interest rate over the next ten years was in the area of 5 percent. One could easily argue that it should be substantially lower, which would result in a substantially higher present value of those future items of income.

Q. Dr. Vagris, looking at this last ten years of data, do you agree with me that there is no year in which the interest rate was as low as 5 percent?

A. Yes, that's true.

Q. And do you also agree that there was considerable fluctuation in the rates over these ten years?

A. Yes, I can see that the high was 16 percent and the low was 4.5 percent.

Q. And you would also agree that there is no way to be sure that the rate will stay as low as 5 percent for the next ten years?

A. Yes, I agree that I cannot be absolutely certain.

Q. Because you cannot be certain, you have to make assumptions?

A. Yes, that's correct.

Q. And some assumptions increase the amount you say the plaintiff deserves?

A. Yes, that's true.

Q. And other assumptions decrease the amount you say the plaintiff deserves?

A. Yes, that's true too.

Q. Did you have discussions with the attorneys for the plaintiff before you selected 5 percent as the discount rate?

A. Yes, of course we had discussions.

Q. All right, Dr. Vagris, let me show you some tables we have prepared using discount rates of 6 percent and 7 percent.

Of course, your own expert will have prepared such tables for you before the deposition (and worked through this whole line of questioning with you), and the range of alternative rates should include the rate used by your expert. If your expert is going to testify that she is most comfortable with 7 percent, you should highlight that rate in your case; but if 10 percent is within what your expert will describe as a reasonable range, you should include that figure, and the resulting calculations, on your trial exhibits.

The principle here is the same whether we are discussing discount rates or automobile speeds or the tensile strength of suture material: try to lead the opposing expert into admitting that he has rather arbitrarily selected a value out of a range of apparently reasonable values; show that he was aware of the impact of his selection on the ultimate result; then have your expert present more favorable results by using other values within the range. (Of course, if your own expert believes that the value chosen by the opposing expert is the most reasonable, this line of cross-examination may not be open to you.)

Knowing the expert can be examined in this way, leading to what is normally a reasonably effective piece of cross-examination, you must prepare your expert for deposition on such assumptions. Your preparation must include a thorough review of the expert's bases for choosing the assumptions that she chose and for rejecting the others. Where a calculated result is not particularly sensitive to or changes much in the assumptions, consider asking the expert to select the most conservative assumption, that is, the one that favors the opponent the most. That approach completely eliminates your opponent's opportunity to use, or defuse, this line of cross-examination at trial.

19.4 OTHER EXPERTS

By the time you depose the opposing expert, you will almost certainly have hired your own expert who has worked to prepare you for the deposition and for the trial. Nevertheless, because of the wonderful opportunities offered by Fed.R.Evid. 803(18) to use learned treatises as the "testimony" of additional experts whom you do not have to pay, you should take advantage of the deposition of the opposing expert to try to identify experts who disagree with him and agree with your expert. Indeed, these other experts need not disagree directly with the opposing expert; it may be that they merely suggest alternative approaches, or note limitations in the use of certain methods. In any event, the deposition of the opposing expert is the best time for you to gain information about these other experts. So, with an eye on the requirements of Rule 803(18), ask questions like the following:

Q. Dr. Vagris, is there any literature in the field of financial accounting that discusses present value calculations such as those you use to do your work in this case?

A. Well, yes, certainly, but it is a very basic calculation and concept.

Q. Did you consult any of this literature in doing your work in this case?

A. Yes. I took a quick look at the text that I use in teaching my advanced accounting students.

Q. What text is that, Doctor?

A. That is a book entitled *Accounting and Beyond*.

Q. Did you look at any other literature on this question or method?

A. No, that was entirely sufficient.

Q. Do you recall what portion of that text you looked at?

A. Yes; there's a chapter that deals with present value calculations and all of the factors, like interest rates, discount rates, uncertainty, that must be considered.

Q. Can you tell me some other books that deal with present value calculations?

A. Yes, certainly. There's *What's It Worth to You*, *Accounting for Beginners*, and *Check That Rate*.

Q. Are these books that you have used at one time or another in your work or teaching?

A. Yes, I have consulted all three.

Q. When you have used them in the area of present value calculations, have you found them to be reliable?

A. Yes, I think that I have.

Q. Are you familiar with an author in this field named Vasys?

A. Yes, I have seen his work.

Q. He has a book entitled *Present Value Accounting.* Are you familiar with it?

A. Yes, I have read portions of it.

Q. Do you consider him to be a reliable authority in this area of financial accounting?

A. I am not able to answer that in the abstract. Some of his writing is certainly reliable, but I can't say that all of it is, unless we sat here and reviewed it all.[2]

Q. Dr. Vagris, are there experts in financial accounting who have criticized the approach to present value calculation that you have used?

A. Yes. Some, not many, believe that instead of trying to calculate future income streams by allowing for appreciation and inflation, and then discounting the results back to present value by applying a discount rate, it makes more sense to assume that the discount rate and the interest or inflation rate will be approximately equal, and therefore effectively cancel each other out. As a result, they recommend using the non-inflated, and non-discounted future income or revenue numbers. Essentially, what they are saying is that, since you cannot know either number precisely, you may introduce less error by assuming that the rates are equal and can therefore be ignored.

Q. Where is this literature reported, Doctor?

A. The article that I am recalling is entitled, "It's a Wash," and it appeared in the *Journal of Applied Economics.*

---

2. It would be nice if opposing experts always admitted that the treatise or text that supports you was reliable, or written by a reliable author; then you would have the proper foundation in the deposition and could lay it out during your cross-examination. But, where the opposing expert will not give that to you in the deposition, do not despair. If you are the plaintiff, your own expert can lay that foundation during his direct examination, so that you can use the text later, during the cross-examination, without any problem. If you represent the defendant, so that your expert testifies second, the court may allow you to use the text during cross-examination if you make a proffer that your expert will lay the foundation when he testifies. In any event, you lose nothing by raising the question of "reliable authority" during the deposition.

19.5 THINGS LEFT TO BE DONE

Rarely will the opposing expert have finished all of her work on the project by the time that you take her deposition. Even if all of the work is in fact done, it is unlikely that the expert will admit it without qualification. Everybody wants a little bit of "wiggle room," and experts are no exception. The goal at an expert deposition is, in a sense, to attach costs to the expert's insistence upon that wiggle room by demonstrating to the expert that the expert's need to do more work is a manifestation of uncertainty in her opinions. Let's examine the kinds of questioning that tie up loose ends; we will use a materials failure case as our model.

Q. Professor Daunis, what additional work do you intend to do before you testify in this case?

A. Well, I haven't actually planned any further tests or examinations of the materials used in the building, if that's what you mean.

Q. No, I am merely asking whether you intend to do any additional work, of any kind, on this matter before you testify?

A. Okay. I suppose that I may do some further reading in the area of metal fatigue, and I may look for state agency records on similar failures in support members in scaffolds or similar structures.

Q. Why do you feel it necessary to do further reading in the area of metal fatigue?

A. I just want to be certain that I have not overlooked anything.

Q. You are not certain now that you haven't overlooked anything?

A. Well, I'm reasonably certain, but it won't hurt to check a bit further.

Q. Are there particular aspects of the question of metal fatigue that you want to check?

A. No; I just want to review the files to make sure that I have seen all of the most current information in the area.

Q. What do you intend to check?

A. I'll check my department's computer database of the literature, looking for "metal fatigue" and "swing sets" or "scaffolds" or "play equipment," entries like that. And I'll probably contact the state agencies again, by telephone, and ask about the same kinds of information.

Q. When do you intend to do this?

A. Within the next two or three weeks.

Q. Will you tell us, or ask your counsel to tell us, after you have finished that review?

A. Yes, certainly, that's fine with me; I don't know what the legal requirements are, but I have no objection.

Q. Counsel, you will, of course, advise us, either by an amendment to your Rule 26(a)(2)(B) report or by supplementation of this deposition, when Professor Daunis has finished this additional work, and of the scope of the work, so that we can determine whether additional deposition time will be needed?

A. Well, if we conclude that our 26(a)(2)(B) report needs revision or supplementation is required, we will certainly do so. Beyond that, we will respond in an appropriate way to whatever discovery requests you make.[3]

Q. Professor Daunis, aside from checking with the state agencies and doing the literature search you just told us about, is there anything else that you feel you need to do, or to complete, before you testify in this matter?

A. Well, I have been thinking about obtaining some SEM—I'm sorry, scanning electron micrographs—of the site of the failure on the overhead support.

Q. Why have you been thinking about that?

A. It might provide some further information about the failure mechanism. I mean, I am comfortable right now with my opinion that the failure was caused by the manufacturer's decision to build the set with three-inch diameter tubing, providing an inadequate safety factor, but the SEM photos may make that even more apparent.

Q. Why haven't you obtained these SEM photos before now?

A. I didn't really think that they were necessary.

Q. But now you feel that they might be necessary?

---

3. This response may seem rather clever, putting the burden back on the questioning party to propound a discovery request to determine whether further work was done. And it may work exactly that way in jurisdictions following the pre-1993 amendments to the Federal Rules of Civil Procedure. In those jurisdictions, no hard and fast rule controls whether and when a party must advise another of further work by its expert. The questioning attorney must therefore be careful in this area, and follow-up interrogatories are probably appropriately cautious. Fortunately, Rule 26(e)(1) now solves this problem by stating that the duty to supplement extends to information contained in the 26(a)(2)(B) report and to information provided through a deposition. Thus, if the expert is asked what further work was done, that work must be revealed even if occurring after the deposition.

A. No, not necessary, but useful.

Q. Professor, can we agree that you will provide us with copies of any SEM photos that you obtain, so that we can have a chance to ask you some more questions about the information that those photos provide?

A. Sure; again, that's fine with me, but it's really up to my lawyer.

Q. Counsel, I presume that you will agree to provide us with those photographs as soon as they are received by Professor Daunis?

A. Yes, we'll send you copies of any photos that he reviews.

Q. Prof. Daunis, is there anything else that you would like to do, or any other line of research that you would like to complete, before you testify in this case?

A. No, I can't think of anything at this time.

Q. Will you let us know if you do decide to do something further, after this deposition is over so that we can all decide whether we need to schedule further deposition time with you?

A. Again, that's fine with me, if my lawyer agrees.

And so on. The expert is probably unaware, at this point, that he has walked into a trap with his last answers—a trap that is more fully discussed in the next section of this chapter. He has indicated that the scanning electron micrographs might provide further information; now, if he does not request them, he can be asked on cross-examination at trial:

Q. Professor Daunis, you are familiar with a photographic technique using an electron microscope, aren't you?

A. Yes.

Q. Those photographs can provide microscopic details about something like the point at which this metal bar fractured, isn't that true?

A. Yes, that's true.

Q. Those photographs could provide additional information about what caused the bar to fracture in this case?

A. Yes.

Q. But you decided not to request those photographs, didn't you?

A. Well, I didn't think that they would add much.

Q. Professor, my question is simply, you decided not to request those photographs, isn't that right?

A. Yes, that's right.

Q. And you made that decision after talking about those photographs with the plaintiff's counsel?

A. Yes, we talked about it.

The other goals of this examination, beyond determining what else the expert intends to do, have also been met. The expert is aware that further work may subject him to further deposition, a prospect that all experts abhor; and the idea has been planted in his mind that doing further work is evidence that he is uncertain of his opinions, at least on their current bases.

19.6 THINGS NOT DONE

As we have discussed earlier, you can always cross-examine experts about their assumptions and about things they did not do. Because experts simply cannot do everything, there is always more that can be done. Your goal at trial is to make the trier of fact think that it was unreasonable that the expert did not do these other things. Often, the expert will defend himself by arguing, at least on redirect examination, that he had enough information from other sources, or that he probably would not have obtained reliable information by doing these other things. Such responses, however, often come out sounding like excuses and not explanations.

At the expert's deposition, you obviously cannot just ask, "What haven't you done that ought to be done?" The expert will give you nothing in response. Instead, you must ask exhaustively about what the expert has done, and then, at trial, extrapolate to what could have been done. Here your own expert can be helpful in identifying additional work that could have been done. If those additional items seem logical and reasonable, the cross-examination may have some effect on the jury. Let's look first at a deposition scenario, and then at the trial cross- examination which is based upon it. We will use a factual situation involving the alleged failure of a medical product used in a hospital.

Q. Dr. Sujis, you have told us about the tensile strength tests you performed on the suture material, and about your conclusion that the material lost too much of its tensile strength when it was tied by surgeons during operations. In addition to your own tensile strength tests, what else did you do to come to this conclusion?

A. I reviewed the literature in the field, primarily in medical journals.

Q. What did you learn from that literature?

A. Well, there have been a number of such suture failures reported with this type of suture, although not from this manufacturer. In each case, the location of the break, near the knot, suggests a deterioration in the tensile strength of the material at that point.

Q. Will you provide us with a list of the articles or books that you looked at?

A. Yes, I can do that tomorrow morning.

Q. What else did you do in coming to your conclusion that the cause of the failure was inadequate tensile strength?

A. I did my tests and I reviewed the literature. Nothing else was really necessary. Oh, I have been reading the depositions in this case, of the defendant doctor and the manufacturer of the suture.

Q. Who have you talked to about the suture, or the cause of its failure?

A. Just my lawyer here, and my laboratory assistants.

Q. Where have you traveled in conducting your investigation of this suture material?

A. Well, I really haven't traveled anywhere; just to my own laboratory and the lawyer's offices, and here, I suppose, if this deposition is included as part of my investigation.

Q. Have you talked to anyone else, in person or by telephone, other than your lab assistants and your lawyer?

A. No, not about this suture material and the failure.

Q. To whom have you written about this suture material and the failure?

A. No one; I mean, I keep my lab notebook, for my own use and that of my assistants, but I haven't written to anyone outside of the laboratory.

Q. You have already described the tensile strength tests to us; did you do anything other than those tests to examine the strength of the suture material?

A. No, those are the standard tests, and their results were very clear to me.

Although you could do more at the deposition, let's look at the cross-examination at trial now, so that we can see how much fun it is to question an expert on things that he did not do.

Q. Dr. Sujis, as you came to your opinion about the cause of the break in the suture material, you wanted to be reasonably certain that you were right, didn't you?

A. Yes, of course.

Q. So you did what was necessary to gather the appropriate information about the suture material, didn't you?

A. Yes.

Q. You read the deposition testimony of the people who manufacture this suture material?

A. Yes, I did.

Q. So you know that there are four or five scientists out at the plant who are concerned with quality control, right?

A. Yes, I remember reading that.

Q. I presume then that you went out to the suture manufacturing plant and talked to those four or five scientists, before you came to your final opinion?

A. No, I did not.

Q. Did you talk with two or three of them?

A. No.

Q. Did you talk with any of them?

A. No.

Q. Who did you talk to when you visited the plant where the material was manufactured?

A. I never visited the plant. I didn't feel that it was necessary.

Q. Did the plaintiff's lawyers tell you that you could not visit the plant?

A. No.

Q. Did you ask them if you could visit the plant?

A. No.

Q. From reading the depositions, you are aware that the hospital receives, handles, and stores the suture material, and then provides it to the surgical team, is that correct?

A. Yes, I remember reading about that procedure.

Q. In coming to your conclusion about the cause of the suture break, did you visit the room where the suture material was stored, to see if it was too warm or too cold?

A. No.

Q. Did you check the storage room to make sure that the boxes of suture material weren't being crushed by boxes of other, heavier supplies?

A. No, I never visited the storage room.

Q. Did you talk to the hospital employees who handled the boxes of suture material from the time that they were delivered to the hospital until they were brought up to be used in surgery?

A. No, I read the depositions of the hospital administrator and the scrub nurse who stocked the supply closets in the surgical suite.

Q. How many operations did you observe to see how the surgeon handled the suture material?

A. None.

Q. Did your lawyers tell you that you couldn't observe any operations?

A. No, I actually never asked them. I didn't think that it would help me.

Q. Please tell us, in total, how many doctors and nurses, people who actually used this kind of suture, you talked to before you came to your final conclusion that the suture failed because it had inadequate tensile strength?

A. Well, I didn't talk to any; that wasn't the kind of information I was relying on.

All of this examination is based upon the deposition answers where the expert indicated he had spoken only to his lab assistants and lawyer, and that he had not traveled anywhere in his investigations. By carefully framing the questions at trial and stretching them out, you can show the jury the significance of the "rejection" of apparently available and relevant information. While the expert may argue that the information is not relevant from his expert point of view, the jury may well disagree.

To conclude with a word of caution, if what the expert could have done is doable between the time of the deposition and the time of trial, asking these questions at the deposition may only alert the witness to what additional work should be undertaken before trial. Some attorneys therefore recommend that this portion of the deposition be confined to pinning the expert down to what was done without asking about what further investigations could have been undertaken.

19.7 EVALUATION OF OWN EXPERT

One of the important tasks during the deposition of the opposing party's expert is to identify how your own expert's opinions will be attacked. In short, why is this expert concluding that her approach and conclusions are more reliable than those of your expert. This information is being elicited for three reasons. First, it permits your expert to anticipate and respond to the opposing expert's criticisms. Second, it may be possible for your expert to correct any errors or omissions before trial. For example, assume the opposing expert states that your expert's work in defining the geographic market in an antitrust monopolization case is flawed because customer leakage to all potential competing geographic markets has not been accounted for. With this information and time permitting, your expert can now conduct further analysis of the market to account for the alleged customer leakage. Finally, finding out the opposing expert's criticisms of your expert allows you to develop potential lines of cross-examination that will discredit these criticisms.

Q. Have you had an opportunity to review Mr. Bernstein's report in this case?

A. Yes.

Q. Do you agree with the opinions that Mr. Bernstein reached in his report?

A. I do not. I think that Mr. Bernstein's analysis accounted only for one potentially competing market, but ignored any other competing markets.

Q. What do you mean?

A. Well, Mr. Bernstein identified how many potential customers were shifting their business from Lansing to Detroit, but he ignored how many were also switching from Lansing to Grand Rapids or Chicago.

Q. How does that affect Mr. Bernstein's opinions and conclusions?

A. Well, obviously that failure to account for customer defections to adjacent markets seriously affects the reliability of the market analysis.

Q. Have you accounted for these markets in your analysis of the markets?

A. No I haven't. The data just wasn't available for examining those markets.

Q. How does that affect your analysis?

A. Well, I have some problems for the same reasons with my own conclusions.

Q. Why isn't that data available?

A. It's hard to say, but probably because the number of customers going to those markets is so small that the government doesn't bother to collect that sort of information.

A final thought is that it never hurts to ask an expert what he or she thinks of your expert's qualifications. Professional experts are easily able to deal with this ploy and will respond in some noncommittal way. "Amateur" experts, that is those who do not make their living by testifying in court, but have other positions, such as professors, are often unwilling to disparage a professional colleague. Whether a favorable answer can be brought out on cross-examination at trial depends on the judge.

19.8 QUALIFICATIONS

We come to deposition questioning on an expert's qualifications last because this area is least likely to provide material for cross-examination, and because it is the area most easily checked without using deposition time. The expert has been chosen by your opponent because he has some qualifications; rarely is an expert disqualified completely from testifying. In general, then, we advise that you postpone questioning on qualifications until the end of the deposition, so that if time is short you can omit or truncate this area.

One useful technique is to review the expert's education and work experience, proceeding in chronological order, asking at each stage how the experience relates to her work in the present case. Thus, with education, the expert should be asked:

Q. Dr. Vagris, what do your studies of accounting in undergraduate college have to do with the calculations of discounted present value that you performed in this case?

Q. What did your master's thesis on the causes of inflation in the 1970s have to do with the calculations of discounted present value that you performed in this case?

Examine each job in the area of expertise in the same way, and ask the witness how her writings relate to the matter at hand. A good direct examination at trial will demonstrate exactly these kinds of connections; you should prepare for that testimony at the deposition.

One area in which the courts have not achieved agreement is the extent to which they require an expert to divulge approaches used and results obtained for other clients in unrelated matters which are not yet public. Suppose, for example, that an expert has analyzed the pricing behavior in an industry in preparation for testifying that there was no price-fixing. If the prosecution could determine that, in other engagements, on similar data, he found price-fixing, or that in those other engagements he looked at different data or used different approaches, they could impeach his testimony at trial. On the other hand, there could be a substantial imposition on the expert, and on the court's time, of allowing inquiry into other cases, other engagements, and other opinions. In response to a motion *in limine* or a request for a protective order, the court should probably allow deposition questioning of the expert at least to the extent necessary to determine whether she has performed similar analyses in other engagements. If she has, then further inquiry about methodology and results could be permitted, perhaps with some confidentiality safeguards if the other client does not agree to allow disclosure. The court may need to hold a pretrial evidentiary hearing[4] to determine the relevance of the other work to the jury's decision on whether to credit the expert's work in the current case. After such a hearing, the court could decide whether the expert's two engagements are so clearly related that the deposing party would be unfairly disadvantaged by having its discovery limited.

Of course, with each category of information—courses, jobs, societies, writings, speeches, and other engagements—you need to do follow up and corral as we have described throughout this book: how did that course relate to the work you did for this case; what sources did you use for the data; what conclusions did you reach in that paper; what methodology did you employ in that other engagement?

19.9 A FINAL THOUGHT

Many trials develop into a battle of the experts. Each side is asking the judge or jury to accept the testimony of that side's experts and to reject the testimony of the other side's. One way of looking at an expert's deposition is that this is an opportunity for you to develop reasons that the judge or jury should accept your expert's testimony as correct and should reject the testimony of the opposing expert. Expert's depositions make much more sense if viewed in this light—finding out what is wrong with the opposing expert's opinion—than as merely an opportunity to find out what the opposing expert is likely to say at trial.

---

4. Because this issue essentially raises the question of whether such information is admissible at trial, you can handle it under Fed.R.Evid. 104(b) or the state equivalent, which permits such a hearing where admissibility is conditioned on certain facts.

There are many possible reasons for the opposing expert to have come up with the wrong opinion: The expert may not be qualified or experienced; the expert may be relying on incorrect or wrong facts; the expert may be making selective use of the available facts; the expert may be making incorrect assumptions; the expert may be using the wrong methodology; the expert may have failed to carry out an important step in the investigation; the expert may be biased; the expert's judgment may be subjective or the judgment may be bad; and the expert, as a result, has come to a wrong opinion or conclusion. The expert's deposition is your chance to explore these possible reasons and more.

AFTERWORD

As we traveled from town to town and jurisdiction to jurisdiction since the publication of the first edition of this book taking and defending depositions and teaching courses on depositions, we have met with almost uniform agreement that deposition practice is very frustrating in today's "hardball litigation" environment. No one professes to believe that the now-traditional, eyeball-to-eyeball, macho style of taking and defending depositions is efficient or what the authors of the rules intended. Yet hundreds or thousands of attorneys must be practicing that style if everyone has encountered it.

Our book and our lectures emphasize the need to change our deposition styles if lawyers want to be efficient in discovery and if the bar is to retain the right to conduct oral depositions. Many courts have already limited *voir dire*; they count and limit the number of interrogatories (including subparts); they limit the number and length of depositions; and they limit the amount of time spent overall in discovery. Some state courts are even more restrictive than federal courts.

These restrictions are not the fault of the courts; they are our fault. Lawyers make a serious mistake if they think that the opportunity to take depositions is a right which cannot be abridged. If depositions can be limited to four hours, they could be limited to two hours or one hour. If they can be limited to five in number, they could be limited to one (as they are in some courts in Canada, we are told). If they can be confined to two months, they could be confined to one week. We have reached the point where even magistrate judges, who in a very real sense owe their jobs to the existence of discovery disputes, are complaining about having to arbitrate deposition and other discovery problems.

Clearly, aggressive trial lawyers have seized upon depositions as an outlet for their aggressive instincts because "combat by trial" is so infrequently available. But, equally clearly, the system is approaching the point at which even the staunchest advocates of the adversarial system are seeking more efficient alternatives. If the bar does not police itself—by returning to (or adopting) the premise that the discovery of new information is the goal in taking a deposition, and protecting the witness from confusion, harassment, and loss of privileged information is the goal of the defense—then the privilege will be lost. Depositions are the most effective, most efficient, and most satisfying means of obtaining information in litigation. Let all of us behave ourselves and preserve this tool for the lawyers who come after us. We hope that the practice advice we offered in this book will assist you in taking and defending depositions which promote the just resolution of your clients' cases.

APPENDIX

FEDERAL RULES OF CIVIL PROCEDURE
As amended to December 1, 2000

V. DEPOSITIONS AND DISCOVERY

Rule 26. General Provisions Governing Discovery; Duty of Disclosure

(a) Required Disclosures; Methods to Discover Additional Matter.

(1) Initial Disclosures. Except in categories of proceedings specified in Rule 26(a)(1)(E), or to the extent otherwise stipulated or directed by order, a party must, without awaiting a discovery request, provide to other parties:

(A) the name and, if known, the address and telephone number of each individual likely to have discoverable information that the disclosing party may use to support its claims or defenses, unless solely for impeachment, identifying the subjects of the information;

(B) a copy of, or a description by category and location of, all documents, data compilations, and tangible things that are in the possession, custody, or control of the party and that the disclosing party may use to support its claims or defenses, unless solely for impeachment;

(C) a computation of any category of damages claimed by the disclosing party, making available for inspection and copying as under Rule 34 the documents or other evidentiary material, not privileged or protected from disclosure, on which such computation is based, including materials bearing on the nature and extent of injuries suffered; and

(D) for inspection and copying as under Rule 34 any insurance agreement under which any person carrying on an insurance business may be liable to satisfy part or all of a judgment which may be entered in the action or to indemnify or reimburse for payments made to satisfy the judgment.

(**E**) The following categories of proceedings are exempt from initial disclosure under Rule 26(a)(1);

(**i**) an action for review on an administrative record;

(**ii**) a petition for habeas corpus or other proceeding to challenge a criminal conviction or sentence;

(**iii**) an action brought without counsel by a person in custody of the United States, a state, or a state subdivision;

(**iv**) an action to enforce or quash an administrative summons or subpoena;

(**v**) an action by the United States to recover benefit payments;

(**vi**) an action by the United States to collect on a student loan guaranteed by the United States;

(**vii**) a proceeding ancillary to proceedings in other courts; and

(**viii**) an action to enforce an arbitration award.

These disclosures must be made at or within 14 days after the Rule 26(f) conference unless a different time is set by stipulation or court order, or unless a party objects during the conference that initial disclosures are not appropriate in the circumstances of the action and states the objection in the Rule 26(f) discovery plan. In ruling on the objection, the court must determine what disclosures—if any—are to be made, and set the time for disclosure. Any party first served or otherwise joined after the Rule 26(f) conference must make these disclosures within 30 days after being served or joined unless a different time is set by stipulation or court order. A party must make its initial disclosures based on the information then reasonably available to it and is not excused from making its disclosures because it has not fully completed its investigation of the case or because it challenges the sufficiency of another party's disclosures or because another party has not made its disclosures.

(**2**) **Disclosure of Expert Testimony.**

(**A**) In addition to the disclosures required by paragraph (1), a party shall disclose to other parties the identity of any person who may be used at trial to present evidence under Rules 702, 703, or 705 of the Federal Rules of Evidence.

(**B**) Except as otherwise stipulated or directed by the court, this disclosure shall, with respect to a witness who is retained or specially employed to provide expert testimony in the case or whose duties as an employee of the party regularly involve giving expert testimony, be accompanied by a written report prepared and signed by the witness. The report shall contain a complete statement of all opinions to be expressed and the basis and reasons therefor; the data or other information considered by the witness in forming the opinions; any exhibits to be used as a summary of or support for the opinions; the qualifications of the witness, including a list of all publications authored by the witness within the preceding ten years; the compensation to be paid for the study and testimony; and a listing of any other cases in which the witness has testified as an expert at trial or by deposition within the preceding four years.

(**C**) These disclosures shall be made at the times and in the sequence directed by the court. In the absence of other directions from the court or stipulation by the parties, the disclosures shall be made at least 90 days before the trial date or the date the case is to be ready for trial or, if the evidence is intended solely to contradict or rebut evidence on the same subject matter identified by another party under paragraph (2)(B), within 30 days after the disclosure made by the other party. The parties shall supplement these disclosures when required under subdivision(e)(1).

(**3**) **Pretrial Disclosures.** In addition to the disclosures required by Rule 26(a)(1) and (2), a party must provide to other parties and promptly file with the court the following information regarding the evidence that it may present at trial other than solely for impeachment:

(**A**) the name and, if not previously provided, the address and telephone number of each witness, separately identifying those whom the party expects to present and those whom the party may call if the need arises;

(**B**) the designation of those witnesses whose testimony is expected to be presented by means of a deposition and, if not taken stenographically, a transcript of the pertinent portions of the deposition testimony; and

(**C**) an appropriate identification of each document or other exhibit, including summaries of other evidence, separately identifying those which the party expects to offer and those which the party may offer if the need arises.

Unless otherwise directed by the court, these disclosures must be made at least 30 days before trial. Within 14 days thereafter, unless a different time is specified by the court, a party may serve and promptly file a list disclosing (i) any objections to the use under Rule 32(a) of a deposition designated by another party under Rule 26(a)(3)(B), and (ii) any objection, together with the grounds therefor, that may be made to the admissibility of materials identified under Rule 26(a)(3)(C). Objections not so disclosed, other than objections under Rules 402 and 403 of the Federal Rules of Evidence, are waived unless excused by the court for good cause.

(4) Form of Disclosures. Unless the court orders otherwise, all disclosures under Rules 26(a)(1) through (3) must be made in writing, signed, and served.

(5) Methods to Discover Additional Matter. Parties may obtain discovery by one or more of the following methods: depositions upon oral examination or written questions; written interrogatories; production of documents or things or permission to enter upon land or other property under Rule 34 or 45(a)(1)(C), for inspection and other purposes; physical and mental examinations; and requests for admission.

(b) Discovery Scope and Limits. Unless otherwise limited by order of the court in accordance with these rules, the scope of discovery is as follows:

(1) In General. Parties may obtain discovery regarding any matter, not privileged, that is relevant to the claim or defense of any party, including the existence, description, nature, custody, condition, and location of any books, documents, or other tangible things and the identity and location of persons having knowledge of any discoverable matter. For good cause, the court may order discovery of any matter relevant to the subject matter involved in the action. Relevant information need not be admissible at the trial if the discovery appears reasonably calculated to lead to the discovery of admissible evidence. All discovery is subject to the limitations imposed by Rule 26(b)(2)(i), (ii), and (iii).

(2) Limitations. By order, the court may alter the limits in these rules on the number of depositions and interrogatories or the length of depositions under Rule 30. By order or local rule, the court may also limit the number of requests under Rule 36. The frequency or extent of use of the discovery methods otherwise permitted under these rules and by any local rule shall be limited by the court if it determines that: (i) the discovery sought is unreasonably cumulative or duplicative, or is obtainable from some other source that is more convenient, less burdensome, or less expensive; (ii) the party seeking discovery has had ample opportunity by discovery in the action to obtain the information sought; or (iii) the burden or expense of the proposed discovery outweighs its likely benefit, taking into account the needs of the case, the amount in controversy, the parties' resources, the importance of the issues at stake in the litigation, and the importance of the proposed discovery in resolving the issues. The court may act upon its own initiative after reasonable notice or pursuant to a motion under Rule 26(c).

(3) Trial Preparation: Materials. Subject to the provisions of subdivision (b)(4) of this rule, a party may obtain discovery of documents and tangible things otherwise discoverable under subdivision (b)(1) of this rule and prepared in anticipation of litigation or for trial by or for another party or by or for that other party's representative (including the other party's attorney, consultant, surety, indemnitor, insurer, or agent) only upon a showing that the party seeking discovery has substantial need of the materials in the preparation of the party's case and that the party is unable without undue hardship to obtain the substantial equivalent of the materials by other means. In ordering discovery of such materials when the required showing has been made, the court shall protect against disclosure of the mental impressions, conclusions, opinions, or legal theories of an attorney or other representative of a party concerning the litigation.

A party may obtain without the required showing a statement concerning the action or its subject matter previously made by that party. Upon request, a person not a party may obtain without the required showing a statement concerning the action or its subject matter previously made by that person. If the request is refused, the person may move for a court order. The provisions of Rule 37(a)(4) apply to the award of expenses incurred in relation to the motion. For purposes of this paragraph, a statement previously made is (A) a written statement signed or otherwise adopted or approved by the person making it, or (B) a stenographic, mechanical, electrical, or other recording, or a transcription thereof, which is a substantially verbatim recital of an oral statement by the person making it and contemporaneously recorded.

(4) Trial Preparation: Experts.

(A) A party may depose any person who has been identified as an expert whose opinions may be presented at trial. If a report from the expert is required under subdivision (a)(2)(B), the deposition shall not be conducted until after the report is provided.

(B) A party may, through interrogatories or by deposition, discover facts known or opinions held by an expert who has been retained or specially employed by another party in anticipation of litigation or preparation for trial and who is not expected to be called as a witness at trial only as provided in Rule 35(b) or upon a showing of exceptional circumstances under which it is impracticable for the party seeking discovery to obtain facts or opinions on the same subject by other means.

(C) Unless manifest injustice would result, (i) the court shall require that the party seeking discovery pay the expert a reasonable fee for time spent in responding to discovery under this subdivision; and (ii) with respect to discovery obtained under subdivision (b)(4)(B) of this rule the court shall require the party seeking discovery to pay the other party a fair portion of the fees and expenses reasonably incurred by the latter party in obtaining facts and opinions from the expert.

(5) Claims of Privilege or Protection of Trial Preparation Materials. When a party withholds information otherwise discoverable under these rules by claiming that it is privileged or subject to protection as trial preparation material, the party shall make the claim expressly and shall describe the nature of the documents, communications, or things not produced or disclosed in a manner that, without revealing information itself privileged or protected, will enable other parties to assess the applicability of the privilege or protection.

(c) Protective Orders. Upon motion by a party or by the person from whom discovery is sought, accompanied by a certification that the movant has in good faith conferred or attempted to confer with other affected parties in an effort to resolve the dispute without court action, and for good cause shown, the court in which the action is pending or alternatively, on matters relating to a deposition, the court in the district where the deposition is to be taken may make any order which justice requires to protect a party or person from annoyance, embarrassment, oppression, or undue burden or expense, including one or more of the following:

(1) that the disclosure or discovery not be had;

(2) that the disclosure or discovery may be had only on specified terms and conditions, including a designation of the time or place;

(3) that the discovery may be had only by a method of discovery other than that selected by the party seeking discovery;

(4) that certain matters not be inquired into, or that the scope of the disclosure or discovery be limited to certain matters;

(5) that discovery be conducted with no one present except persons designated by the court;

(6) that a deposition, after being sealed, be opened only by order of the court;

(**7**) that a trade secret or other confidential research, development, or commercial information not be revealed or be revealed only in a designated way; and

(**8**) that the parties simultaneously file specified documents or information enclosed in sealed envelopes to be opened as directed by the court.

If the motion for a protective order is denied in whole or in part, the court may, on such terms and conditions as are just, order that any party or other person provide or permit discovery. The provisions of Rule 37(a)(4) apply to the award of expenses incurred in relation to the motion

(**d**) **Timing and Sequence of Discovery.** Except in categories of proceedings exempted from initial disclosure under Rule 26(a)(1)(E), or when authorized under these rules or by order or agreement of the parties, a party may not seek discovery from any source before the parties have conferred as required by Rule 26(f). Unless the court upon motion, for the convenience of parties and witnesses and in the interests of justice, orders otherwise, methods of discovery may be used in any sequence, and the fact that a party is conducting discovery, whether by deposition or otherwise, does not operate to delay any other party's discovery.

(**e**) **Supplementation of Disclosures and Responses.** A party who has made a disclosure under subdivision (a) or responded to a request for discovery with a disclosure or response is under a duty to supplement or correct the disclosure or response to include information thereafter acquired if ordered by the court or in the following circumstances:

(**1**) A party is under a duty to supplement at appropriate intervals its disclosures under subdivision (a) if the party learns that in some material respect the information disclosed is incomplete or incorrect and if the additional or corrective information has not otherwise been made known to the other parties during the discovery process or in writing. With respect to testimony of an expert from whom a report is required under subdivision (a)(2)(B) the duty extends both to information contained in the report and to information provided through a deposition of the expert, and any additions or other changes to this information shall be disclosed by the time the party's disclosures under Rule 26(a)(3) are due.

(**2**) A party is under a duty seasonably to amend a prior response to an interrogatory, request for production, or request for admission if the party learns that the response is in some material respect incomplete or incorrect and if the additional or corrective information has not otherwise been made known to the other parties during the discovery process or in writing.

(f) Conference of Parties; Planning for Discovery. Except in catagories of proceedings exempted from initial disclosure under Rule 26(a)(1)(E) or when otherwise ordered, the parties must, as soon as practicable and in any event at least 21 days before a scheduling conference is held or a scheduling order is due under Rule 16(b), confer to consider the nature and basis of their claims and defenses and the possibilities for a prompt settlement or resolution of the case, to make or arrange for the disclosures required by Rule 26(a)(1), and to develop a proposed discovery plan that indicates the parties' views and proposals concerning:

(1) what changes should be made in the timing, form, or requirement for disclosures under Rule 26(a), including a statement as to when disclosures under Rule 26(a)(1) were made or will be made;

(2) the subjects on which discovery may be needed, when discovery should be completed, and whether discovery should be conducted in phases or be limited to or focused upon particular issues;

(3) what changes should be made in the limitations on discovery imposed under these rules or by local rule, and what other limitations should be imposed; and

(4) any other orders that should be entered by the court under Rule 26(c) or under Rule 16(b) and (c).

The attorneys of record and all unrepresented parties that have appeared in the case are jointly responsible for arranging the conference, for attempting in good faith to agree on the proposed discovery plan, and for submitting to the court within 14 days after the conference a written report outlining the plan. A court may order that the parties or attorneys attend the conference in person. If necessary to comply with its expedited schedule for Rule 16(b) conferences, a court may by local rule (i) require that the conference between the parties occur fewer than 21 days before the scheduling conference is held or a scheduling order is due under Rule 16(b), and (ii) require that the written report outlining the discovery plan be filed fewer than 14 days after the conference between the parties, or excuse the parties from submitting a written report and permit them to report orally on their discovery plan at the Rule 16(b) conference.

(g) Signing of Disclosures, Discovery Requests, Responses, and Objections.

(1) Every disclosure made pursuant to subdivision (a)(1) or subdivision (a)(3) shall be signed by at least one attorney of record in the attorney's individual name, whose address shall be stated. An unrepresented party shall sign the disclosure and state the party's address. The signature of the attorney or party constitutes a certification that to the best of the signer's knowledge, information, and belief, formed after a reasonable inquiry, the disclosure is complete and correct as of the time it is made.

(2) Every discovery request, response, or objection made by a party represented by an attorney shall be signed by at least one attorney of record in the attorney's individual name, whose address shall be stated. An unrepresented party shall sign the request, response, or objection and state the party's address. The signature of the attorney or party constitutes a certification that to the best of the signer's knowledge, information, and belief, formed after a reasonable inquiry, the request, response, or objection is:

(A) consistent with these rules and warranted by existing law or a good faith argument for the extension, modification, or reversal of existing law;

(B) not interposed for any improper purpose, such as to harass or to cause unnecessary delay or needless increase in the cost of litigation; and

(C) not unreasonable or unduly burdensome or expensive, given the needs of the case, the discovery already had in the case, the amount in controversy, and the importance of the issues at stake in the litigation.

If a request, response, or objection is not signed, it shall be stricken unless it is signed promptly after the omission is called to the attention of the party making the request, response, or objection, and a party shall not be obligated to take any action with respect to it until it is signed.

(3) If without substantial justification a certification is made in violation of the rule, the court, upon motion or upon its own initiative, shall impose upon the person who made the certification, the party on whose behalf the disclosure, request, response, or objection is made, or both, an appropriate sanction, which may include an order to pay the amount of the reasonable expenses incurred because of the violation, including a reasonable attorney's fee.

Rule 27.   Depositions Before Action or Pending Appeal

(a) Before Action.

(1) Petition. A person who desires to perpetuate testimony regarding any matter that may be cognizable in any court of the United States may file a verified petition in the United States district court in the district of the residence of any expected adverse party. The petition shall be entitled in the name of the petitioner and shall show: 1, that the petitioner expects to be a party to an action cognizable in a court of the United States but is presently unable to bring it or cause it to be brought, 2, the subject matter of the expected action and the petitioner's interest therein, 3, the facts which the petitioner desires to establish by the proposed testimony and the reasons for desiring to perpetuate it, 4, the names or a description of the persons the petitioner expects will be adverse parties and their addresses so far as known, and 5, the names and addresses of the persons to be examined and the substance of the testimony which the petitioner expects to elicit from each, and shall ask for an order authorizing the petitioner to take the depositions of the persons to be examined named in the petition, for the purpose of perpetuating their testimony.

(2) Notice and Service. The petitioner shall thereafter serve a notice upon each person named in the petition as an expected adverse party, together with a copy of the petition, stating that the petitioner will apply to the court, at a time and place named therein, for the order described in the petition. At least 20 days before the date of hearing the notice shall be served either within or without the district or state in the manner provided in Rule 4(d) for service of summons; but if such service cannot with due diligence be made upon any expected adverse party named in the petition, the court may make such order as is just for service by publication or otherwise, and shall appoint, for persons not served in the manner provided in Rule 4(d), an attorney who shall represent them, and, in case they are not otherwise represented, shall cross-examine the deponent. If any expected adverse party is a minor or incompetent the provisions of Rule 17(c) apply.

(3) Order and Examination. If the court is satisfied that the perpetuation of the testimony may prevent a failure or delay of justice, it shall make an order designating or describing the persons whose depositions may be taken and specifying the subject matter of the examination and whether the depositions shall be taken upon oral examination or written interrogatories. The depositions may then be taken in accordance with these rules; and the court may make orders of the character provided for by Rules 34 and 35. For the purpose of applying these rules to depositions for perpetuating testimony, each reference therein to the court in which the action is pending shall be deemed to refer to the court in which the petition for such deposition was filed.

(4) Use of Deposition. If a deposition to perpetuate testimony is taken under these rules or if, although not so taken, it would be admissible in evidence in the courts of the state in which it is taken, it may be used in any action involving the same subject matter subsequently brought in a United States district court, in accordance with the provisions of Rule 32(a).

(b) Pending Appeal. If an appeal has been taken from a judgment of a district court or before the taking of an appeal if the time therefor has not expired, the district court in which the judgment was rendered may allow the taking of the depositions of witnesses to perpetuate their testimony for use in the event of further proceedings in the district court. In such case the party who desires to perpetuate the testimony may make a motion in the district court for leave to take the depositions, upon the same notice and service thereof as if the action was pending in the district court. The motion shall show (1) the names and addresses of persons to be examined and the substance of the testimony which the party expects to elicit from each; (2) the reasons for perpetuating their testimony. If the court finds that the perpetuation of the testimony is proper to avoid a failure or delay of justice, it may make an order allowing the depositions to be taken and may make orders of the character provided for by Rules 34 and 35, and thereupon the depositions may be taken and used in the same manner and under the same conditions as are prescribed in these rules for depositions taken in actions pending in the district court.

(c) Perpetuation by Action. This rule does not limit the power of a court to entertain an action to perpetuate testimony.

Rule 28. Persons Before Whom Depositions may be Taken

(a) Within the United States. Within the United States or within a territory or insular possession subject to the jurisdiction of the United States, depositions shall be taken before an officer authorized to administer oaths by the laws of the United States or of the place where the examination is held, or before a person appointed by the court in which the action is pending. A person so appointed has power to administer oaths and take testimony. The term officer as used in Rules

30, 31 and 32 includes a person appointed by the court or designated by the parties under Rule 29.

(b) In Foreign Countries. Depositions may be taken in a foreign country (1) pursuant to any applicable treaty or convention, or (2) pursuant to a letter of request (whether or not captioned a letter rogatory), or (3) on notice before a person authorized to administer oaths in the place where the examination is held, either by the law thereof or by the law of the United States, or (4) before a person commissioned by the court, and a person so commissioned shall have the power by virtue of the commission to administer any necessary oath and take testimony. A commission or a letter of request shall be issued on application and notice and on terms that are just and appropriate. It is not requisite to the issuance of a commission or a letter of request that the taking of the deposition in any other manner is impracticable or inconvenient; and both a commission and a letter of request may be issued in proper cases. A notice or commission may designate the person before whom the deposition is to be taken either by name or descriptive title. A letter of request may be addressed "To the Appropriate Authority in [here name the country]." When a letter of request or any other device is used pursuant to any applicable treaty or convention, it shall be captioned in the form prescribed by that treaty or convention. Evidence obtained in response to a letter of request need not be excluded merely because it is not a verbatim transcript, because the testimony was not taken under oath, or because of any similar departure from the requirements for depositions taken within the United States under these rules.

(c) Disqualification for Interest. No deposition shall be taken before a person who is a relative or employee or attorney or counsel of any of the parties, or is a relative or employee of such attorney or counsel, or is financially interested in the action.

Rule 29. Stipulations Regarding Discovery Procedure

Unless otherwise directed by the court, the parties may by written stipulation (1) provide that depositions may be taken before any person, at any time or place, upon any notice, and in any manner and when so taken may be used like other depositions, and (2) modify other procedures governing or limitations placed upon discovery, except that stipulations extending the time provided in Rules 33, 34, and 36 for responses to discovery may, if they would interfere with any time set for completion of discovery, for hearing of a motion, or for trial, be made only with the approval of the court.

Rule 30. Depositions Upon Oral Examination

(a) When Depositions May Be Taken; When Leave Required.

(1) A party may take the testimony of any person, including a party, by deposition upon oral examination without leave of court except as provided in paragraph (2). The attendance of witnesses may be compelled by subpoena as provided in Rule 45.

(2) A party must obtain leave of court, which shall be granted to the extent consistent with the principles stated in Rule 26(b)(2), if the person to be examined is confined in prison or if, without the written stipulation of the parties.

(A) a proposed deposition would result in more than ten depositions being taken under this rule or Rule 31 by the plaintiffs, or by the defendants, or by third-party defendants;

(B) the person to be examined already has been deposed in the case; or

(C) a party seeks to take a deposition before the time specified in Rule 26(d) unless the notice contains a certification, with supporting facts, that the person to be examined is expected to leave the United States and be unavailable for examination in this country unless deposed before that time.

(b) Notice of Examination: General Requirements; Method of Recording; Production of Documents and Things; Deposition of Organization; Deposition by Telephone.

(1) A party desiring to take the deposition of any person upon oral examination shall give reasonable notice in writing to every other party to the action. The notice shall state the time and place for taking the deposition and the name and address of each person to be examined, if known, and, if the name is not known, a general description sufficient to identify the person or the particular class or group to which the person belongs. If a subpoena duces tecum is to be served on the person to be examined, the designation of the materials to be produced as set forth in the subpoena shall be attached to, or included in, the notice.

(2) The party taking the deposition shall state in the notice the method by which the testimony shall be recorded. Unless the court orders otherwise, it may be recorded by sound, sound-and-visual, or stenographic means, and the party taking the deposition shall bear the cost of the recording. Any party may arrange for a transcription to be made from the recording of a deposition taken by nonstenographic means.

(3) With prior notice to the deponent and other parties, any party may designate another method to record the deponent's testimony in addition to the method specified by the person taking the deposition. The additional record or transcript shall be made at that party's expense unless the court otherwise orders.

(4) Unless otherwise agreed by the parties, a deposition shall be conducted before an officer appointed or designated under Rule 28 and shall begin with a statement on the record by the officer that includes (A) the officer's name and business address; (B) the date, time, and place of the deposition; (C) the name of the deponent; (D) the administration of the oath or affirmation to the deponent; and (E) an identification of all persons present. If the deposition is recorded other than stenographically, the officer shall repeat items (A) through (C) at the beginning of each unit of recorded tape or other recording medium. The appearance or demeanor of deponents or attorneys shall not be distorted through camera or sound-recording techniques. At the end of the deposition, the officer shall state on the record that the deposition is complete and shall set forth any stipulations made by counsel concerning the custody of the transcript or recording and the exhibits, or concerning other pertinent matters.

(5) The notice to a party deponent may be accompanied by a request made in compliance with Rule 34 for the production of documents and tangible things at the taking of the deposition. The procedure of Rule 34 shall apply to the request.

(6) A party may in the party's notice and in a subpoena name as the deponent a public or private corporation or a partnership or association or governmental agency and describe with reasonable particularity the matters on which examination is requested. In that event, the organization so named shall designate one or more officers, directors, or managing agents, or other persons who consent to testify on its behalf, and may set forth, for each person designated, the matters on which the person will testify. A subpoena shall advise a non-party organization of its duty to make such a designation. The persons so designated shall testify as to matters known or reasonably available to the organization. This subdivision (b)(6) does not preclude taking a deposition by any other procedure authorized in these rules.

(7) The parties may stipulate in writing or the court may upon motion order that a deposition be taken by telephone or other remote electronic means. For the purposes of this rule and Rules 28(a), 37(a)(1), and 37(b)(1), a deposition taken by such means is taken in the district and at the place where the deponent is to answer questions.

(c) Examination and Cross-Examination; Record of Examination; Oath; Objections. Examination and cross-examination of witnesses may proceed as permitted at the trial under the provisions of the Federal Rules of Evidence except Rules 103 and 615. The officer before whom the deposition is to be taken shall put the witness on oath or affirmation and shall personally, or by someone acting under the officer's direction and in the officer's presence, record the testimony of the witness. The testimony shall be taken stenographically or recorded by any other method authorized by subdivision (b)(2) of this rule. All objections made at the time of the examination to the qualifications of the officer taking the deposition, to the manner of taking it, to the evidence presented, to the conduct of any party, or to any other aspect of the proceedings shall be noted by the officer upon the record of the deposition; but the examination shall proceed, with the testimony being taken subject to the objections. In lieu of participating in the oral examination, parties may serve written questions in a sealed envelope on the party taking the deposition and the party taking the deposition shall transmit them to the officer, who shall propound them to the witness and record the answers verbatim.

(d) Schedule and Duration; Motion to Terminate or Limit Examination.

(1) Any objection during a deposition must be stated concisely and in a non-argumentative and non-suggestive manner. A person may instruct a deponent not to answer only when necessary to preserve a privilege, to enforce a limitation directed by the court, or to present a motion under Rule 30(d)(4).

(2) Unless otherwise authorized by the court or stipulated by the parties, a deposition is limited to one day of seven hours. The court must allow additional time consistent with Rule 26(b)(2) if needed for a fair examination of the deponent or if the deponent or another person, or other circumstance, impedes or delays the examination.

(3) If the court finds that any impediment, delay, or other conduct has frustrated the fair examination of the deponent, it may impose upon the persons responsible an appropriate sanction, including the reasonable costs and attorney's fees incurred by any parties as a result thereof.

(4) At any time during a deposition, on motion of a party or of the deponent and upon a showing that the examination is being conducted in bad faith or in such manner as unreasonably to annoy, embarrass, or oppress the deponent or party, the court in which the action is pending or the court in the district where the deposition is being taken may order the officer conducting the examination to

cease forthwith from taking the deposition, or may limit the scope and manner of the taking of the deposition as provided in Rule 26(c). If the order made terminates the examination, it may be resumed thereafter only upon the order of the court in which the action is pending. Upon demand of the objecting party or deponent, the taking of the deposition must be suspended for the time necessary to make a motion for an order. The provisions of Rule 37(a)(4) apply to the award of expenses incurred in relation to the motion.

(e) Review by Witness; Changes; Signing. If requested by the deponent or a party before completion of the deposition, the deponent shall have 30 days after being notified by the officer that the transcript or recording is available in which to review the transcript or recording and, if there are changes in form or substance, to sign a statement reciting such changes and the reasons given by the deponent for making them. The officer shall indicate in the certificate prescribed by subdivision (f)(1) whether any review was requested and, if so, shall append any changes made by the deponent during the period allowed.

(f) Certification and Delivery by Officer; Exhibits; Copies.

(1) The officer must certify that the witness was duly sworn by the officer and that the deposition is a true record of the testimony given by the witness. This certificate must be in writing and accompany the record of the deposition. Unless otherwise ordered by the court, the officer must securely seal the deposition in an envelope or package indorsed with the title of the action and marked "Deposition of [here insert name of witness]" and must promptly send it to the attorney who arranged for the transcript or recording, who must store it under conditions that will protect it against loss, destruction, tampering, or deterioration. Documents and things produced for inspection during the examination of the witness must, upon the request of a party, be marked for identification and annexed to the deposition, and may be inspected and copied by any party, except that if the person producing the materials desires to retain them the person may (A) offer copies to be marked for identification and annexed to the deposition and to serve thereafter as originals if the person affords to all parties fair opportunity to verify the copies by comparison with the originals, or (B) offer the originals to be marked for identification, after giving to each party an opportunity to inspect and copy them, in which event the materials may then be used in the same manner as if annexed to the deposition. Any party may move for an order that the original be annexed to and returned with the deposition to the court, pending final disposition of the case.

(2) Unless otherwise ordered by the court or agreed by the parties, the officer shall retain stenographic notes of any deposition taken stenographically or a copy of the recording of any deposition taken by another method. Upon payment of reasonable charges therefor, the officer shall furnish a copy of the transcript or other recording of the deposition to any party or to the deponent.

(3) The party taking the deposition shall give prompt notice of its filing to all other parties.

(g) Failure to Attend or to Serve Subpoena; Expenses.

(1) If the party giving the notice of the taking of a deposition fails to attend and proceed therewith and another party attends in person or by attorney pursuant to the notice, the court may order the party giving the notice to pay to such other party the reasonable expenses incurred by that party and that party's attorney in attending, including reasonable attorney's fees.

(2) If the party giving the notice of the taking of a deposition of a witness fails to serve a subpoena upon the witness and the witness because of such failure does not attend, and if another party attends in person or by attorney because that party expects the deposition of that witness to be taken, the court may order the party giving the notice to pay to such other party the reasonable expenses incurred by that party and that party's attorney in attending, including reasonable attorney's fees.

Rule 31. Depositions Upon Written Questions

(a) Serving Questions; Notice.

(1) A party may take the testimony of any person, including a party, by deposition upon written questions without leave of court except as provided in paragraph (2). The attendance of witnesses may be compelled by the use of subpoena as provided in Rule 45.

(2) A party must obtain leave of court, which shall be granted to the extent consistent with the principles stated in Rule 26(b)(2), if the person to be examined is confined in prison or if, without the written stipulation of the parties,

(A) a proposed deposition would result in more than ten depositions being taken under this rule or Rule 30 by the plaintiffs, or by the defendants, or by third-party defendants;

(B) the person to be examined has already been deposed in the case; or

(C) a party seeks to take a deposition before the time specified in Rule 26(d).

(3) A party desiring to take a deposition upon written questions shall serve them upon every other party with a notice stating (1) the name and address of the person who is to answer them, if known, and if the name is not known, a general description sufficient to identify the person or the particular class or group to which the person belongs, and (2) the name or descriptive title and address of the officer before whom the deposition is to be taken. A deposition upon written questions may be taken of a public or private corporation or a partnership or association or governmental agency in accordance with the provisions of Rule 30(b)(6).

(4) Within 14 days after the notice and written questions are served, a party may serve cross questions upon all other parties. Within 7 days after being served with cross questions, a party may serve redirect questions upon all other parties. Within 7 days after being served with redirect questions, a party may serve recross questions upon all other parties. The court may for cause shown enlarge or shorten the time.

(b) Officer to Take Responses and Prepare Record. A copy of the notice and copies of all questions served shall be delivered by the party taking the deposition to the officer designated in the notice, who shall proceed promptly, in the manner provided by Rule 30(c), (e), and (f), to take the testimony of the witness in response to the questions and to prepare, certify, and file or mail the deposition, attaching thereto the copy of the notice and the questions received by the officer.

(c) Notice of Filing. When the deposition is filed the party taking it shall promptly give notice thereof to all other parties.

Rule 32.   Use of Depositions in Court Proceedings

(a) Use of Depositions. At the trial or upon the hearing of a motion or an interlocutory proceeding, any part or all of a deposition, so far as admissible under the rules of evidence applied as though the witness were then present and testifying, may be used against any party who was present or represented at the taking of the deposition or who had reasonable notice thereof, in accordance with any of the following provisions:

(1) Any deposition may be used by any party for the purpose of contradicting or impeaching the testimony of deponent as a witness, or for any other purpose permitted by the Federal Rules of Evidence.

(2) The deposition of a party or of anyone who at the time of taking the deposition was an officer, director, or managing agent, or a person designated under Rule 30(b)(6) or 31(a) to testify on behalf of a public or private corporation, partnership or association or governmental agency which is a party may be used by an adverse party for any purpose.

(3) The deposition of a witness, whether or not a party, may be used by any party for any purpose if the court finds:

(A) that the witness is dead; or

(B) that the witness is at a greater distance than 100 miles from the place of trial or hearing, or is out of the United States, unless it appears that the absence of the witness was procured by the party offering the deposition; or

(C) that the witness is unable to attend or testify because of age, illness, infirmity, or imprisonment; or

(D) that the party offering the deposition has been unable to procure the attendance of the witness by subpoena; or

(E) upon application and notice, that such exceptional circumstances exist as to make it desirable, in the interest of justice and with due regard to the importance of presenting the testimony of witnesses orally in open court, to allow the deposition to be used.

A deposition taken without leave of court pursuant to a notice under Rule 30(a)(2)(C) shall not be used against a party who demonstrates that, when served with the notice, it was unable through the exercise of diligence to obtain counsel to represent it at the taking of the deposition; nor shall a deposition be used against a party who, having received less than 11 days' notice of a deposition, has promptly upon receiving such notice filed a motion for a protective order under Rule 26(c)(2) requesting that the deposition not be held or be held at a different time or place and such motion is pending at the time the deposition is held.

(4) If only part of a deposition is offered in evidence by a party, an adverse party may require the offeror to introduce any other part which ought in fairness to be considered with the part introduced, and any party may introduce any other parts.

Substitution of parties pursuant to Rule 25 does not affect the right to use depositions previously taken; and, when an action has been brought in any court of the United States or of any State and another action involving the same subject matter is afterward brought between the same parties or their representatives or successors in interest, all depositions lawfully taken and duly filed in the former action may be used in the latter as if originally taken therefor. A deposition previously taken may also be used as permitted by the Federal Rules of Evidence.

(b) Objections to Admissibility. Subject to the provisions of Rule 28(b) and subdivision (d)(3) of this rule, objection may be made at the trial or hearing to receiving in evidence any deposition or part thereof for any reason which would require the exclusion of the evidence if the witness were then present and testifying.

(c) Form of Presentation. Except as otherwise directed by the court, a party offering deposition testimony pursuant to this rule may offer it in stenographic or nonstenographic form, but, if in nonstenographic form, the party shall also provide the court with a transcript of the portions so offered. On request of any party in a case tried before a jury, deposition testimony offered other than for impeachment purposes shall be presented in nonstenographic form, if available, unless the court for good cause orders otherwise.

(d) Effect of Errors and Irregularities in Depositions.

(1) As to Notice. All errors and irregularities in the notice for taking a deposition are waived unless written objection is promptly served upon the party giving the notice.

(2) As to Disqualification of Officer. Objection to taking a deposition because of disqualification of the officer before whom it is to be taken is waived unless made before the taking of the deposition begins or as soon thereafter as the disqualification becomes known or could be discovered with reasonable diligence.

(3) As to Taking of Deposition.

(A) Objections to the competency of a witness or to the competency, relevancy, or materiality of testimony are not waived by failure to make them before or during the taking of the deposition, unless the ground of the objection is one which might have been obviated or removed if presented at that time.

(B) Errors and irregularities occurring at the oral examination in the manner of taking the deposition, in the form of the questions or answers, in the oath or affirmation, or in the conduct of parties, and errors of any kind which might be obviated, removed, or cured if promptly presented, are waived unless reasonable objection thereto is made at the taking of the deposition.

(C) Objections to the form of written questions submitted under Rule 31 are waived unless served in writing upon the party propounding them within the time allowed for serving the succeeding cross or other questions and within 5 days after service of the last questions authorized.

(4) As to Completion and Return of Deposition. Errors and irregularities in the manner in which the testimony is transcribed or the deposition is prepared, signed, certified, sealed, indorsed, transmitted, filed, or otherwise dealt with by the officer under Rules 30 and 31 are waived unless a motion to suppress the deposition or some part thereof is made with reasonable promptness after such defect is, or with due diligence might have been, ascertained.

Rule 33.   Interrogatories to Parties

(a) Availability. Without leave of court or written stipulation, any party may serve upon any other party written interrogatories, not exceeding 25 in number including all discrete subparts, to be answered by the party served or, if the party served is a public or private corporation or a partnership or association or governmental agency, by any officer or agent, who shall furnish such information as is available to the party. Leave to serve additional interrogatories shall be granted to the extent consistent with the principles of Rule 26(b)(2). Without leave of court or written stipulation, interrogatories may not be served before the time specified in Rule 26(d).

(b) Answers and Objections.

(1) Each interrogatory shall be answered separately and fully in writing under oath, unless it is objected to, in which event the objecting party shall state the reasons for objection and shall answer to the extent the interrogatory is not objectionable.

(2) The answers are to be signed by the person making them, and the objections signed by the attorney making them.

(3) The party upon whom the interrogatories have been served shall serve a copy of the answers, and objections if any, within 30 days after the service of the interrogatories. A shorter or longer time may be directed by the court or, in the absence of such an order, agreed to in writing by the parties subject to Rule 29.

(4) All grounds for an objection to an interrogatory shall be stated with specificity. Any ground not stated in a timely objection is waived unless the party's failure to object is excused by the court for good cause shown.

(5) The party submitting the interrogatories may move for an order under Rule 37(a) with respect to any objection to or other failure to answer an interrogatory.

(c) Scope; Use at Trial. Interrogatories may relate to any matters which can be inquired into under Rule 26(b)(1), and the answers may be used to the extent permitted by the rules of evidence.

An interrogatory otherwise proper is not necessarily objectionable merely because an answer to the interrogatory involves an opinion or contention that relates to fact or the application of law to fact, but the court may order that such an interrogatory need not be answered until after designated discovery has been completed or until a pretrial conference or other later time.

(d) Option to Produce Business Records. Where the answer to an interrogatory may be derived or ascertained from the business records of the party upon whom the interrogatory has been served or from an examination, audit or inspection of such business records, including a compilation, abstract or summary thereof, and the burden of deriving or ascertaining the answer is substantially the same for the party serving the interrogatory as for the party served, it is a sufficient answer to such interrogatory to specify the records from which the answer may be derived or ascertained and to afford to the party serving the interrogatory reasonable opportunity to examine, audit or inspect such records and to make copies, compilations, abstracts or summaries. A specification shall be in sufficient detail to permit the interrogating party to locate and to identify, as readily as can the party served, the records from which the answer may be ascertained.

Rule 34. Production of Documents and Things and Entry Upon Land for Inspection and Other Purposes

(a) Scope. Any party may serve on any other party a request (1) to produce and permit the party making the request, or someone acting on the requestor's behalf, to inspect and copy, any designated documents (including writings, drawings, graphs, charts, photographs, phonorecords, and other data compilations from which information can be obtained, translated, if necessary, by the respondent through detection devices into reasonably usable form), or to inspect and copy, test, or sample any tangible things which constitute or contain matters within the scope of Rule 26(b) and which are in the possession, custody or control of the party upon whom the request is served; or (2) to permit entry upon designated land or other property in the possession or control of the party upon whom the request is served for the purpose of inspection and measuring, surveying, photographing, testing, or sampling the property or any designated object or operation thereon, within the scope of Rule 26(b).

(b) Procedure. The request shall set forth, either by individual item or by category, the items to be inspected, and describe each with reasonable particularity. The request shall specify a reasonable time, place, and manner of making the inspection and performing the related acts. Without leave of court or written stipulation, a request may not be served before the time specified in Rule 26(d).

The party upon whom the request is served shall serve a written response within 30 days after the service of the request. A shorter or longer time may be directed by the court or, in the absence of such an order, agreed to in writing by the parties, subject to Rule 29. The response shall state, with respect to each item or category, that inspection and related activities will be permitted as requested, unless the request is objected to, in which event the reasons for the objection shall be stated. If objection is made to part of an item or category, the part shall be specified and inspection permitted of the remaining parts. The party submitting the request may move for an order under Rule 37(a) with respect to any objection to or other failure to respond to the request or any part thereof, or any failure to permit inspection as requested.

A party who produces documents for inspection shall produce them as they are kept in the usual course of business or shall organize and label them to correspond with the categories in the request.

(c) Persons Not Parties. A person not a party to the action may be compelled to produce documents and things or to submit to an inspection as provided in Rule 45.

Rule 35. Physical and Mental Examinations of Persons

(a) Order for Examination. When the mental or physical condition (including the blood group) of a party, or of a person in the custody or under the legal control of a party, is in controversy, the court in which the action is pending may order the party to submit to a physical or mental examination by a suitably licensed or certified examiner or to produce for examination the person in the party's custody or legal control. The order may be made only on motion for good cause shown and upon notice to the person to be examined and to all parties and shall specify the time, place, manner, conditions, and scope of the examination and the person or persons by whom it is to be made.

(b) Report of Examiner.

(1) If requested by the party against whom an order is made under Rule 35(a) or the person examined, the party causing the examination to be made shall deliver to the requesting party a copy of the detailed written report of the examiner setting out the examiner's findings, including results of all tests made, diagnoses and conclusions, together with like reports of all earlier examinations of the same condition. After delivery the party causing the examination shall be entitled upon request to receive from the party against whom the order is made a like report of any examination, previously or thereafter made, of the same condition, unless, in the case of a report of examination of a person not a party, the party shows that the party is unable to obtain it. The court on motion may make an order against a party requiring delivery of a report on such terms as are just, and if an examiner fails or refuses to make a report the court may exclude the examiner's testimony if offered at trial.

(2) By requesting and obtaining a report of the examination so ordered or by taking the deposition of the examiner, the party examined waives any privilege the party may have in that action or any other involving the same controversy, regarding the testimony of every other person who has examined or may thereafter examine the party in respect of the same mental or physical condition.

(3) This subdivision applies to examinations made by agreement of the parties, unless the agreement expressly provides otherwise. This subdivision does not preclude discovery of a report of an examiner or the taking of a deposition of the examiner in accordance with the provisions of any other rule.

Rule 36. Requests for Admission

(a) Request for Admission. A party may serve upon any other party a written request for the admission, for purposes of the pending action only, of the truth of any matters within the scope of Rule 26(b)(1) set forth in the request that relate to statements or opinions of fact or of the application of law to fact, including the genuineness of any documents described in the request. Copies of documents shall be served with the request unless they have been or are otherwise furnished or made available for inspection and copying. Without leave of court or written stipulation, requests for admission may not be served before the time specified in Rule 26(d).

Each matter of which an admission is requested shall be separately set forth. The matter is admitted unless, within 30 days after service of the request, or within such shorter or longer time as the court may allow or as the parties may agree to in writing, subject to Rule 29, the party to whom the request is directed serves upon the party requesting the admission a written answer or objection addressed to the matter, signed by the party or by the party's attorney. If objection is made, the reasons therefor shall be stated. The answer shall specifically deny the matter or set forth in detail the reasons why the answering party cannot truthfully admit or deny the matter. A denial shall fairly meet the substance of the requested admission, and when good faith requires that a party qualify an answer or deny only a part of the matter of which an admission is requested, the party shall specify so much of it as is true and qualify or deny the remainder. An answering party may not give lack of information or knowledge as a reason for failure to admit or deny unless the party states that the party has made reasonable inquiry and that the information known or readily obtainable by the party is insufficient to enable the party to admit or deny. A party who considers that a matter of which an admission has been requested presents a genuine issue for trial may not, on that ground alone, object to the request; the party may, subject to the provisions of Rule 37(c), deny the matter or set forth reasons why the party cannot admit or deny it.

The party who has requested the admissions may move to determine the sufficiency of the answers or objections. Unless the court determines that an objection is justified, it shall order that an answer be served. If the court determines that an answer does not comply with the requirements of this rule, it may order either that the matter is admitted or that an amended answer be served. The court may, in lieu of these orders, determine that final disposition of the request be made at a pretrial conference or at a designated time prior to trial. The provisions of Rule 37(a)(4) apply to the award of expenses incurred in relation to the motion.

(b) Effect of Admission. Any matter admitted under this rule is conclusively established unless the court on motion permits withdrawal or amendment of the admission. Subject to the provision of Rule 16 governing amendment of a pretrial order, the court may permit withdrawal or amendment when the presentation of the merits of the action will be subserved thereby and the party who obtained the admission fails to satisfy the court that withdrawal or amendment will prejudice that party in maintaining the action or defense on the merits. Any admission made by a party under this rule is for the purpose of the pending action only and is not an admission for any other purpose nor may it be used against the party in any other proceeding.

Rule 37. Failure to Make Disclosure or Cooperate in Discovery; Sanctions

(a) Motion For Order Compelling Disclosure or Discovery. A party, upon reasonable notice to other parties and all persons affected thereby, may apply for an order compelling disclosure or discovery as follows:

(1) Appropriate Court. An application for an order to a party shall be made to the court in which the action is pending. An application for an order to a person who is not a party shall be made to the court in the district where the discovery is being, or is to be, taken.

(2) Motion.

(A) If a party fails to make a disclosure required by Rule 26(a), any other party may move to compel disclosure and for appropriate sanctions. The motion must include a certification that the movant has in good faith conferred or attempted to confer with the party not making the disclosure in an effort to secure the disclosure without court action.

(B) If a deponent fails to answer a question propounded or submitted under Rules 30 or 31, or a corporation or other entity fails to make a designation under Rule 30(b)(6) or 31(a), or a party fails to answer an interrogatory submitted under Rule 33, or if a party, in response to a request for inspection submitted under Rule 34, fails to respond that inspection will be permitted as requested or fails to permit inspection as requested, the discovering party may move for an order compelling an answer, or a designation, or an order compelling inspection in accordance with the request. The motion must include a certification that the movant has in good faith conferred or attempted to confer with the person or party failing to make the discovery in an effort to secure the information or material without court action. When taking a deposition on oral examination, the proponent of the question may complete or adjourn the examination before applying for an order.

(3) Evasive or Incomplete Disclosure, Answer, or Response. For purposes of this subdivision an evasive or incomplete disclosure, answer, or response is to be treated as a failure to disclose, answer, or respond.

(4) Expenses and Sanctions.

(A) If the motion is granted or if the disclosure or requested discovery is provided after the motion was filed, the court shall, after affording an opportunity to be heard, require the party or deponent whose conduct necessitated the motion or the party or attorney advising such conduct or both of them to pay to the moving party the reasonable expenses incurred in making the motion, including attorney's fees, unless the court finds that the motion was filed without the movant's first making a good faith effort to obtain the disclosure of discovery without court action, or that the opposing party's nondisclosure, response, or objection was substantially justified, or that other circumstances make an award of expenses unjust.

(B) If the motion is denied, the court may enter any protective order authorized under Rule 26(c) and shall, after affording an opportunity to be heard, require the moving party or the attorney filing the motion or both of them to pay to the party or deponent who opposed the motion the reasonable expenses incurred in opposing the motion, including attorney's fees, unless the court finds that the making of the motion was substantially justified or that other circumstances make an award of expenses unjust.

(C) If the motion is granted in part and denied in part, the court may enter any protective order authorized under Rule 26(c) and may, after affording an opportunity to be heard, apportion the reasonable expenses incurred in relation to the motion among the parties and persons in a just manner.

(b) Failure to Comply With Order.

(1) Sanctions by Court in District Where Deposition is Taken. If a deponent fails to be sworn or to answer a question after being directed to do so by the court in the district in which the deposition is being taken, the failure may be considered a contempt of that court.

(2) Sanctions by Court in Which Action is Pending. If a party or an officer, director, or managing agent of a party or a person designated under Rule 30(b)(6) or 31(a) to testify on behalf of a party fails to obey an order to provide or permit discovery, including an order made under subdivision (a) of this rule or Rule 35, or if a party fails to obey an order entered under Rule 26(f), the court in which the action is pending may make such orders in regard to the failure as are just, and among others the following:

(A) An order that the matters regarding which the order was made or any other designated facts shall be taken to be established for the purposes of the action in accordance with the claim of the party obtaining the order;

(B) An order refusing to allow the disobedient party to support or oppose designated claims or defenses, or prohibiting that party from introducing designated matters in evidence;

(C) An order striking out pleadings or parts thereof, or staying further proceedings until the order is obeyed, or dismissing the action or proceeding or any part thereof, or rendering a judgment by default against the disobedient party;

(D) In lieu of any of the foregoing orders or in addition thereto, an order treating as a contempt of court the failure to obey any orders except an order to submit to a physical or mental examination;

(E) Where a party has failed to comply with an order under Rule 35(a) requiring that party to produce another for examination, such orders as are listed in paragraphs (A), (B), and (C) of this subdivision, unless the party failing to comply shows that that party is unable to produce such person for examination.

In lieu of any of the foregoing orders or in addition thereto, the court shall require the party failing to obey the order or the attorney advising that party or both to pay the reasonable expenses, including attorney's fees, caused by the failure, unless the court finds that the failure was substantially justified or that other circumstances make an award of expenses unjust.

(c) Failure to Disclose; False or Misleading Disclosure; Refusal to Admit.

(1) A party that without substantial justification fails to disclose information required by Rule 26(a) or 26(e)(1), or to amend a prior response to discovery as required by Rule 26(e)(2), is not, unless such failure is harmless, permitted to use as evidence at a trial, at a hearing, or on a motion any witness or information not so disclosed. In addition to or in lieu of this sanction, the court, on motion and after affording an opportunity to be heard, may impose other appropriate sanctions. In addition to requiring payment of reasonable expenses, including attorney's fees, caused by the failure, these sanctions may include any of the actions authorized under Rule 37(b)(2)(A), (B), and (C) and may include informing the jury of the failure to make the disclosure.

(2) If a party fails to admit the genuineness of any document or the truth of any matter as requested under Rule 36, and if the party requesting the admissions thereafter proves the genuineness of the document or the truth of the matter, the requesting party may apply to the court for an order requiring the other party to pay the reasonable expenses incurred in making that proof, including reasonable attorney's fees. The court shall make the order unless it finds that (A) the request was held objectionable pursuant to Rule 36(a), or (B) the admission sought was of no substantial importance, or (C) the party failing to admit had reasonable ground to believe that the party might prevail on the matter, or (D) there was other good reason for the failure to admit.

(d) Failure of Party to Attend at Own Deposition or Serve Answers to Interrogatories or Respond to Request for Inspection. If a party or an officer, director, or managing agent of a party or a person designated under Rule 30(b)(6) or 31(a) to testify on behalf of a party fails (1) to appear before the officer who is to take the deposition, after being served with a proper notice, or (2) to serve answers or objections to interrogatories submitted under Rule 33, after proper service of the interrogatories, or (3) to serve a written response to a request for inspection submitted under Rule 34, after proper service of the request, the court in which the action is pending on motion may make such orders in regard to the failure as are just, and among others it may take any action authorized under subparagraphs (A), (B), and (C) of subdivision (b)(2) of this rule. Any motion specifying a failure under clause (2) or (3) of this subdivision shall include a certification that the movant has in good faith conferred or attempted to confer with the party failing to answer or respond in an effort to obtain such answer or response without court action. In lieu of any order or in addition thereto, the court shall require the party failing to act or the attorney advising that party or both to pay the reasonable expenses, including attorney's fees, caused by the failure unless the court finds that the failure was substantially justified or that other circumstances make an award of expenses unjust.

The failure to act described in this subdivision may not be excused on the ground that the discovery sought is objectionable unless the party failing to act has a pending motion for a protective order as provided by Rule 26(c).

(e) [Abrogated]

(f) [Repealed. Pub.L 96-481, Title II, § 205(a), Oct. 21, 1980, 94 Stat. 2330]

(g) Failure to Participate in the Framing of a Discovery Plan. If a party or a party's attorney fails to participate in good faith in the development and submission of a proposed discovery plan as required by Rule 26(f), the court may, after opportunity for hearing, require such party or attorney to pay to any other party the reasonable expenses, including attorney's fees, caused by the failure.

INDEX

Index

Index